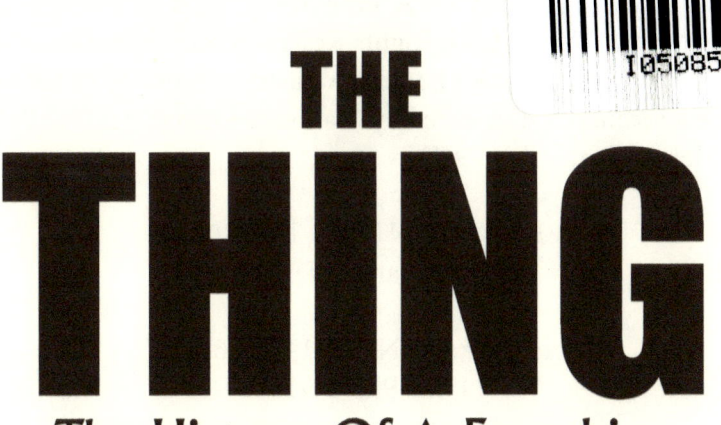

THE THING

The History Of A Franchise

Phil Hore

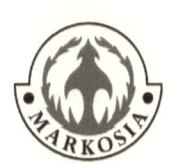

THE THING: The History Of A Franchise TM & © 2023 Phil Hore & Markosia Enterprises, Ltd. All Rights Reserved. Reproduction of any part of this work by any means without the written permission of the publisher is expressly forbidden. Published by Markosia Enterprises, PO BOX 3477, Barnet, Hertfordshire, EN5 9HN.

FIRST PRINTING, May 2023.
Harry Markos, Director.

Paperback: ISBN 978-1-915860-21-7
eBook: ISBN 978-1-915860-22-4

Book design by: Ian Sharman

www.markosia.com

First Edition

PART ONE
Who Goes There?

Who Goes There? (ASTOUNDING SCIENCE-FICTION, Aug., 1938) dealt with an alien thing from outer space that enters the camp of an Antarctic research party and blends alternately into the forms of the various men and dogs in the camp.

The job is to find the host and kill "it" before, in the guise of some human or other creature, it gets to civilization. Who Goes There? was in a sense one of the most thrilling detective stories ever written...RKO, altering the story considerably, produced it as a profitable horror picture titled The Thing (1951)...

To be clear, this book isn't a definitive look into John Carpenter's 1982 film THE THING, we are investigating the entire THING franchise that has grown from the original 1938 novella. There were comics, songs, computer and board games, tv shows and more. Unlike most of The Thing fans of my generation I didn't discover the story by watching the 1982 movie or even catching the 1951 film with my dad during the late Friday night feature on TV. Nope, I read 'Who Goes There?' first in a Sci-Fi anthology I bought from Scholastic for schoolbook club called 'Starstreak'. I think I would have been eleven or twelve at the time and the story freaked me out.

Arguably the most important science fiction novella ever written, 'Who Goes There?' was penned by John W. Campbell jr., and it not only initiated one of the longest movie franchises in Hollywood history, as we'll see it influenced many of the most popular movies and TV shows ever made.

John Campbell edited ASTOUNDING SCIENCE FICTION for thirty-three years, surely a record among editors of almost all magazines...ASTOUNDING led the way repeatedly for the entire field...raising the tone of SF from that of adolescent extravaganzas to meaningful adult fiction and packaging. For the last decade, ASTOUNDING has been ANALOG, a title change which reflected this growing maturity for the magazine and the field. The number of major-name authors whom John Campbell discovered or encouraged is legion. "I have no plans for retirement," he told me recently. "I intend to go on editing ANALOG until I die." His wish was unfortunately prophetic. He died in his sleep on a Sunday evening, apparently of a heart-attack. He almost certainly died a happy man, satisfied with what he had made of his life and at the same time full of plans for the future. May he rest in peace.

To tell the history of The Thing we need to know more about its author, and the most respectful way I could think to do this was to highlight what an opposition magazine wrote after his death. The above quotes appeared in Ted White's 1971 remembrance of the editor in Amazing Stories.

Campbell's own Astounding Magazine also published a biography of their famous editor by Sam Moskowitz, first printed in 1963.

JOHN Wood Campbell, Jr., was born in a two-family frame house at 16 Tracey Ave., Newark, N. J., on June 8, 1910. His father was an electrical engineer with New Jersey Bell Telephone… After seven years in Newark the family moved to Maplewood, N. J., where John attended public school. Precociously intellectual, young John had virtually no friends. At home, his relationship with his parents was emotionally difficult. According to Campbell, his father carried impersonality and theoretical objectivity in family matters to the brink of fetish ; he almost never used the pronoun "I;" all statements were in the third person: "It is necessary," "one must," "it appears that," "one should." Not only was the senior Campbell an authoritarian but he was also a self-righteous disciplinarian who concealed whatever affection he felt for his son.

An emotionally absent father is a sad thing for a son to handle, but to find the source of one of the most disturbing, imaginative horror stories ever put to paper we have to go deeper. For that kind of psychological manipulation, you need a mother…and in Campbell's case, two mothers.

His mother was Dorothy Strahern …[whose] *changeability baffled and frustrated the youngster. Campbell recalls her as self-centred and flighty, her moods unpredictable moment to moment. While not deliberately cruel, her gestures of warmth appeared so transitory and contrived to him as to be quickly discounted. Complicating the situation was the fact that Campbell's mother had an identical twin sister. John could tell them apart. The sisters, Campbell says, were in psychological conflict because John's mother had married first. He thought he was being used as a pawn by his mother to subtly taunt her twin.*

No matter which form, the main theme that threads through all versions of Who Goes There? is paranoia. The largest fear is not knowing who could be trusted because the enemy was hiding in plain sight – in fact could be hiding within the ones you know the best.

The result was, Campbell says, that his aunt treated him with such abruptness he was convinced she hated him. This created a bizarre situation. The boy would come running into the house to breathlessly impart something to a woman he thought was his "mother." He would be jarred by a curt rebuff from her twin, his aunt. This situation became a continuing and insoluble nightmare. Was the woman standing in front of him "friend" or "foe"?...

Paranoia. Deep seated paranoia. Imagine coming home and not knowing if you were talking to your mother or the one person on the planet who seemed to hate you and looked exactly like her? Was this the true origin of his story?

Things were not all bad though, as Campbell grew older, he began to show a precocious intelligence and a serious fondness for science fiction.

Loneliness directed young Campbell's alert and curious mind into everything. He blew up the basement with his chemistry experiments. Manually dexterous, he repaired bicycles for other kids. For their parents he revitalized electrical appliances. He read omnivorously, particularly myths, legends, folklore, and anthropology. Edgar Rice Burroughs' Tarzan and John Carter of Mars were discovered by Campbell when he was seven. At eight he was perusing Jeans, Eddington and astronomy texts. At 14 he was sent to Blair Academy, an exclusive boys' school in Blairstown, N.J. He succeeded in making only a few friends there; he infuriated the instructors by correcting their "errors" in class. Sports did not attract him, though he developed a good game of tennis and a mild interest in football. Despite four years at Blair, he never obtained a diploma.

Sure, he had no diploma, but he was still accepted at the Massachusetts Institute of Technology in 1928. He also managed to read the first issue of Amazing Stories and began writing.

Painfully aware that SF writers frequently repeated obvious scientific errors, Campbell's own first attempt, a short story titled Invaders from the Infinite, was aimed at correcting the misconception that there would be a problem in heating an interplanetary ship in space. The story was sent to amazing stories, and accepted. Elated, Campbell pounded out a longer story titled When the Atoms Failed. That, too, was accepted. His enthusiasm waned, however, as months passed and neither story appeared. Home on vacation in the summer of 1929, Campbell visited T. O'Conor Sloane, the editor.

I think this says a lot about Campbell. Not only was he confident in his own abilities, even as a young man he wasn't willing to just sit around and wait for things to happen.

Now six-foot one, with hawk-like features, Campbell presented a formidable appearance as he was ushered into Sloane's editorial offices. Sloane, 80, had a flowing white beard. But despite his appearance, the old man was anything but a stuffed shirt. He quickly admitted that the manuscript of Invaders From the Infinite had been lost. Did the author, perhaps, have a carbon? He did not? Well, his career would then have to be launched with When The Atoms Failed.

Sloane more than made up for the disappointment by giving When the Atoms Failed the cover of the Jan., 1930, issue, and beginning the blurb of the story: "Our new author, who is a student at the Massachusetts Institute of Technology, shows marvellous ability at combining science with romance, evolving a piece of fiction of real scientific and literary value."

School, graduation, marriage, the Great Depression and the various odd jobs a young man takes to feed his family, during all this Campbell continued to write and sell his stories. Thanks to his MIT background and the benefit of teachers who seemed to like the man, these stories were always based on real science, no matter how fantastic they became.

His growing popularity and distinct style meant editors began contacting the writer for more. This led to a small issue. Some of these new stories were so unique and different from his usual fare there was a fear they'd cause confusion and perhaps even resentment when readers, looking forward to the standard type of Campbell tale, got one of these new stories instead.

The problem was solved with a pen name, Don A. Stuart, derived from the maiden name of Campbell's wife, Dona Stuart." This new writing style proved such a winner: *DON A. Stuart at once bid fair to eclipse Campbell in popularity.* Because the Stuart stories were so different and had become so popular, editors stopped buying work submitted by 'Campbell' as they felt these strictly science-based tales had become old fashioned. The author was being overshadowed by his pseudonym. For example, 'Stuarts' story Twilight is considered a true classic and helped change science fiction forever as it showed a maturity often lacking in earlier works. It also inspired future superstars like Arthur C. Clark.

Despite selling several tales, life hadn't been easy during the depression years. However, everything changed when Campbell was hired as the editor of Astounding Science Fiction in 1937. This was an important moment for the medium as, in many ways, you could say sci-fi grew up under Campbell's influence.

He immediately instituted strict rules for submissions to the popular magazine. The new editor wanted stories where…*the protagonist solves a technical problem through scientific or engineering training or outwits one or more aliens because humans are the toughest, smartest kids on the block.* In 1980, Fantastic Science Fiction magazine explained how: *John W. Campbell once said he often asked his authors to write as though their stories were appearing in non-fiction magazines to be read in a future world.*

The champion of sci fi, Harlan Ellison, later noted Campbell: *set the parameters of the genre as consistent with his own concerns.* This desire to have accurate science in all stories would get the editor and the magazine into a little trouble in 1944 when he published 'Deadline'. The author, Cleve Cartmill, suggested a story about a super-bomb, and Campbell thought it was a great idea and sent the writer material from unclassified articles and science papers about atomic research. In one of these was the suggestion of using Uranium-235 to create a nuclear fission device. The story not only caught the eye of the scientists creating just such a bomb for the Manhattan Project at Los Alamos, it also came under the scrutiny of the FBI. The agency immediately began investigating everyone involved with Deadline to uncover if there had been a wartime security breach.

You can imagine how many warning lights went off when the story was pulled apart by US codebreakers to see if it contained any hidden messages to the countries enemies. Something highly suspicious seemed to be going on as the evil nations in the story were the Sixa, Ynamre and Ytal, who'd developed the bomb at Nilreq. To destroy the bomb before it could be used, the Seilla sent a commando called Ybor Sebrof.

Those words backwards roughly spelt Axis, Germany, Italy, Berlin and Allies. Worried the magazine was sending coded messages to foreign powers, the FBI paid a visit to Campbell. The editor clarified what had happened, how he'd been to M.I.T. and could even be considered a physicist and how he'd got the information. It seems his explanation was believed as the FBI soon moved on, though not before asking Campbell to hold off on publishing atomic weapon stories until after the war.

The FBI wasn't done though, as they still had suspicions about the stories author. Apparently, they decided to find out more by one of the strangest sting operations I've ever heard of. They approached Cartmill's postman and asked for his help, explaining they needed someone to make small talk with the writer and at some stage bring up his story and find out if he was a secret agent without letting him know this was part of an interrogation...

...what could go wrong?

Apparently, nothing. The postman intercepted the author one day and asked him about his work, claiming he was a sci-fi fan. He later repeated everything back to his FBI handlers, explaining not only did Cartmill not seem to be a foreign agent, he was apparently so displeased with the story that he'd claimed: "It stinks."

Legend has it this affair led to the former M.I.T. student also completing a little detective work of his own that would have really had warning alarms ringing at the FBI. Campbell had noticed that a lot of the physicists whose names appeared in the science articles and papers he'd been reading – and also happened to be Astounding Magazine subscribers - had all recently changed their postal address to the same small town, Los Alamos. Here he guessed was the location of the government team trying to make the bomb – though this time Campbell kept his suspicions to himself.

Astounding wasn't the only publisher to fall under such suspicions either. In my last book 'HORROR', about the war on comic books in the 1950s, I recount the time the same thing happened to DC comics.

Campbells' new rules and belief in realism was not only causing him trouble with the FBI, complaints had surfaced that the magazines' stories were becoming too formulaic. Yet the rules meant authors had to think a problem through – there'd be no more magical salvation, with an improbable technology or alien suddenly appearing to help solve an issue. Characters now had to solve things in a way that made scientific sense.

Campbell, Wells and Welles

Right up front I'm going to point out there's a blog on this subject by Alec Nevala-Lee, so please check it out, it's a great read. In 'Falls the Shadow' the author records that Campbell in 1938 saw Orson Welles': *famous modern-dress production of Julius Caesar with the writer L. Sprague de Camp, of which he wrote in a letter:*

It represented, in a way, what I'm trying to do in the magazine. Those humans of two thousand years ago thought and acted as we do—even if they did dress differently. Removing the funny clothes made them more real and understandable. I'm trying to get away from funny clothes and funny-looking people in the pictures of the magazine. And have more humans.

It's rare to find anything personal written by Campbell, so it's nice to highlight even just this small paragraph about something he was striving to achieve. The real treasure though was what the blog discovered about Campbell's thoughts on arguably Welles' most controversial production.

Astounding was asked to sponsor Welles radio company, the Mercury Theatre, and their radio show of 'War of The Worlds'. Famously this caused wide-spread panic in the states, and Astounding's latest editor explained his thoughts on what happened and again, perhaps we have another insight into his most famous story.

Campbell was less pleased by Welles's most notable venture into science fiction, which he must have seen as an incursion on his turf. He wrote to his friend Robert Swisher: "So far as sponsoring that War of [the] Worlds thing—I'm damn glad we didn't! The thing is going to cost CBS money, what with suits, etc., and we're better off without it." In Astounding, he said that the ensuing panic demonstrated the need for "wider appreciation" of science fiction, in order to educate the public about what was and wasn't real:

I have long been an exponent of the belief that, should interplanetary visitors actually arrive, no one could possibly convince the public of the fact. These stories wherein the fact is suddenly announced and widespread panic immediately ensues have always seemed to me highly improbable, simply because the average man did not seem ready to visualize and believe such a statement.

If we look at the reaction of the Antarctic crew to the presence of The Thing in their midst, the one thing they don't do is panic. They're scared, they fight and they work the problem and find a scientific solution…but they never panic.

Sadly, though his new editor duties meant Campbell had a consistent pay-packet, they also meant he no longer had the time for his own writing.

Few authors made their literary exit more magnificently. From the memories of his childhood he drew the most fearsome agony of the past. The doubts, the fear, the shock and then the frustration of repeatedly discovering that the woman who looked so much like his mother, was not. Who goes there? Friend or foe? He had attempted the theme once before with a light touch in Brain Stealers of Mars. This time it was for real.

The earlier 1936 tale 'Brain Stealers of Mars' also dealt with shapeshifting aliens, but today has been all but forgotten while 'Who Goes there?' continues to win accolades. Years later the novelette was highlighted in Campbell's collected works, and reading this book's blurb it made the same point as above.

When John Campbell gave up writing for editing, science-fiction lost at least two of its best writers—for under his own name and the pen-name of Don A. Stuart he had produced a number of memorable yarns.

What Did You Think?

The first mention of Campbell's popular story was in Astounding Science Fiction (July 1938). On page 99 of the magazine is the 'In Times To Come' section, and here was a small notice about what stories were going to appear in future issues. Halfway down the page was the somewhat jokey/mysterious blurb:

DON A. STUART has a long novelette. It's placed in Antarctica — for a reason. It had to be there for that is the only place on the face of the Earth where there is no animal life whatever — and Stuart discusses a thing that must be isolated. A deadly imitation. The story's problem lies in the title — Who Goes There?

Its location on the page's bottom half indicates this wasn't thought to be anything special. In fact the story being promoted heavily as the must-read for the issue was Hell-Ship.

This was a time before the internet or really anyway of tracking how popular a story was. Yet a little research into the only true source available, the magazines letter page, reveals that when Who Goes There? was first published, it hit hard and really grabbed fans, who realised they were reading something special.

...the story...was in my estimation the best in the issue. It was admirably written, and it held my interest throughout the entire story. The idea of an animal having the ability to convert its shape into that of any other form perfectly is a novel idea... (Don Thielke).

Dear Mr Campbell:
I respectfully submit that you are being unfair to your readers. You ask for

suggestions as to how to improve the stories – and then, in the same issue, you print one like "Who Goes There?" The very idea of a better story than that!

For, wonder of wonders, it is a literary work of art, equal to a Stevensons short story...in this one, thank the Lord, there is not only an idea, but an honest-to-goodness plot, worthy of Edgar Wallce or Conan Doyle at this best. In fact it does have a strong resemble to a detective story.

But, its main attraction, and the reason why you will be getting floods of letters on praise of it, in that the fellows who win the battle are human beings with fully normal intelligence, present day equipment, and nothing else. I have no objections to a ray gun or a spaceship, but for goodness' sake, give the characters some brains. The plot should be a struggle of intelligence, not weapons (Donald West).

This letter points out something often ignored, that Who Goes There? is a very strong detective story. Yes, there's horror and suspense, and could also be considered a classic haunted house tale, but it's the ongoing mystery of what's going to happen, whose been infected and how can they find a way of uncovering and dealing with such a creature that's the engine driving the plot onward. This was recognised in a 1979 article in Asimov Magazine called 'On Science Fiction Detective Stories' by Jon L. Breen. The article notes the strong similarities between many sci-fi and detective stories, and notes *John W. Campbell, Jr...tried something of the kind in "Who Goes There?"*.

The story also gives us evidence that Campbell was writing what he believed in. The tale is all about humans thinking an issue confronting them through and coming up with a plausible solution to save them. Perhaps because of this new style the praise kept coming in.

...of the stories in this month's magazine, I thought Don Stuarts "who Goes There?" to be the best. Suspense was the strong point of the story, yet it didn't keep me that way too long. I always appreciate a happy ending, with the menace vanquished and the secrets of science saved for the benefit of mankind (Robert V. Woodings).

I especially enjoyed "Who Goes There?" It was a sort of melange of "The Living Death", Lovecraft's "Mountains of Madness" and the well-known werewolf takes. However, it was written in such a style that it was altogether engrossing, interesting and new. John, if you can get around to it, you may pat Don on the back for me (L. M. Jensen).

Remember, more like "Who Goes There?", which was good both for its idea and for the character (Allan Ingvald).

Why don't you have Don a Stuart write ...more stories, Mr. Campbel? "Who Goes There?" is tops for the year as far as I'm concerned (J. J. D.).

...your expanding circulation is bringing in many new readers whose imagination is not so well developed as yet, compared to we readers who have been reading science-fiction since it began. For them you must publish stories with a standardized science-background and with the type of action and story for which they are looking. We also enjoy such stories when they are well written...for their entertainment value...Nevertheless, do not entirely forget us! We constantly crave something new... and more, ever more, of the human, spellbinding atmosphere of "Who Goes There?" After all that advance publicity about "Hell Ship", the story let me down. If I had read "Hell Ship" and "Who Goes There?" without having read the praises for the former, I probably would have had a different reaction (Grady L. McMurtry).

This is an interesting point. As Campbell was the magazine's editor, had he played down the quality of his own story by highlighting another author? Then again, as it wasn't all praise for his story, maybe he thought Hell Ship was the better tale?

Anyone who writes sci-fi is aware their audience is highly educated and are going to call you out if they think you've made a mistake. Campbell's audience was no different.

Don A Stuart slipped a bit on page 70. He said "A Man's muscle cells live many hours after he had died. Just because they live, and a few things like hair and fingernail cells still live, you wouldn't accuse a corpse of being a Zombie, or something? Now, you may be wrong, but isn't it now a proven fact that the hair and fingernails do not grow after death, according to a popular superstition? I stand to be corrected. Well, playing devil's advocate, the story says these cells remain alive, not necessarily pointing out that they continued growing (Tony Strother).

I did uncover a surprising resource that had tracked exactly how popular the tale was becoming. The magazine occasionally surveyed their readers on their favourite articles, ranking with a simple number system of first to fifth. Although not all the readers were complimentary, even their criticisms were often underlined by a certain respect.

First Place: Stuart's "Who Goes There?" Mr Stuarts "science" might trouble the soul of a biologist, I have no doubt it would. He does not attempt to make his incredible premise credible – even conceivable. But – Given the premise, he is utterly convincing. If the situation should happen, the human beings he had drawn would, I think, feel and act just like that. Refreshing Good suspense too (W. K. Veriaud).

You will note that I put Don Stuart's "Who Goes There?" a poor last. This is not on the account of the mechanics of his writing, but only that the tale was highly repulsive to me personally. I just didn't like it. However, I think Mr Stuart is one of your better writers and he has written stories that rank with the best (R. R. Dawson).

Don A. Stuart...was good enough to hold my interest...Good solid reading – not too new in plot, but all right for my Twenty cents (Patricia Evans).

At the end of this process Campbell collated all the votes and wrote:
It is spoken! Your decisions are made and here recorded...every story was voted in first place at least once: every story was voted terrible at least once...
Who Goes There? 93% Don A. Stuart
The terrible Sense 55% Calvin Peregory
Hell SHIP 52% Arthur J. Burks
Jason Comes Home 4% A. B. L Macfadyen, Jr.

Stuart's story was the clear winner – but few reading this pole (and I wonder if the authors on the list themselves knew) that the winner was just a pseudonym of the editor? I have no doubt the stats are correct because later it was voted in numerous publications as one of the most important sci-fi stories of the 20th century. Locust Magazine voted it #4 in Best Novellas, and it tied 1st on the 1971 'Astounding/Analog All-Time Poll - Pre-1940 Short Fiction'. It was apparently also voted the #1 story by the SF Writers of America.

Reprints and The Movie

For Stuart fans it was the sentence that could be heard around the world. In the September 1950 issue of Astonishing this letter from Dean McLaughlin also hinted that readers knew both authors were the same man. *I heard that Hollywood has latched onto "Who Goes There" by a fellow named Campbell. Know him?*

When a major Hollywood studio buys your story and one of the most important movie directors ever 'produces' the film, things surely must change. It's a chance to cash in and maybe not have to struggle for a while as an artist.

Later we'll go into Howard Hawks discovering Campbell's story in 1947, but we do have an idea about what Campbell was paid from a surprising source. In 'Before the Golden Age; a science fiction anthology of the 1930s' Isaac Asimov recounted the first story he sold to Campbell, and how he finally felt: *I was there. Like science fiction itself, I had moved up to a higher level.*

When it came to his interaction with Astounding's editor, Asimov recalled:
"Who Goes There?" was eventually made into the financially successful but

science fictionally contemptible motion picture The Thing, for which John was paid a mere few hundred dollars in total. When I expressed indignation at this, Campbell characteristically shrugged it off. He said, "It helps spread science fiction among the outsiders. That's all that counts."

TRIVIA: Did you know that in interviews Asimov always held to the claim it was Campbell who created the Three laws of Robotics? Campbell always argued that Asimov already had the idea for the laws, he just helped him focus them. Asimov disagreed with this and explained Campbell had created them during their many conversations.

Thanks to the upcoming Howard Hawks helmed 'The Thing From Another World' Campbell's story was reprinted in various collections. A 1948 book carried the famous image of a three-eyed Thing on the cover by Hannes Bok, beating the movie image by three years. Fantasy Annual magazine listed this as their top fantasy book for the year. Another reprint appeared a short time later that really leaned into the link between story and film, and was so blatant even Amazing Science Fiction's review in 1952 had to admit was...*a collection of Campbell stories first published some four years ago, said reprinting apparently being based on the inclusion of the short novel Who Goes There, which as almost everybody knows was the basis of that 1951 movie called The Thing. At any rate, this fact is highly blurbed on the jacket cover.* Hey, if I wrote the story a popular movie was based on, I think I'd blurb it all over the place too.

A decade after the Thing From Another World hit movie screens, one seemingly forgotten reprint of Campbell's story appeared in issue #12 and 13 of Famous Monsters of Filmland Magazine (FM). Edited down to a more manageable size, let's just say reviews 'varied'.

Having read the complete story already at first I wasn't going to read your version of "Who Goes There?" but I decided to start it and find out if you skilfully condensed it. Superb, in both issues it was a fresh and vivid account of the overpowering fear that accompanied it (John Clark).

You stated in the editor's note that you stayed up till 5 in the morning editing "Who Goes There?"...After I had read 2 paragraphs it was obvious. You somehow, with your abridgment, managed to make it unreadable and completely confused. I was sick with disappointment...

This last letter of bitter disappointment was written by one Daniel O'Bannon of St Louis Missouri. Funnily enough a Dan O'Bannon - the man who penned the original script for ALIEN, a movie heavily influenced by 'Who Goes There?' - also once lived in St. Louis Missouri. I wonder if they're related?

The Comedy

> For the story starts by stating
> That some guys investigating
> The Antarctic are debating
> On exactly what to do
> With a monster they've found frozen
> Near the campsite they have chosen,
> And the quarrel grows and grows, un-
> 'Til they're in an awful stew.
>
> And so then the men are tested
> To see who has been digested,
> And who's been left unmolested,
> But the test doesn't work! It's hexed!
> So each man just sits there, shrinking
> From the others, madly thinking,
> As he watches with unblinking
> Gaze, and wonders—Who Goes Next?

You can find the entire 'Who Rhymes There?' online, and it was clearly a love letter to Campbell's original story. It first appeared with the title, 'Parodies Tossed' in Science Fiction Stories, May 1956, then reprinted with the title of 'All About the Thing' in SF: The Year's Greatest Science Fiction and Fantasy, Second Annual Volume, published by Gnome Press (1957) and Dell (June 1957). I did read somewhere another historian believed it was based on the film – but clearly the mention of the blood test proves its based-on Campbell's novelette (Sorry, during editing I could not find the original source where I read that historian's comment).

Recent love

The story continued to astound and scare for decades after it was published – as I said at the start, I first read it in Primary school in 1979 or 1980. In 1983 The Twilight Zone Magazine printed a list of the 13 scariest stories, and sitting at #6 was 'Who Goes there?'

In 2014, Famous Monsters carried several articles on the history of Sci-Fi and its article 'Pulp Science Fiction' noted:

While pulps continued in popularity and influence for the next several years, it was the arrival of writer and editor John W. Campbell in 1938 as the editor…that would usher in Sci-Fi's Golden Age...In Campbell's first year as editor, he would publish his own short story, "Who Goes There", that would eventually be named as Howard Hawks THE THING FROM ANOTHER WORLD and later by John Carpenter as the Sci-Fi/monster masterpiece THE THING. The revolution had begun.

In 2021 the host of the Tonight Show, Stephen Colbert was interviewing Quentin Tarantino. By their banter its obvious they knew each other and were just having fun. Things got interesting when the host asked:

Colbert: I want to ask you, as long as I have a movie master here and a guy who knows a lot about movies. We might enjoy a few movies in common. Do you have a favourite adaptation?

Tarantino: I do.

Colbert: And I wanted to ask you. I'm a huge fan of the original short story or novella of 'The thing'.

Tarantino: Who Goes There?

Colbert: Do you love the Thing?

Tarantino: I love both of them.

...but we'll get back to this interview later.

The Forgotten Man

Before we move on there's just one more person we need to talk about, the artist from the original story. Born in Graudenz, Germany (a future part of Poland), Hans Waldemar Wessolowski studied art in Berlin and made a living by selling funny caricatures of people. Later he joined the merchant navy in 1911 and saw the world, however, when his ship was sailing past New Orleans the artist leapt overboard, swam ashore and successfully applied for US citizenship. Married and living in New York, Wessolowski began doing interior art and cover paintings for various magazines published in the city, including Astounding Science Fiction. His art is easy to spot as it has 'H. Wesso' somewhere on the image. This fact was noticed by the magazine's readers, with one fan, Russel Morris Wood, writing:

More power to Wesso. His 'mutant' covers are swell. And the artwork on the inside of the magazine had been steadily improving the past few months.

There's very little information about the artist, like his artistic method – though one source noted he could do a cover painting in a few days, seemed to use very little black in his art and really went for whatever colours he was feeling at the time as his paintings are routinely bright.

The cover on the first Astounding was the work of ... Wesso, who illustrated "The Beetle Horde" in a fashion that was typically his own. Wesso did all thirty-four of the Clayton Astounding covers; his medium being watercolours, his style garish. Wesso's covers were a joy to behold—brilliantly colourful and jammed with action, they were so awful as to be positively beautiful. His first science fiction cover was for the September, 1929 Amazing Stories and illustrated "The Red Peril" by Captain S. P. Meek, his last for the March, 1942 Astonishing (A Requiem For Astounding - Alva Rogers, 1964).

The Internet Speculative Fiction Database webpage is a handy site for such things as sci-fi artists, and for Wessolowski they list literally hundreds of magazines he produced during a career that spanned several decades before he died aged 53 in 1948.

Though his covers are popular, there's little argument the work he'll be most remembered for was the stark, thickly inked interior images for 'Who Goes there?'

The Last Word

As for Campbell, I think it's appropriate we let his biographer Ted White have the last word on him, followed by my interview with Campbell's family.

...for all practical purposes, Campbell's writing career ended at the age of 28 with Who Goes There? As one of the first of the modern science fiction writers, he had a profound influence on the field. A few who owe him a direct debt have been noted. Many others are obvious. For the more than a quarter-century since he ceased writing, older readers have been haunted by half remembered echoes in the plot structure of hundreds of stories. It is not strange if sometimes readers shake the hypnotic wonder of the wheeling cosmos from their minds and demand: "Who goes there?"

Can you name another sci-fi story from nearly a century ago that's still being wildly distributed and remade today?

Researching this book is one reason why I'll always argue the worth of Facebook. Now Campbell died in 1971, but when I first mentioned this book on FB I received the following message from John Campbell Hammond. *Hello there, I just came across a few of your posts. Curious about the project. Anything I can add I would be happy to help. Name is no coincidence, John W Campbell was my grandfather.*

Well, that's cool. I sent some questions to find out what John's family remembers about the story and its release.

Are you a fan? If so, do you have a go-to, the film or book? *Yes, I am a fan. My go to is the movie over the book.* How did you first see John Carpenter's The Thing? *When the movie was released in 1982 I was 10 yrs old. My mother, daughter of JWCjr, took me and a friend to the matinee on opening day. I absolutely love it! It's what fueled my love for SciFi/Horror movies.*

You're named after your grandfather. Did you know him? *Unfortunately he passed a year before I was born and never got to meet him.*

There is a legend your grandfather came up with the story when he thought back to his childhood about never knowing if he was talking to his mother or her exact twin. Does the family know if this is true? *Yes, there are some funny...not so funny stories about his mother and her twin. I think we will keep those personal.*

In Antarctica, when the station there closes for the winter, the remaining skeleton crew watch all versions of The Thing. Has the family ever watched the movies together? *Watching the movie together? I'm not aware, but when the prequel came out my sister and a group of friends went to see it in the theater.*

One important part of Sci-Fi history was the creation of the laws of Robotics. Are you aware Isaac Asimov always claimed it was John Campbell who created them? *As the story was told to me, Grandpaw was "proof reading" ... I-Robot and asked Isaac if he realizes what he had written. Not knowing, he then explained to him the that he just wrote the 3 laws of robots, and they were written into the story.*

One of the more interesting facts I found was when your grandfather was interviewed by the FBI as a possible spy during WW2. Does the family know about this incident? *As told to me...men in black suits entered his office and told him he had to stop writing the things he was. He asked "Why", they replied "Because we're doing them". Had to do with Manhattan project and atomic research. I believe the story in reference was "The Atomic Age"?* Often famous writers have their papers stored and catalogued. Recently the book length 'Who Goes There?' story appeared from Cambell's records. Was the family part of this process? *He did in fact have some of his work saved in different moratoriums. During research for a book titled 'Astounding: the golden age of scifi' written by Alec Nevela Lee, he discovered an old file with Frozen Hell written on it which turned out to be the original manuscript of Who Goes there. During this time we were in the midst of negotiations for a new film and our publisher, John Bettoncourt, took it to the press and had it published. It's been a whirlwind the last cpl years. The franchise has exploded with 3 "sequels" planned. 1st one will hit Kickstarter mid April of this year.*

Thank you for helping keep the legacy alive. Any other questions feel free to ask.

Chapter Two – The Song

Baby Shark, Do Do De Do

At the start of the 50's a science fiction phenomenon took hold of the public's imagination. No, it wasn't a book or a movie, it was a novelty song written by Charles Randolph Grean, and within the year it had mutated and taken over the world.

The musician had got his start working for big bands like Glen Miller, before moving to RCA records to help record the company's growing stable of country and western artists. Here Grean arranged 'The Christmas Song' for Nat King Cole, then in the 60s he produced and wrote a large percentage of the music for a series of albums based around a new TV Sci-Fi phenomena first broadcast on September 6, 1966.

Recently an old video on You Tube made the rounds to the delight/horror of the world's hordes of geeks and nerds. Everyone's favourite pointy eared Vulcan - dressed in snazzy white jeans and a white turtleneck (skivvy to those not American) - sat on a rock surrounded by a bevy of dancing 60s beauties wearing printed sweatshirts. From here he belted out a song about that other famous pointy eared icon of fantasy and the bravest hobbit of them all, Bilbo Baggins.

Released in 1968 by Dot Records, the single was part of an album called 'Two Sides of Leonard Nimoy'. Leaning heavily into the actor's presence on Star Trek with songs like 'Highly Illogical' and 'Spock Thoughts', it also sported a cover with dual images of Nimoy, one as himself and the other as Spock. If this doesn't sound bizarre enough, astonishingly the album reached 97 on the US album chart.

We are going to take a brief station break while those of you who haven't heard the song now google it…go ahead, we'll wait for you…

…Well? How bizarre is that? Welcome to the world of novelty songs. Often humorous, novelty songs are generally based on a gimmick, and a great example is Weird Al Yankovic doing an almost note for note remake of a popular song of the day like Michael Jackson's 'Beat It' - just with new words (Eat It). Another example, if you survived the 90s you recall all those horrendous frog songs that were immediately snapped up and respawned as ring tones. Recently, we had the global phenomena 'Baby Shark'.

Novelty songs have been around since the first caveman hummed a tune, but recorded novelties began appearing in the 1800s, were big in the 20s and 30s, but really hit their stride in the 50s and early 60s. I was lucky enough to write a few articles for Famous Monsters magazine, and one was based around monsters, music and the best novelty songs featuring certain horror creatures. We're talking 'The Monster Mash' or my personal favourite, Buck Owens 'It's a Monster's Holiday.'

A book on how to create an attention-grabbing novelty single called "The Manual (How to Have a Number One the Easy Way)", was written by 90s band, The KLF. Famous for burning a million pounds - and not having anyone believe they'd actually done it - The KLF had released a #1 single under the name 'The Timelords' called 'Doctorin' the Tardis' in 1988. The book claims their remix of the Doctor Who TV theme proves that anyone could achieve a number one single by simply doing a little research on what people would respond to - preferably something nostalgic with a gimmick - then pair it with a catchy groove.

Could it work? Well, you bought this book for almost the same reason...and I bet when I mentioned the KLF song some of you recalled the tune instantly with warm feelings.

Novelty songs made a comeback in the late 60s, and Grean was responsible for many of these. He not only wrote Bilbo Baggins for Nimoy, but most of the songs that appeared on his albums... yes... albums! In the three years Star Trek was on TV Nimoy released FIVE albums. Most contain covers of hits songs of the day and I've had them running non-stop for the entire time I've been writing this chapter... and they are glorious. Go on, give them a listen, I guarantee you won't be disappointed. This is called sharing the pain!

There's a number of original songs on the albums as well as the covers, often with a sci-fi theme, and Grean wrote most of them. Now before we move on, I'd like to ask, how is it we've been mocking William Shatner's 'singing' performances for years (as he was clearly having fun at his own expense), yet no one has roasted Nimoy for these more sincere efforts?

Grean later broke into the charts himself when he released his own sci-fi hit, a cover of the theme from the long running Canadian supernatural soap opera, Dark Shadows. 'Quentin's Theme' by the Charles Randolph Grean Sound would reach #13 on the Billboard charts and #3 on the easy listening charts...and it was a cover...from a monster-based soap opera. What were people taking in the 60s? Oh right, everything!

And finally we get to why we're here. These were not Grean's first hits. Two decades earlier he released a horror novelty tune that not only made #1 - it stayed there for eight weeks.

BOOM BOOM BOOM

The Thing is one of those pieces of musical novelty nonsense... that flash across the musical firmament from time to time and then, just as quickly disappear... is how one Australian newspaper described the song by Grean, with a tune likely based on an old English folk song 'The Lincolnshire Poacher'. Though he wrote the song, it was actually performed by several artists who released a number of versions in a very short time. This includes Danny Kay and Australian orchestra leader Les Welch. Years later Ray Charles and Batman himself, Adam West, also recorded their own covers. Yet it was the initial Phil Harris release, recorded on October 13, 1950, that would reach #1.

Though the top 100 hadn't really begun yet, records show THE THING reached the top spot on many lists like the Best Sellers in Stores, Most played by Jockeys, and Most Played in Jukeboxes. This success is astonishing as it was taking on some serious heavy weights at the time. In the same charts were songs by Bing Crosby, Frank Sinatra and Eddie Fisher (Princess Leia's dad).

> While I was walkin' down the beach one bright and sunny day
> I saw a great big wooden box a-floatin' in the bay
> I pulled it in and opened it up and much to my surprise
> Ooh, I discovered a, right before my eyes
> Ooh, I discovered a, right before my eyes

I was surprised how many versions were recorded of this silly song in such a short time. The reason? Grean had peddled the song's rights to a publication house, which in turn sold the song to anyone with coin to spend as the original version rocketed up the charts.

New novelty tune, "The Thing"...by RCA Victor's artists and repertory chief Charles Grean, has been picked up for publication by Howie Richmond following bids for the song from several major pubs. It's understood that Richmond, who has had a string of novelty tracks ranging from "Music, Music, Music" to "Goodnight Irene" since he opened shop early this year, gave Grean a $4,000 advance for the tune (Variety, November 1950).

This explains why so many other artists were able to release their own version so soon after the Harris single hit the airwaves.

The Song

Soon everyone was dancing to the #1 song on the pop charts, a tune about an indescribable (possible Alien?) horror that a man finds in a box on the beach one day. In fact, every time the song goes to mention what's in the box, the singer stops, and all the listener can hear is a drumbeat: BOOM BOOM BOOM.

The man then carries the box to someone he knows who buys odd stuff, but when the shopkeeper see's the THING he threatens the man with the cops unless he takes it away. Next the man goes home, where his wife won't allow him inside while he has the Thing in the box. The story goes on, with the man constantly trying to rid himself of THE THING, but everyone sends him away. Finally, the man dies and heads to meet St Peter, who takes one look in the box and orders the man 'down below'.

> The moral of this story is, if you're out on the beach
> And you should see a great big box, and it's within your reach
> Don't ever stop and open it up, that's my advice to you
> 'Cause you'll never get rid of the, no matter what you do
> Oh, you'll never get rid of the, no matter what you do
> BOOM BOOM BOOM

For about a year the song seemed to be everywhere, and for a simple reason. It was fun and it allowed other companies to attach themselves to the tune and try and cash in on its popularity, which in turn drove its presence during 1950/51 to even greater heights.

The song is interesting but for us why the tune has its own chapter is what it spawned. The numerous publicity stunts initiated to cash in on the song's popularity are legion and began with the record company itself.

Cashbox (or Cash box) Magazine was an entertainment publication that ran from 1942 to 1996 – and has recently been revived as an online tabloid. Though it concentrated on music production, the magazine also covered items such as Jukebox charts and the amusement arcade industry. The cover of the Dec 9th, 1950, issue carried a photo with three men standing in front of a TWA passenger airliner. In front of the three is a large box with the RCA record label logo stencilled across the front. Painted in rough white letters over this, however, were the words THE THING, with a ghostly question mark hovering over the entire box. Attached was a small label.

Phil Harris looks mighty curious as he gets his first glimpse of "The Thing"... Shipped from New York by Victor A & R Director, Charles Grean, creator of that amazing Thing, the box was transported under armoured guard to the airport, and then flown by TWA to Hollywood in a sealed plane. Waiting at the west coast terminal, prepared to brave whatever arrived, were (left to right), Henri Rene, A & R man for victor, Phil Harris, and Bill Bullock....No one who saw "The Thing" is telling what it is but there's a malicious rumour going about the country that Phil has been trying to get rid of a box containing----"

And so began an avalanche of promotions across the world to promote the song and whatever could be attached to it. DISPLAY WORLD magazine – yes, a magazine for stores and businesses who needed to create window displays - wrote glowingly about a new exhibit in California.

...Capitalizing on the popularity of "The Thing" of musical fame, the store camouflaged a main floor counter to simulate a large crate with an open top. A big black lock hung at the front, and fishermen's netting draped at one side of the cover gave the effect of the box having just been dragged up from the ocean deep with all its buried treasure. "The Thing," in this case, was an unusual little item, a "tie full of hidden fashion tricks,"... Lettered on the inside of the crate's cover was the legend "We've opened the box and here's The Thing!" (Vol 58 Iss 3).

In Massachusetts, a local paper described how a: *WFGM disk jockey, is shown with the winning entries in his "Thing" contest in which he asked contestants to draw pictures of what their imaginations led them to believe "The Thing" was. In five days over three hundred drawings, ranging from juvenile scrawls to professional pen and ink drawings were received. The prize was —you guessed it—a record of Phil Harris' "The Thing".*

NBC-TV ran a campaign over Christmas indicating the Thing in the box was everyone's goodwill to help people in need, hoping they could boost the Christmas Spirit that season. To back this spot up Harris was slated to appear on as many TV Christmas shows as possible.

The channel kept up the pressure, with NBCs Dan Seymour interviewing the man who'd bought the song from Grean. Howard Richmond: *explained how frenzied he has been driven by people wanting him to identify the 'thing,' and songwriter Charles Grean...whom the cameras found cowering behind a couch to avoid curious 'Thing' singers. The show then brought on Leo Sunnee, who played the tune on a bass fiddle while standing on his head, and Salvadore Dali, the surrealist artist, who was... supposedly on the edge of a tall building* (Variety, December 1950). Dali then refused to reveal what The Thing was when asked and jumped off the set.

Cashbox Magazine also carried the results of other such promotions, announcing the winner of a DC radio station's competition to describe what the box held was Mrs. Dorothy Davis, who identified The Thing as Chloe. This was an old jazz song about someone searching for their lost love in a swamp.

Chloe was written in 1927 and has been recorded by numerous jazz singers over the years, including Louis Armstrong. I'm not sure if there's any real link between both songs... but I'm willing to make one. If you listen to the early versions of Chloe - they begin with very spooky music and the heavy thud on the beat by the orchestra. To my ear this echoes the later BOOM BOOM BOOM describing the Thing and potentially was the reason the winner had associated both songs. Armstrong's version also hit the radio waves in 1952, perhaps cashing in on this new horror novelty song craze created by The Thing a year earlier and the similarities of both tunes? Mrs. Davis won $75 worth of prizes and two parrot feathers...so that's kinda' weird.

In LIFE magazine readers guessed what was in the box in their letter section, claiming the Thing was *a television set/a stack of Goodnight Irene records/Stalin's moustache/A Texan...*

During halftime at the 1951 Rose Bowl the University of Michigan Marching Band claimed they knew what the Thing was in the box, and as one of the musicians announced it was Christmas presents, the other band members formed a train and began choo-chooing down the field.

In Australia the Sun Newspaper reported in December 1950 that *nearly 300,000 records of America's newest hit, The Thing, have been sold in a week... The* same article later explained that as part of an on-air promotion, a *disc jockey... asked listeners to identify the object and send it in."* To the radio stations people sent *"two truckloads of things, including a piece of an old mast, part of an old prow, oil paintings, junk jewellery.* I could not find any follow up report to explain what they did with all these 'Things' once they arrived.

The Daily News also reported a similar story but added how the song had thousands: *especially teenagers — worried. But nobody knows what it is. The thing that is worrying people is a "pop" tune known as The Thing (which doesn't help much in identifying it). The tune has swept Perth with an air of mystery. People who have heard the number — it is played several times a day — ask each other. "What is the Thing?" ... A local radio "disc jockey"... last week asked listeners to telephone the station to say what they thought the Thing was. Dozens of replies were received...An unkind listener suggested that it could have been the "disc jockey" himself. Other suggestions: A skunk, a boxful of mothers-in-law, a barrel of beer, or the Harry Lime theme — played, of course, on the zither.*

The song was becoming so famous that record stores sold out. This led to an unusual event when shops like Hollis Music in New York took out ads in Variety Magazine, announcing when they had the single back in stock. One article from Down Under really brought home just how big a sensation the song had become, heralding its arrival like it was the second coming of Jesus.

Look out for The Thing... the paper explained in a way only an Aussie newspaper could. *Aired for the first-time last Saturday and played over several stations since, the new novelty song, The Thing, is likely to sweep Australia like a plague of measles.*

The Thing is one of those pieces of musical novelty nonsense... that flash across the musical firmament from time to time and then, just as quickly disappear. The article then noted something interesting. *Les Welch has recorded it for Pacific, and it will be several weeks before the Phil Harris recording is heard here.* And a final note. *The song 'has little to recommend it musically' and 'several radio stations are cooperating in a 'The Thing' competition, in aid of the Crippled Children's Society.* Well, that's nice.

This means in Australia the local version was released before the original Harris single arrived. This was later followed by a French language version called 'L Objet, sung incredibly cheerfully (when you think what happens in the song) by Maurice Chevalier. At the same time in London Teresa Brewer was working *fast to get its version of "The Thing" to the counters.*

A 1985 book called 'Million selling records from the 1900s to the 1980s' explains The Thing by Harris *reached 1,000,000 by 1951... and Variety reported it sold 400,000 in ten days, then an all-time record for Victor... This disc was No 1 for four weeks in the USA and four weeks in the bestsellers...RCA Victor ordered a gold-plated disk of 'The Thing', proof that the Phil Harris etching had passed the 1,000,000 mark.*

The song had become a global phenomenon and THING mania was creeping into almost every aspect of life. For example, Fire Engineering Magazine reported in 1951 the White Plains fire department had announced that everyone could stop worrying, they knew what The Thing was. It was the weld on an old fire truck's ladder. In Melbourne the ARGUS newspaper disclosed that the Army will troop The Thing at the 4th Field Ambulance annual ball as its...*said to be a valuable aid in field dressing.*

Forbes Magazine declared The Thing was a new television devise from CROSLEY that allowed a set to pick up UHF signals. The Coronet magazine announced the US Airforce *wheeled the "Thing" out. Except that it had no propeller, it was an airplane... ...in fact it was their first jet aircraft.* The Riverine Herald announced: *There had been "two blockages in the sewerage mains during the past month... 'One blockage had been caused by tree roots but out of the second had come the "thing".*

The mysterious creature had also made its way into schools and hospitals. The Northern Neck News (9 March 1951) explained at the local school's yearly variety show *the identity of "The Thing" was revealed at the show when a group of high school students sang the song and did the pantomime.* The West Australian newspaper noted that victims of poliomyelitis [Polio] were having *instruction on the machine...nicknamed 'The Thing',* which incorporated, *leg exercises with chest and stomach massage and has a hand-operated vibrator for deep seated massage.*

The A.P.O.A Mental Hospital Service Bulletin announced: *ST. ELIZABETHS HOSPITAL...were entertained in February by...Essentially a talent show for the patients...In the first scene of the fantasy, the hero finds on the beach a box which contains "The Thing."... A series of adventures follows in which he attempts unsuccessfully to sell "The Thing" and then rid himself of it, first in a pawn shop, then in Hell and in Heaven.*

Helping some of the more vulnerable of societies individuals is great and it sounds like everyone had fun – they even moved the show throughout the hospital for those who were incapable of attending – HOWEVER - considering what subject this book is about, one line caught me as distinctly troubling. *During the process ample opportunity was provided for demonstration of a variety of talents among the patients, particularly their capacity for mimicry of some of the better known staff physicians...* I wonder if any of their patients were survivors from Outpost #31?

The song was also showing up in sports. In 1952 the Saturday Evening Express announced golfer Eric Cremin had 'The Thing': *He refers, of course, to the new centre-shafter putter.* The Suffolk News-Herald recounted: *North Caroline U. track coaches are experimenting with music as an aid in training their runners, claiming it improves their cadence... With a tongue in cheek tone, the newspaper noted the university could probably "create some sprint records by having a juke box playing "The Thing" at the starting line.*

Though clearly a joke, this single line suggests not everyone was a fan, an issue with all such novelties songs. Think Baby Shark, techno frog, Aga Doo, Barbie Girl and Disco Duck - these songs when they catch the public's imagination can seemingly be everywhere, on the radio, as part of a TV ad, as muzak in an elevator or supermarket, and that bombardment of annoying, often ludicrous lyrics can often cause a visceral, guttural reaction to the tune. Some newspapers had already warned that the song was likely to spread like measles, and just like the measles, people were not happy when they caught the tune. The Daily News noted: *this song was barred in England...Since this was not done for moral reasons, it is quite probable that authorities feared a rising of Scottish nationalism, and that this song was part of their propaganda.*

I'm not sure if this is true by the way as I've found no record of the song being banned in the UK. What I did find was the song was released in 1951 on the label His Masters Voice, so if it was banned it was likely the UK version, and not the original.

It wasn't just the Phil Harris single that people hated either, famous singers like Bing Crosby/Fred Astaire recorded their own, and in 1951 Down Beat Magazine wrote a backhanded compliment about Danny Kayes version: *This Thing is the least obnoxious of all the Things because it does not attempt to be anything other than a disc to cover Decca when a request is made for popular music's latest blight tune...the reverse is strictly a children's record and indicates the mind age Decca feels is susceptible to The Thing.*

Talking about the song could also be dangerous. *An argument over the identity of "The Thing" chilled conjugal love...In Toronto, a...Canadian...told her husband "The Thing" was a song; he told her "The Thing" was her face; whereupon she attacked him with a butcher knife* (America: A Catholic Review of the Week 1951).

Other than the moronic husband who called his wife's face 'The Thing' there are a few more victims of the song's popularity. One of the longest running plays on Broadway was HARVEY, that tale of Elwood P Dowd and his invisible friend, the giant rabbit-like sprite, Harvey. Written by Mary Chase, in 1949 the playwright had been rehearsing her new piece *"Mr. Thing" at her Denver home, and hies to Broadway shortly to submit it to producers, It has no connection with her first legit hit, "Harvey", or with the currently popular song and shooting film, both titled "The Thing".*

When the play reached Broadway in 1954 it was renamed 'Mrs. McThing?' Perhaps the growing fame of the song and recent hit movie (first promoted with the same name) made the play's producers change the title?

It wasn't just companies either that were cashing in on the growing Thing craze. Comics were big business for newspapers and magazines in the 50s, and many started to fill with jokes and cartoons based around the song. Dagwood talked about the Thing… and the infamous horror cartoonist Charles Addams did a Thing joke in his ongoing Addams Family. The cartoon is set on a beach with a grinning Fester opening a mysterious box and a crowd of people and beasts all fleeing in terror.

The cartoon would later be converted into the Addams Family TV show and several films. Now is it a coincidence that just a few years later the series suddenly contained a new character that would grow into a real fan favourite, the disembodied hand called Thing T. Thing? Weirdly, Thing was originally not just a hand but a hideous creature always seen out of focus in the background of the cartoons, so I'm calling it…everyone's favourite disembodied hand is now firmly placed in the Thing franchise. I bet in the upcoming Thing film there'll be a scene of the discarded hand creeping around like some demonic alien spider to prove my theory correct.

It's impossible to explain today just how big the song was becoming. Numerous sources claim 'The Thing' as a common phrase even entered the language thanks to the tune (and possibly the movie). I've looked and cannot find any evidence this was the case, though doing a phrase search by date shows it most certainly wasn't a common saying before the 1950s. You know something has had a serious impact when it becomes an everyday common phrase.

Grean became a very minor celebrity, but Harris became something of a movie star, with studios immediately cashing in on the song's popularity. Within a year Harris appeared in Thunder Across the Pacific, and in one scene he sang The Thing, meaning the song was highlighted in a movie during the same year that The Thing From Another World was released. Now this was a war movie, so watching Harris sing dressed in a military uniform, inside a military building, surrounded by military equipment, well, knowing how Hollywood works, surely someone at some point must have suggested the song should have been in the Hawks film? A few years later Harris appeared alongside the Duke himself, John Wayne, in The High and the Mighty. Arguably he then reached even greater fame when he became a voice actor for Disney, and in 1967 voiced Baloo in The Jungle Book. I'd argued The Thing wasn't Harris's most famous song, it was 'The Bare Necessity'.

Was The Thing The Thing?

The one missing piece of this puzzle is the possibility that the song's author, Charles Grean, had been inspired by news of an upcoming Howard Hawks movie called The Thing for his song? Hawks film was to be based on Campbell's story 'Who Goes There?', so did Grean write and rush out his ditty before the movie (which clearly takes some time to film and distribute) hit the silver screen? Honestly, I have no idea.

As we'll see in the next chapter, the 1951 Howard Hawks film was being heavily promoted and talked about by the world's various media, so it's entirely possible this is exactly what Grean did, meaning the song should officially be part of the 'Who Goes There' library of inspired works…but there's just no letter or interview from the song's author admitting that's what happened. That being said, I'd like to put the argument forward that this is exactly the case, and for evidence I present an odd occurrence that happened just a few years later.

In the 1950s a new exercise craze was sweeping Australia. Women were being encouraged to take a bamboo hoop and swing it around their hips to help them stay in shape. Joan Anderson brought one of these hoops back from Australia in 1957 and called it a 'Hula-Hoop' after the way Hawaiian girls danced with their hips. This hoop was shown to Arthur Melin, owner of Wham-o toys, who stole the idea, cutting the Anderson family out of any profits and unleashing the plastic Hula Hoop on the world. Within a year the world went Hula crazy – with millions of hoops being sold (an estimated 100 million in two years).

An article called 'Hula Balloo' in the September 1958 issue of TIME magazine takes up the story.

On Labor Day weekend, a pop lyricist named Charles Grean (The Thing, Sweet Violets) was placidly cruising Long Island Sound in his 2-ft skiff when he was struck by an inspiration. "With this hoop craze," he thought, "there's bound to be a song. Somebody ought to move fast!" Grean raced ashore and started to move. Next day he took his already completed lyrics around to his pal, Composer Bob Davie, and within an hour the two of them had batted out 'a simple little teenage song with a good rock 'n' roll melody," named it Hoopa Hoola.

That was Monday. Tuesday morning the song was accepted by Atlantic Records. Tuesday night Grean flew to Chicago to have his touring wife, Singer Betty Johnson, record it. Rushing the Dubs. She learned the song in 15 minutes, recorded it in a dozen takes in the early hours of Wednesday morning. Atlantic rushed the tapes into production, cutting enough "dubs" (sample acetate disks for immediate use, good for 15 to 20 plays) to give the New York disk jockeys a preview hearing (Grean also dispatched a pretty secretary to demonstrate the hoop motion to local deejays).

Two days later the completed records started coming into Atlantic's New York offices, were promptly funnelled out to a list of 2,500 key disk jockeys about the country. Atlantic distributors started setting up deejay hoop contests through the Middle West. Scarcely more than a week after Lyricist Grean landed, his song was on the market ahead of the competition, and the painful fruits of his inspiration were assaulting ears across the land...

Three more songs based on hula hoops hit the airways within weeks, but Grean had beaten everyone to the punch...and that's my point. Grean was clearly looking for pop-culture fads to attach a novelty song to and cash in, and he repeated this exact process numerous times...as previously mentioned, FIVE Nimoy albums during the Star Trek years.

Here we have evidence of his process just a few years after he wrote 'The Thing'. I believe the music producer heard that a new, big budget Sci-Fi film - the first in some years - was about to be released by of all people, Howard Hawks. The film was called 'The Thing' and was about some mysterious alien creature. Inspired by the name and premise Grean wrote a song to cash in on the alien craze he hoped would be following.

The TIME article also pointed out the results if you were slow cashing in on such fads, explaining the last hula song to be released: *trailed the field by about five days...A production push of the kind the hula hoopsters have been engaged in can send costs soaring to five times what they usually are. To absorb that kind of expense requires a major hit... and none of the hula songs yet recorded seem likely to go that far. "It's beginning to look," said one weary A. & R. man last week, "like everybody got carried away with the whole thing".*

It's my opinion Grean's song was based on the upcoming film that, as we shall soon see, was already being heavily publicised. Therefore, we need to add yet another product to The Thing franchise before we get to Hawk's movie, one that cashed in on not only the song's popularity but another growing fad.

Though we think of them as a 70s phenomenon, pinball machines in one shape or another have been around for centuries. They really took off though when electronic coin-operated machines appeared in the 1930s. Just a few years before the song hit, the games became even more popular when the first flippers appeared, changing everything. Reading some of the magazines produced at the time to promote these games to buyers, it's amazing to read how they advertised hot machines with special features at specific locations, as though hordes of pinball players were scouting such periodicals for the best machines and then hunted them down to play.

With the popularity of the song, a Chicago based pinball company released THE THING – a game with artwork hinting at the story in the song and not the movie about to premier. Looking at the pinball artwork, there isn't a lot to suggest an alien, instead it's about the mystery of what's in the box, with a little devil ducking about, seemingly tempting everyone to open the crate.

Numerous magazines crowed about the game, explaining how many flippers and bumpers it had, and that when a player got their ball into the box they'd hear BOOM BOOM BOOM. It's clearly based on the song, in turn inspired by the movie.

PART TWO
The Film

It's hard to understand today just what society was like after the Second World War. People had been beaten and bruised, loved ones killed, with the horrors of the conflict flickering across their movie screens and blaring out of their radios. Newspapers had been full of doom and gloom and most of the world was either rebuilding their lives and homes or still under strict restrictions.

Cinema in the post war years was equally bleak – full of noir and crime. People were starting to look for something to distract themselves with, and the news that one of Hollywood's top directors was putting some serious effort into a beloved science fiction property had a lot of people excited.

The entire Thing franchise began with Campbell, but for many of us of a certain age our first encounter with the story was on a tv watching an old black and white movie. Today Howard Hawks name is slipping from memory, and that's criminal. The man is as important as Spielberg, Nolan, Ephron, Scott, Mann, Ford, Fincher, Bigelow, Scorsese, Hitchcock, Cameron, Lee, Tarantino, Kubrick and a hundred others whose name means quality and excitement. The fact that you recognise those names and know intimately the films they made tells you how important these directors are – and Hawks deserves to be lauded along with them.

A little research shows that Parade.com has a list of their top 75 directors (their #1 is Spielberg), the Guardian UK's top 40 begins with David Lean (a great choice), Screenrant's top 10 has Hitchcock at #1 and Filmlifestyle's Best Movie Directors of All Time: The Essential Guide starts with Kubrick. Scouring through these lists, almost every single one forgot to mention Howard Hawks.

Why is this a crime? Well, between 1926 and 1970 Hawks filmed forty movies – and many of these are considered the very pinnacle of their genre. You want a screwball comedy? How about His Girl Friday or I Was a Male War Bride? How about a western, we have Rio Bravo/Rio Lobo (they're the same film after all) or Red River. Up for a war movie? Well, there's Sergeant York...or how about the gold standard of classic Hollywood, a Film Noir? There's Bogart in The Big Sleep – a story I love so much I based my first novel Brotherhood of the Dragon on it.

This man defined and tops so many genres, yet his name is melting away like the block-of-ice encasing a certain alien. Let's change that because there's another genre that Hawks also topped.

Late in 1950 RKO Radio announced it had three 'exploitation specials' for release, with *one in April, May and June will be given extensive campaigns, based on maximum use of publicity, advertising and local showmanship*. Shortly after, the world's tabloids filled with reports that one of Hollywood's most respected directors was heading one of these projects. In November, The Suffolk News-Herald announced they had the: *low-down on Howard Hawks' hush-hush scientific adventure story. It's about a creature from another planet captured at an army scientific laboratory near the north pole. The Thing – only Hawks knows what it looks like, and he won't talk.*

'Exploitation' is a strange term that doesn't seem to fit well in a modern mind. To me exploitation suggests a 70s film with an African American sporting a wicked afro, karate kicking some bad-mamma-jamma in the mamma-jammas. 70s Blaxploitation films are obvious exploitation films...it's in the name after all.

As a rule, exploitation films attempt to find success by associating themselves with a current trend, highlight a very specific and often overlooked genre, or contains fetish content for a specific market. They often include subjects like drug use, gore, sex, destruction and more often than not, are international films made cheaply.

For example, there's a whole genre called Ozplotation, covering many films made in Australia in the 70s and 80s – and according to the documentary 'Not Quite Hollywood' - a real favourite of Quentin Tarantino. Giallo films are Italian-made slasher flicks, Chop-socky are Hong Kong martial arts movies. The most famous are Spaghetti Westerns - so named because they were Italian - and slasher films, which seem to have overtaken the entire horror genre recently. The most profitable exploitation films are from this latter genre. Evil dead, Mad Max – and one of the most profitable independent/exploitation films ever made, John Carpenter's Halloween.

We'll come back to exploitation films later, but even the highest quality of these movies are considered 'B' pictures – meaning Hollywood considers them something less than their best. Many are placed under more generalised categories – some nice like 'cult' or 'arthouse', while other labels were deliberately far worse to create backlash and fear against a film. Words like obscene and pornography eventually morphed into new labels such as England's 'video-nasties'.

Often because of their material or because they weren't constrained by the rigid structure many studios insisted on, exploitation films became important milestones triggering whole new genres or 'waves' of similar, but larger budgeted films in response to their sudden popularity. As early as 1951 Variety's Jay Allen recognised this pattern.

CYCLE EVIL

Literary agents are frantically beating the bushes in Hollywood to uncover stories along the line of RKO's "the Thing"... in order to meet the "demand" for films of that ilk that has sprung up in the wake of...[its]... great box office success...A leading agent declares that he has been so deluged by requests for such story properties that he can sell them almost sight unseen. In other words, Hollywood once again has come to the erroneous conclusion that because one picture is a success, all other pictures of a like nature will be equally enthusiastically received by the paying customers.

Instead of concluding, because "The Thing" made money when other films were dying on the vine, that the public wants to see horror films...it would be wise to examine ALL of the pictures which have earned big profits during this time of business doldrums and set about determining one important fact. What one essential trait do those money-making pictures have in common?"

The answer the article concluded? Each successful film *has been or promised to be, different*. A great example of this cycle was the cheaply made Halloween. When the film hit the screen its popularity grew and the money poured in. We know other studios were enviously watching this success, especially against plummeting ticket sales at the time.

It's not that the studios were making bad films, but thanks to the rise in popularity of TV, music – even pinball – the future was looking bleak, and that doesn't include the coming tsunami called home video on the horizon. The established studios needed quick money and were soon producing their own horror films. They were cheap to make as you didn't need to spend big bucks on an established movie star because these films didn't require that kind of publicity to succeed. It was the hook that got the kids to buy a ticket – often literally, all bloody and dangling from the stump of a physically deformed serial killer.

For decades the world had been censored. TV had rigid rules and edited scenes out of movies they deemed inappropriate, even comic books had been strangled by the Comics Code Authority since the early 1950s. Yet suddenly there was a wave of seemingly dangerous, unfiltered movies at the cinema (and video store) that parents seemed to be oblivious too – and the kids devoured them.

Halloween spawned massive franchises like Friday the 13th and Nightmare on Elm St., but I'd argue this horror cycle began with Howard Hawks and The Thing From Another World (which from now on I'll just call Thing '51). Yes, there'd been earlier examples of exploitation films like the Universal monsters, but these had long since disappeared, or they were cheaply made social issue titles like 1936's Reefer Madness. What Hawks did was make a seemingly mainstream exploitation film that sparked a generation of similar movies.

Today an 'A' director stepping into the sci-fi genre wouldn't get a second glance, but in the 1950s this was unheard of. Hawks clearly knew he was taking a chance and would later explain why.

During WW2, no matter where he went he encountered young soldiers devouring quickly disposable media in the form of comic books and pulp novels. I covered the effects of this flood of American media to the rest of the world in my book 'Horror'. The deluge of American culture into countries like England and Australia had caused serious concern and many governments had taken steps to end their import. Bans on US magazines, comics, books and movies were growing, evidence why a director like Hawks taking on such a property was raising eyebrows.

Hawks had an unnatural ability to pick stories the public enjoyed, and later explained by producing Thing '51 he was aware this was likely starting something new.

The trick of this type of film opens a vast story market. Because the subject matter is involved with that which is unknown, science fiction stories permit the use of new and different plot structures in the writing of screenplays…It is important that we don't confuse the Frankenstein-type of film with the science-fiction picture.

Hawks then explained the difference.

The first film is an out-and-out horror thriller based on that which is impossible. The science-fiction film is based on that which is unknown, but given credibility by the use of scientific facts… Forgetting that almost every Hollywood studio has at least one science-fiction story on its production agenda, one need only check the growing popularity of the science-fiction magazines to learn of the ever-increasing demand for this type of literature (American Cinematographer, January 1991).

Coming from the war and seeing what young soldiers were reading, Hawks sensed the next big thing was science fiction. In 1948 he found himself in Heidelberg filming 'I was a Male War Bride' and surrounded by the US army occupying Germany. One day as Hawks trolled through everything the local PX offered (an army base store that offered US goods to soldiers stationed overseas) he discovered a copy of Astounding Science Fiction magazine containing John W. Campbell, Jr's 'Who Goes There?' He later recounted what happened next to film director and Hawks protégé – Peter Bogdanovic.

I bought the story; it was just four pages long, and we took about a week to write it. We had trouble the first two days finding a way of telling the story. Finally, we got the idea of the reporter and we told it through his eyes.

'Who Goes There' is not four pages long, it's a large novelette, so that's a weird description. Maybe the tyranny of time had played a trick on the directors' memory? Things became clear though when I found an interview Hawks gave the French magazine, Cahiers du cinema.

We wrote the script in four and a half days. I had read the story...in Heidelberg... We only used four pages from it. I bought the rights and hired two good screenwriters. The story interested me because I thought it was an adult treatment of an often-infantile subject.

The last part of that statement is a little weird until you understand the pressure Hollywood had been placing on Hawks when he first announced the project. Here was one of the industries greatest directors, who'd brought to screen numerous beloved films such as The Big Sleep and Bringing up Baby, and he was about to embark on a project that was considered beneath such an artist.

Richard Keinen was Hawks script clerk on the film, and when he was interviewed in 1982 he recalled: *We all thought this was the dumbest thing we'd ever heard of. We thought, 'What is Howard Hawks doing making this stupid horror film?'*

Part of the issue was sci-fi films were cheaply made 'B' films. In December 1951, the Suffolk News-Herald reported on how just this classification system had begun to fail Hollywood.

NOT "B" NOR "A" —JUST GOOD B-MOVIES, the studios are yelling, must be eliminated because of TV competition. Only super colossal A's can keep the box office jingling. Yet many of the great box office hits of the last few years were B pictures.... "The Thing" and numerous others. As the Screen Producers Guild contends so rightly: "To arbitrarily class these as B pictures because the people who made them used their heads and didn't waste money is unfair. It's a budgetary terminology and nothing more." Isn't it time for Hollywood to eliminate both A and B pictures —and produce just GOOD pictures?

Getting back to Hawks work on the film. The director claimed they only used four pages from the original Campbell story, and that's obvious to anyone who saw the movie and read the book. Hawks and his writers Charles Lederer - with some uncredited work done by long time Hawks collaborator, Ben Hecht – harvested just the basic elements they wanted from the novelette and then wrote their own story on top of this.

Now I'm going to admit there's some speculation following, simply because there's so few firsthand documents out there and almost no one left alive that had anything to do with the film. There's also a lot of articles and interviews that either directly contradict each other or hint at information and answers to questions we may have – but I'll make sure I highlight the difference between fact and possibility when we get there.

For example, there's a suggestion it was the scriptwriters, Hecht and Lederer, who knew the quality of Campbell's story, and it was they who showed it to Hawks. Lederer wrote the script for 'I Was a Male War Bride', so he was likely on hand in Germany to hand it to Hawks, but was far as I can see Hecht played no part in finding the book...

...however, there's an odd biography by William MacAdams called 'Ben Hecht: the man behind the legend'. In this Williams records Hawks asking Hecht about their next project.

"How about doing a science-fiction story?"

Hecht said no.

"But what if we call it The Thing from Another World and tell the story of a guy from another planet who's a vegetable that lives on human blood?"

"In that case, okay," Hecht agreed...

We'll come back to Hecht and this strange recounting of how the story began later.

Myth: For years there's been a persistent rumour that one of the kings of all science fiction media – the man himself who terrorised the US with a simple radio program, had helped write part of Thing '51. In 1980, Starburst Magazine #22 wrote an article about '51 and noted: *Orson Welles is also supposed to have lent a hand in the shooting.* Welles certainly had the chops to make the movie a success, but did he have anything to do with the film? There's absolutely no evidence this was the case, and this wasn't even the first time such a relationship was claimed between Hawks and Welles either. In 1973 the Take One Magazine asked Hawks about the director of Citizen Kane.

Q: *Orson Welles claims to have contributed a great deal to the script of I Was a Male War Bride. Is that true?*

HAWKS: *I have no knowledge of any contribution that Orson made. As a matter of fact, the first script that I read was a horrible thing... we (Joe Schenck) completely rewrote the whole script, and I never saw Orson during that time, so I don't think he had anything to do with the final picture.*

If Orson had ever worked with Hawks the director would likely have admitted it here, so its unlikely Welles had any roll making the Thing '51 or any Hawks film.

In a later interview Hawks explained how he worked with his writers to get the strong dialogue that would be the hallmark of his films, as well as some of the odd twists and turns they contain. It also explains why only the core of Campbell's original story is recognisable in the film.

...when Hecht and MacArthur and I used to work on a script, we'd sit in a room and work for two hours and then we'd play backgammon for an hour. Then we'd start again and one of us would be one character and one would be another character. We'd read our lines of dialogue and the whole idea was to try to stump the other people, to see if they could think of something crazier than you could.

Yet none of this explains why Hawks decided The Thing was his next project. I believe for that we need to look at the three-picture deal with RKO he'd recently signed. As Hawks was completing his part of the contract the studio gained a new owner, the infamous Howard Hughes.

Known for designing aircraft, Hughes had been trying to buy a film studio for some time, and the ailing RKO was ripe for the plucking. Known for his hardnose business ethics, everyone employed at the studio was concerned for their jobs if he took over. President of RKO, N. Peter Rathvon, noted: *He had a reputation for firing anybody who disagreed with him.*

This proved prophetic as Hughes immediately ordered massive layoffs. He was likely feeling pressure thanks to the success and failures of the jewel in his company crown, TWA airlines. In 1947 TWA lost eight million dollars and Hughes had just borrowed ten million to buy new passenger craft to increase the routes his airline covered.

Many RKO execs quit in protest, but this didn't stop the new owner, who began firing everyone in sight and cancelling almost every project then underway. RKO had been releasing nearly two dozen (mostly 'B') movies a year at this point, and that number fell to less than ten once Hughes took command. By the time the takeover was complete, nearly three-quarters of RKO's staff had been fired.

The studios fortunes had risen and fallen over the last few years. It had a few successes, but also had its share of failures. There was also the rise of McCarthyism, with a congressional hearing into communism in Hollywood already labelling RKO as: *a hotbed of Red subversion.*

Isadore 'Dore' Schary was one of those still in charge at RKO, and he instantly clashed with the new owner. Hughes was a renowned antisemite, and the Jewish Dore was known for not backing down from a bully. Rumours indicate when employer and employee first met, they both pointed out they'd heard that they didn't like each other. Dore ended the conversation by asking *do you want to talk about rumours or business?* Impressed, Hughes then said Dory was in charge as he had no time and had no intention of interfering with the studio.

This promise didn't even last a single film. Dore reported his next movie would be Battleground and Hughes immediately fired off a memo. *The public's fed up with war...They'd much rather see a romantic comedy. Drop it!*

The man running RKO then knew his time was up when he was called into another face-to-face meeting with Hughes, who was naked and with a young girl in his bedroom. Hughes then did what has to be one of the world's greatest dick power moves by claiming he was constipated and then sat on the toilet for an hour, insisting Dore talk to him through the door.

The head of RKO quit, and within a short time was running RKOs' competitor, MGM, replacing Louis B. Meyer himself.

James Whale, the director famous for filming Frankenstein and the Bride of Frankenstein for Universal, gave his own reason why Hughes had been desperate to buy a film studio – and I think we've just seen an instance that it was far more nefarious. Hughes became notorious in Hollywood for his casting couch, and insisted on meeting many of the youngest upcoming actresses looking for a job. *So many, in fact, that Howard found that these women were taking up too much of his time. At one point, he refused to see all "but the most beautiful and the sexiest".* Whale recalled he was *...like a kid in a candy store* and that *Some of the most gorgeous women in the world were making themselves available to him.*

The Two Howards

The animosity between Hawks and Hughes is legendary and went back to 1933 when the director was filming Dawn Patrol starring Douglas Fairbanks Jr. The movie was being proclaimed *the greatest air epic ever!* Hughes took umbrage with this as he believed he was in the process of filming just that.

'Hell's Angels' was going to be something new – and honestly, the film itself became a true Hollywood horror tale and deserves its own book. Depicting aerial fighting over the Western Front, Hughes insisted the film would accurately portray the sense of being in a cockpit during a dogfight. After filming most of the script Hughes saw the world's first talkie and insisted shooting it all again, this time with sound. He then tried to colour some scenes and insisted on such dangerous stunts that four men, three pilots and a mechanic, were killed. Hughes himself became a victim after pushing for a scene that even his stuntmen considered too dangerous. An accomplished pilot, Hughes jumped in the cockpit, and as everyone predicted he crashed, fracturing his skull and requiring some serious plastic surgery. This wouldn't be his last crash either, possibly explaining his deteriorating mental state in later life. This could stem from the pain and injuries suffered during these accidents.

Injured, over budget, over time and with people dying, this pressure seemed to make Hughes increasingly paranoid and be began to believe that elements of his film were being stolen by Hawks for his similar WW1 film 'Dawn Patrol.' It didn't help that both films were sharing pilots. There were also rumours that Hawks was rushing to get his picture finished so that he "could sweep the field first".

Hughes' began secretly hiring some of Hawks crew to spy on the production – offering $500 for each secret they revealed. He then hired the best pilots away from Dawn Patrol. Hawks later recounted that *I had pilots under 'exclusive' contract, and Hughes also had the same pilots under 'exclusive' contract.* Hughes next bought every single available WW1 era plane – something he continued to do even after his film was finished – just so the aircraft weren't available to Hawks

Now the following has been recounted in several Hughes biographies, so who knows if it really happened. Apparently driven to the wall by paranoia, Hughes showed up at Hawks house in the middle of the night. The director later recounted what happened next.

I suddenly woke up with a start realizing an intruder was also persistently ringing my doorbell. I threw open the door to confront Howard Hughes. His blood vessels were popping out of his skin. That was one mad Texas boy, but I wasn't afraid of him at all.

'Howard Hughes here.'

'As if I didn't know who you are...'

'I'm making an air epic, and I'm told you're making a pale imitation of it.'

'We'll battle it out at the box office.'

After a few more insults Hawks slammed the door on Hughes, who stormed away more determined than ever. Next, he hatched a plan with some of the Hells Angel's staff, they were going to find Hawks secretary and bribe her for a copy of the script. Hawks was ready for this move though and had Hughes staff arrested.

Next Hughes sued, insisting Warner bros. had plagiarized his movie to make Dawn Patrol. While the issue was in court Hawks went into editing overdrive and managed to finish his film and screen Dawn Patrol before the case was resolved...

...and here's where things get weird. Despite all this animosity Hawks and Hughes would work together on numerous projects in the future, and their relationship always seemed to end with one screwing over the other. Yet after a few years of bitter words, they'd bury the hatchet and work together again.

It should be pointed out the two men made some iconic films together. Scarface (1931), The Outlaw (1943) – but always the Howards would end their working relationship in controversy and betrayal. This leads us to 1949, when Hawks found himself with a three-picture deal with RKO that was bought by Hughes – who seemed intent on sticking his finger in every one of the company's pies.

Hawks needed a picture to finish his deal with RKO and get away from Hughes. His writers, Lederer and Hecht, got to work by pulling Campbell's original story. 'Who Goes There?', apart. The most important element they took from the book was the feeling of isolation, with a remote group of Americans trapped in a hostile environment and fending off an alien creature they'd accidentally released from a block of ice after finding and destroying the flying saucer it had apparently crashed to earth in.

The basic premise, humanity vs alien, was nothing new, but then outside influences about them started to filter into the story and the writers began creating something unique.

Paranoia

[The Thing from Another World was] ... *seen at the time as fables based on McCarthyism; communists, like victims of The Thing, looked, sounded, and acted like your best friend, but they were infected with a deadly secret.* Roger Ebert's review sums up what so many have written over the years about the movie. It was a product of the Cold War and reflected what society was feeling at the time – that the government was insisting anyone, even those you knew best, may not be what they seemed. Communism was the real threat they claimed, and we had to be on guard less the Red Menace infected the entire world.

I'm not saying their wrong, but we know paranoia is the main theme of the entire Thing franchise – and it all begins with Campbell's original story. We also know what Hawks had previously gone through with Hughes, so maybe there's something far more personal behind these themes? It would seem the director was constantly being hounded by a man he simply did not trust, yet continually found overseeing his career. That would surely make you feel a little paranoid.

The Director

The stories paranoia is based around the idea of not knowing who to trust and the idea of imitations – that characters were not who you thought them to be. For decades The Thing '51 has suffered from this exact affliction, so let's get this out of the way right now. After reading far too many interviews, books, blogs and listening to podcasts and director's commentaries, I'll plant the flag here and now and proudly stand and salute under its flapping banner. Howard Hawks directed The Thing from Another World!

Officially Hawks was only the producer, and he began by looking for who could direct the film. There are some reports *Hawks considered hiring Lederer to direct the project as he'd been working with the scriptwriter for some time* (America's film legacy, Daniel Eagan, 2010). However, Hawks owed someone a great debt and it was time to pay up.

Christian Nyby had been a film editor for many years and had already worked with Hawks on To Have and Have Not (1944) and The Big Sleep (1946). However, it was on Red River (1948) where Hawks felt he owed the editor a serious debt of gratitude.

There's a fantastic record of Nyby's work on Red River, and if you're interested in such things, you can head over to the Criterion website and read the entire story. The cutter was editing a film called Fighter Squadron for Warner Bros. when he got a call from Hawks, who was shooting a western.

The director made his hellos and then told Nyby flat out that he'd put together a rough cut of his new movie and it was terrible. He knew the cutter was busy, but was there any chance he could pop around, have a look and maybe pass on some notes? Nyby agreed and Hawks organised a viewing of this early Red River cut. Afterwards both men sat down for a drink and Hawks asked, "what do you think?"

"It's terrible." Nyby admitted.

Hawks then asked if he could edit the film for him – and Nyby agreed, but only if Hawks could get permission from Warners for him to leave Fighter Squadron. Hawks later contacted Jack Warner directly and together they managed to work out a loan of the editor. Nyby takes up what happened next.

So what I did was work on Fighter Squadron during the day, at the regular hours, and then drive over to Goldwyn and work at night on Red River, from about 6:00 p.m. to about one or two in the morning...I did that for about six weeks, until I finished Fighter Squadron.

Adding to the problem.

*Hawks was using up to eight cameras...with each camera shooting an entire magazine of film, which is one thousand feet each. Dailies up to that time amounted to about half a million feet...It was just an awful lot of film. And more was coming in every day. There must have been 700,000 to 750,000 feet before Hawks was finished...*and Nyby, after an entire day editing another film, sat there and watched every foot Hawks had shot deep into the night.

Hawks had left Nyby with a mountain of seemingly unrelated shots. While the cutter began scouring the dozens of reels, now free the director jumped onboard the Queen Elizabeth to Europe, then on to Germany to begin filming I Was a Male War Bride.

Part of the problem was the way both men worked. Hawks would change things on the fly, adding dialogue or changing his mind entirely about a scene – so the shooting script was not always accurate. That's why Hawks always asked his editor to be on set, to watch and have a firsthand idea of what was happening. For Red River, however, Nyby came into it cold. He had no idea what was happening or why things had been shot the way they were, and he had no way of asking the absent Hawks. Worse still, it seemed the script supervisor, whose job on set was to record any changes and how each shot was made (wide angle, close up etc), had failed to take accurate notes.

All Nyby could do was sit and watch, take his own notes, scheme and plan, and then start splicing the things he felt belonged together to help create a workable narrative. When Nyby was asked how long it took him to fix Red River, he explained: *All together, I was on the film for about a year...*

...A YEAR!

Nyby ploughed through the film Hawks shot and had created a winning story. Is it any wonder when it came to filming the Thing From another World that the director felt he owed an enormous debt to his friend and editor? Nyby had once admitted desiring a director's card for years and Hawks was more than happy to give him that opportunity, and they now had the perfect project to work together on.

Trivia time: Red River, the movie that Nyby saved and would lead to his 'directing' The Thing, was set in 1851 – and The Thing '51 was released exactly one century later. It's the little things that make me happy.

The following is what we can think of as a series of puzzle pieces that, taken individually may not mean that much, but when all their crazy edges are put together, make the larger image clear.

In 1973, Take One Magazine interviewed Hawks and asked him 'the' question.
Q: Is it true that you, rather than Christan Nyby, directed The Thing?
Hawks: I was the producer, and in charge of casting. Chris had been cutter, and I thought he deserved a chance to direct. I thought he did an awfully good job and should have credit for it.

In 1982, Cinefantastique Magazine interviewed Nyby, and brought up his work on the Thing. *I'd edited so many of Howard's films...Howard felt he owed me a favour...I wanted to be a director, Howard knew this, and he helped me get my first credit with The Thing.* Nyby then proved he was getting tired of the question. In 1982 when he was asked once again who directed the film, the editor had a little snap. *That's one of the most inane and ridiculous questions I've ever heard, and people keep asking, 'that it was Hawks' style. Of course it was, this is a man I studied and wanted to be like. You would emulate and copy the master you're sitting under, which I did. Anyway, if you're taking painting lessons from Rembrandt you don't take the brush out of the master's hands.*

We have the principals involved claiming Nyby was the director, so why do I think otherwise? Well, the answers above are a little ambiguous. Read them again, they don't actually say Nyby directed, they explain why he was listed as the director, and when you go through other interviews the issue of who directed becomes even more cloudy...or crystal clear.

Clem Portman was a soundman on the film and recalled: *Chris (Nyby) was in charge of postproduction. I don't remember Howard being in the dubbing room at all. I assumed Howard had stepped aside and let Chris handle things.* This is seemingly evidence Nyby had directed the film, but as we just learnt Hawks rarely cut and edited his movies. Is this why Nyby took such passionate ownership of the film? Certainly, Roland Gross edited the film, but Nyby would have been sitting on his shoulder making many of the decisions, allowing the cutter to take real ownership of the film more than any other he'd worked on.

The following is a list why I think Hawks directed the film.

1. Years later Nyby suggested in an interview he knew another reason why Hawks had chosen him. *Hawks knew he probably couldn't have controlled Lederer as much as he did me.* Now that's a strange word to use by a director. Control? This may not be the best argument by Nyby to prove he was in charge.

2. William Self played the soldier who first saw The Thing when it escaped from the ice. *The controversy of who directed the Thing is interesting. Chris Nyby generally ran the rehearsal, and Hawks stood on the sideline's with his arms folded and watched and listened. Then Chris would go over to Howard, and they would have their private conversation, and Chris would come back and talk to us.* To me it's clear this explains even when Nyby was directing a scene, it was under Hawks direct instructions.

3. Ed Lasker (associate producer): *Nyby didn't direct a thing. One day Howard was late and Chris said 'why don't we get started? I know what the shot should be.' And I said , "No, Chris, I think we'll wait until Howard gets here.*

4. Bill Self (actor): *Chris Nyby was a very nice, decent fellow, but he wasn't Howard Hawks.*

5. Hawks seemed to have been a fair guy, that's why it's a little strange that in the opening credits the font used for Hawk's name is far larger than the 'director' Nyby. Is that because he was letting us all know subliminally that he'd directed it? This leads to a major piece of evidence against Nyby.

6. In the biography 'Howard Hawks: The Grey Fox of Hollywood', Todd McCarthy explains: *Hawks generosity to Nyby did not extend to the protégé's salary; of the 50,000 the RKO contract specified for a directing fee, Hawks parcelled out just $5,40 to Nyby, keeping the remaining $44,040 for himself.* If Hawks truly felt he owed Nyby so much and the editor had indeed directed The Thing as both men insisted, then how is it Nyby was paid just over 10% of the directors' salary? Is it because he only did 10% of the work? If he had done the majority of directing surely Nyby would have stood up for himself and asked for the full amount? To me this is solid proof Hawks directed the film because that's what he paid himself for doing… and the man always got paid.

7. One of the greatest pieces of evidence that Nyby did not direct the movie was his own career. Yes, the editor did become a director thanks to the opportunity Hawks gave him, allowing Nyby to join the Directors Guild. Yet most of his work would be on TV, directing episodes for The Twilight Zone, Lassie, Perry Mason, The Rockford Files, The Six Million Dollar Man, Kojak, Gunsmoke, Bonanza and Rawhide to name just a few. He also directed a handful of feature films like Hell on Devil's Island, Young Fury, Operation C.I.A., and First to Fight. *As a director, I just hoped that I could be like Hawks. Do work as well as he did. That was my goal. I liked to tell things in a straightforward way, from the eye level. And then I liked the feeling of conversation that his characters had, giving the dialogue a little more natural feeling rather than just exchanging lines. It was more of how you'd experience it in life than in a movie, usually, or in a play* (Criterion).

My point? If Nyby directed The Thing and used everything he'd learnt sitting at the feet of Hawks for all those years, why did this ability appear in Thing '51 but never again? Surely those qualities and techniques Nyby had picked up from his mentor should have continued to shine through, yet after 1951 Nyby directed TV shows and low-grade shlock movies and never again attained the ability shown in The Thing.

Finally, the greatest proof comes from Kenneth Tobey, the actor playing the films main character, Captain Patrick Hendry. This man spent more time on set than anyone except the directors and crew. In 1982 Tobey was asked the same question and answered: *Howard Hawks directed The Thing. I remember who said 'Action' and 'Cut,' and to me that's the director...Howard was having some trouble with one of the guilds at the time, so he put Chris' name on it and let him direct one scene in which we all went through a doorway. Howard worked with us every single moment of the shooting. Chris was there observing, but he didn't know how to direct since he'd never directed before. He didn't even know how to communicate with the actors. I subsequently worked with him several times as a director, and he became very good...*

In a different interview Tobey recounted: *A lot of what was being shot was being somewhat adlibbed by Hawkes. On the set he would tell one character to say a line and another to answer over the top, creating the unique dialogue scene The Thing is known for.* Tom Weaver covered this in more detail in his interviews with various THING talent. As I mentioned at the start of this chapter, because this movie was a mainstream exploitation film Hawks may have wanted to distance his name just in case it failed, thus he'd only be known as the producer of a 'B' horror picture, not the director. Tobey's explanation about Hawks having union trouble only helps strengthen the idea that he'd also removed his name to create plausible deniability if it flopped.

For years a hallmark of the director was the way he had his characters delivers snappy dialogue. In an interview Hawks even pointed out how he did it. Basically, he told his actors to start their line just before their fellows finished theirs, that way only the middle, most important part of the sentence could be heard. This gave it a more naturalistic tone. The standard of '51's dialogue would not go unnoticed by reviewers once the film was released. *Before its appearance there is little more than imaginative science talk and off-screen howling from the 'Thing', but the dialogue is a flashy, interesting, erratic jumble reminiscent of disc-jockey chatter* (The Nation, Vol 172).

Decades later Tobey gave a strange interview to Starlog Magazine about this very issue.

A lot of the picture was ad-libbed by the actors when we were sitting around... Howard would ask: 'Ken, what would you say here?' We improvised a lot of scenes that way. For example, we adlibbed the sequence in which we tried to decide how to destroy the creature. We were saying: 'If it's a vegetable, how do you kill it?' We went on in that vein until Maggie Sheridan came up with the famous line: 'You boil it!'

Tobey then claimed his major contribution was even more significant, that it was his idea for the actors to deliver their lines so rapidly that their dialogue overlapped.

I just did that by instinct...Having been on the stage for a long time, I was used to picking up cues pretty quickly. I've always talked rather rapidly. As soon as I understand what the other person is trying to say I have to convey my idea, and very often that leads to overlapping dialogue. The other actors picked up on it and kind of enjoyed it, although some of them couldn't do it quite as easily. It made the movie more realistic, because that's the way many people speak. With that type of fantastic storyline, the more reality the characters have the more believable the movie is.

I'm a little dubious about Tobey's recounting as another source (Cinefantastique, #13/14 1982) refutes this. On the first day of shooting the *cast sat around with Hawks and Nyby: Hawks outlined scenes made dialogue suggestions, gave lines to one, then another. "Ken, You say that, Bob, then you come in with that."*

We know Hawks switched and edited the script on the fly, taking lines from one actor and giving them to another. At one point the mostly inexperience cast became upset at this until Hawks explained that when Gary Cooper or John Wayne got a script, the first thing they did was edit out as many of the words as possible. A good rule to keep a character interesting is make sure they don't have to say or explain too much and weigh their scenes down with exposition. Again, this leads to the obvious conclusion, Hawks was directing and training his actors how to deal with the way he filmed his movies.

Finally, though Hawks stuck to the same story for years he eventually did come clean, explaining that on: *the very first day of working, Chris came in and said 'Look, I'm in trouble. It's a lot different making scenes than taking the stuff you give me and putting it together. I need help.' So I used to be there. I'd come in and watch him rehearse a scene in the morning and I'd say, 'I think I'd tackle it this way.' People say Nyby didn't have anything to do with it. Well, he did have a lot to do with it. But he needed some help* (Howard Hawks: the grey fox of Hollywood).

The answer is simple. Nyby never directed the movie; it was Hawks all the way. Everything about '51, the tight cinema techniques, the strong sense of male community against adversity. The entire film just drips with a certain quality – and it was Hawks who supplied that quality.

The film was heralded as something new, the first sci-fi tale since WW2 began. Hawks also intended to try a few new techniques, so there was a lot that could go wrong. Worse, it may never have found an audience and the potential for the movie being a flop was a very real one. Repaying a debt and giving yourself a little insurance in case things went wrong, well, why not?

CAST

Hawks was looking to make a high quality, big budget film and asked RKO for 1.6 million, but when he explained he was only producing and not directing the film, this was cut to 1.3 million. That was still a substantial budget for 1950, but for a special effects movie to be filmed in a remote location, changes had to be made.

The team realised there was one way to keep costs down. No Stars! Hawks later explained why he hired no named actors in an unusual place, an Australian newspaper called The World's News (10 Mar 1951).

There are producers in Hollywood who will laugh at doing a picture costing that much without using stars to attract fans to the theatre. But before they laugh too loudly, I would like to point out that the money saved by eliminating marquee names will permit us to add an additional £100,000 or better to the production budget for the purpose of improving the quality of the finished product. I'll match perfection to star power any time!

Hawks Women

The most famous part of the casting began in 1945 when Hawks saw an ad in Vogue and noticed the pretty brunette within, so did a little investigation and discovered the woman's name was Margaret Sheridan. He quickly signed her to a personal contract, allowing him to use the actress no matter what studio he worked for in the future. Hawks had uncovered Lauren Bacall and Ella Raines in the same way and made huge stars out of both.

One complaint that does hang around The Thing franchise is the lack of women in the various versions, and that when there is a woman role its little more than a token. I personally think that's a little unfair. Campbell's original story was of its time, and in the 1930s there were no women working at any Antarctica outpost. In fact, the first woman to reach an Antarctic Island was Caroline Mikkelsen in 1935.

Now most horror films of the day had a brave but dull hero (the monster was the star) and a female lead that was just there to be placed in danger, scream, and be rescued. The Thing '51 was never going to be one of those films! Its director was Howard Hawks, and he'd been changing Hollywood for years with a group of actresses known as the 'Hawksian Women'.

Some of Hollywood's most famous voices during its Golden Age began as a lead in a Hawks film. At a time when men seemed to dominate the Silver Screen, Hawks created roles for strong women who, at the very least, were the equal of their leading men, if not stronger. If you've ever watched His Girl Friday (1940), you know exactly the type of woman we're talking about.

Trivia: When Hollywood was once again dominated by herculean action heroes in the 1980s with oddly nerdy names like Sylvester, Arnold and Bruce, there was one director who brought the idea of the Hawksian woman back, but we'll obviously be getting to John Carpenter later.

After their initial interview, Hawks ensured Sheridan was placed into several drama and dance classes, intending to polish her natural abilities and get her ready to star in his upcoming western, Red River. Sheridan had other ideas, however, and later recounted what happened in 'SECOND CHANCE' (The Mail - Sat 1 Dec 1951).

Margaret Sheridan...has the feminine lead in Howard Hawks' science thriller, 'The Thing.' .... I married a flier. When I had the chance to play the lead in 'Red River' I had to turn it down because I was expecting a baby...I was all set to quit movies and settle down to being a wife and mother, but Mr. Hawks told me to be patient — my chance would come again.

Married and pregnant, Sheridan wasn't available for the western, but by the time The Thing was being cast Hawks called his protégée to the set. However, I wouldn't say everything had been forgiven.

Hawks would later say when Sheridan returned: *She wasn't the same girl, if she'd only done Red River, she'd have been a big star.*

And yet, Hawks will always be Hawks, and we get a short glimpse of the female action heroes to come named Ripley and Sarah when the director creates a moment for his Hawksian Woman. Who comes up with the idea how to kill The Thing? Its Nikki, who offers the suggestion that leads to the creature's destruction.
Just Cook it!

In my research I found several instances of how Hawks helped empower the women who worked for him...and everything was rosy. However, the brightest light can cast the darkest shadow, and the further I looked the more disturbed I became. Just like The Thing, it seems we have a monster hiding in plain sight.

The Voice

One feature that most Hawks women shared was their voice – that deep, husky tone that made actresses like Lauren Bacall a Hollywood favourite. Sure, everyone seemed to have been a smoker back then, helping create that characteristic "throaty purr", but Bacall was only eighteen when she first appeared in 'To Have and Have Not', so how did a teenager achieve that voice? Well, Take One Magazine (1973) revealed truth can be stranger than fiction.

Q: How did you get Bacall to have that voice?

HAWKS: I told her what Walter Huston (who is one of the greatest actors I've ever seen) did to get his voice. Huston told me that he' learned to talk from the stomach by reciting his lines to a tree 125 feet away. By doing that he was able to be heard — he could speak quietly and still be heard. So I told Bacall. She came in three weeks later talking like a bass singer, and we put her in the picture. Originally, she'd had a high, nasal voice, and she couldn't possibly have read the lines that we had in the picture with that voice. She had to keep working all during the movie, and after the movie, but she never stopped until that voice became perfectly natural.

That's a great Hollywood story – however it may not be entirely true. Bacall and Sheridan were asked that same question for an article that appeared in the Barrier Miner (24, April, 1951).

Sultry new movie star Margaret Sheridan says she got her husky voice by screaming. She is following the formula that her discoverer, Howard Hawks, has prescribed for such proteges as Carole Lombard, Jean Harlow, Lauren Bacall, Martha Vickers, and Joanne Dru to give them their voices. "It gives your voice a husky quality," explains the dark-haired beauty, whose throaty tones make their debut in RKO's "The Thing."

"So Mr. Hawks tells all his discoveries to scream." Hawks sent Lauren Bacall to the hills to scream. But Miss Sheridan says she did her yelling at home with a baby

in one hand and a floor mop in the: other. "The husky voice ' doesn't ! last, though," she added. "You have to keep screaming. Hawks thinks I'm home screaming 100 times a day now, but I'm not. I'll have to scream again before I do another picture."

I lean towards Hawks insisting they scream as other actresses admitted to the same issue. In her memoir 'Leading Lady' (2017) Sherry Lansing explained: *He thought I sounded too girly...He told me that to turn my voice from shrill to husky, I needed to practice screaming at the top of my lungs until I developed calluses on my vocal cords.*

Think about that for a second. Imagine going every single day into the woods (or some other location you can be alone) and simply screaming until you become so painfully hoarse you lose your voice. You then show up the next day and do it all over again, and you do it so often you physically destroy your vocal cords and change the natural tone of your voice. That's beyond brutal, that's torture.

Yes, people can change their looks and their voice if they wish – but when it's someone who personally owns your contract and controls your future, that's not a situation that should ever occur. Kudos to Hawks for how he portrayed women in his films, but I really am starting to think he should be damned for how he treated those same actresses under his employ.

The Hero?

Though the average Joe on the street may not know Kenneth Tobey, Hawks sure did. Starlog Magazine #62 recounted:

Tobey had already been in 24 Broadway plays and nine movies when he first worked with Hawks in 1940 in 'I Was A Male War Bride'..."I played a sailor, It was only supposed to be one afternoon's work but Howard got interested and kept adding me to other scenes, so I worked for two weeks. During the shooting he told me: 'Someday I'm going to star you in a picture.' I didn't know what he was talking about, but it excited me. When I read in the Hollywood Reporter that he was going to do another movie I had my agent contact him. I was called in for an interview and was told I had the part. The movie was The Thing. It was the first film role in which I had over 10 lines.

During the interview Tobey also recalled when the owner of RKO made his presence felt during filming.

I got home about 3 a.m. after being out on an all-night drunk...and received a phone call from one of Hughes' representatives, who told me: 'Howard Hughes wants to see you right away.' I answered: 'I can't come over now. I've been out partying.' He said: 'In that case Mr. Hughes wants a picture of you.' They sent a photographer over who took my picture and brought it back to him. So I missed the chance to meet

Hughes, which I've always regretted. I saw him on the back lot once, but I didn't have the nerve to say hello.

At a time when Hollywood movies were generally driven by a single named star, tough-guying it through a wave of bad guys, Tobey was to play a new type of hero, the non-hero, one who rarely did anything heroic. As a captain and leader, it was decided that his character would never make a decision. Instead, when someone offered a suggestion, Captain Hendry simply said something like "that's a good idea", encouraging co-operation between the scientists and the soldiers to defeat their shared enemy.

Even the monster's end had little to do with the film's non-hero. Tobey explained in his interview that even *near the end, where they decided to electrocute the Thing... they all go off and leave me standing in the hall.* This isn't to say Tobey's performance went unnoticed. The Suffolk News-Herald took a specific interest in the actor.

Red-haired Kenneth Tobey's easy acting style in "The Thing" — his smoothness will give Spencer Tracy competition... Grins Tobey through his freckles: "... I waited 10 years for that role in 'The Thing'.

Sadly, Tobey's career after The Thing never took off. Despite having starred in such an acclaimed film he'd never again be the leading man. Indeed, he received only fourth billing two years later in his second feature, The Beast From 20,000 Fathoms.

I was under contract to Hawks and Hughes...My agent advised me to get out of that contract because he had a really good picture for me at 20th Century-Fox. So, I got out of my RKO contract, but the job at Fox didn't pan out. Then I was just a nobody. I have no idea why my career didn't take off from The Thing. I thought it was going to happen, but it never did. Perhaps people thought I was too expensive, or that I wasn't a good enough actor. The result was that I didn't work for quite a while, so I had to take The Beast just to pay the rent. I didn't know what the billing was. I knew it was an 11-day part, and just did it the best I could.

The Heavy

The story goes, one day Hawks and Nyby were having lunch in the RKO commissary when a distinguished looking actor walked past them. Hawks leaned over to his friend and said, *He looks like Abraham Lincoln as painted by C. Aubrey Smith.* Hawks later cast the actor as Dr. Arthur Carrington.

Robert Cornthwaite was a veteran of radio and stage who'd acted in small roles in films before The Thing. He recalled in a 2003 interview with Chiller theatre:

My agent arranged a test with Hawks, but RKO studio head Howard Hughes okayed it because my voice had a convincing intellectual sound to it which the role called for. As I was to play a character 20 odd years older than myself, I had to arrive at the studio hairdresser's department before 5am in order to bleach my hair white. I also had a beard pasted on by makeup man Lee Greenway. I tried my best to present an image of dignity and worldly experience to the role, despite the audiences' sympathy diminishing toward the end when I became 'The Heavy'.

The make-up transformation to turn Cornthwaite into the much older Dr. Carrington was so spectacular the actor would rarely be recognised for his role in the film. Cornthwaite would also share about what happened while he was getting the make-up for the first time, and we get a little glimpse of the superstitions many actors live their lives by.

When they did the screen test for the picture the makeup man, Lee Greenway, bet me $5 that I'd get the part. I didn't want to take the bet. I'm glad I didn't.

The cowboy

There was one giant actor in the film that, though not famous at the time, became beloved when he starred in Gunsmoke, one of the biggest shows ever to hit the TV screen. James Arness was a war veteran who'd wanted to be a pilot in the air force, but at 6ft 7 that was never going to happen. Instead, he became a footslogger in the US army, served in Europe, was wounded and awarded the Bronze Star and the Purple Heart. Sadly, these injuries would trouble him for the rest of his life.

Arness began working in radio, but after hitchhiking to Hollywood, managed to get a few small roles in westerns. Recognising his physical presence, Hawks ensured he was the first actor hired for The Thing. George E. Turner's article in American Cinematographer explained what happened next.

Arness received $750 per week with a four-week guarantee. He was also handed a $1,000 petty cash voucher in advance and a salary extension clause of eight days beyond the completion date as an inducement not to take any other jobs before the starting date of November 18. According to the budget submitted to RKO by Lasker, the arrangement was necessary because Arness had to be *available at all times for fitting his head and costumes... as it will take us some weeks to prepare the moulds for his head, which then cannot be used on any other actor.*

Tobey also recalled how Arness interacted with the rest of the cast, and how he helped Tobey out in later years.

He was absolutely embarrassed beyond words...He wouldn't even have lunch with us, because he had to wear all that green make-up. He's really a dear man, though. I once played a small part on his Gunsmoke, and was only on it for one day. We were getting near the end of the day and he could've finished the scene and gone home, and I'd have been through. Instead he said: 'It's getting too late. I can't work anymore.' He quit at exactly 6 p.m., so I got another day's work out of it. He didn't say anything about it, but I'm positive he did it for me.

NOTE: There is something odd about this Turner article. You can read the entire piece on American Cinematographer's website. Here it mentions the article had originally appeared in a 1991 edition of American Cinematographer Magazine, yet I found the article first in a copy of Cinefantastique #12 from 1982. It seems when it comes to The Thing, nothing is ever what it appears.

Another war veteran in the film was Dewey Martin. A fighter pilot who fought in the Pacific, Martin returned to the states after the war and worked several odd jobs until heading to Hollywood. The Truth (29 Jul 1951) wrote an article about Dewey, who admitted this film was his second chance. *There is quite a story behind Dewey Martin's getting the next most important role to Kirk Douglas in 'The Big Sky.' The 24-years-old Texan started off big with Humphrey Bogart in 'Knock On Any Door' and then didn't get another picture for 18 months. What do struggling actors do when they aren't acting? They struggle. But he really hit bottom when he found himself taking tickets at the theatre where he had been featured on the screen with Bogart. When Howard Hawks remembered him, and actually scouted the town to give him a role in 'The Thing,' Martin wasn't even sure he wanted to get back in the heart-break-game. 'Don't worry kid,' Hawks told him, 'you're on your way this time.'*

To prove not everything was smooth sailing with the cast, Tobey recounted: *Hawks took great interest in Dewey Martin, who played Bob, the crew chief. He subsequently gave him starring roles in The Big Sky and Land of the Pharaohs. Then I understand he thought Dewey got too big for his britches, and they didn't end up too well. Frankly he wasn't that good an* actor.

The Frankenstein

One of the largest complaints against The Thing '51 is the monster, well, I've a theory why Hawks moved his alien away from Campbell's iconic shapeshifter and into a large, hulking humanoid. It's clear when the team began the idea was to create a monster like the one in the book. A well-known Hollywood portrait artist, Nicholas Volpe, was hired to make concept sketches for the film, and several were based on Campbell's alien. A budget of $10,000 was then set aside for makeup experimentation. Stuntmen Bob Morgan, Chuck Moreland and Sol Gorss took turns standing in for Arness, while Lee Greenway tried to develop a monster that not only met Hawks' approval but could be physically developed and filmed.

Rumour #1 – there's unsubstantiated accounts the crew were so close to creating a less human-shaped alien that they hired a one-legged man to help create that shape-shifting effect from the book. Its suggested they never went with this because it simply didn't look menacing enough. If true, I'm positive that was not the reason.

Rumour #2 – There's apparently a cut scene of The Thing prowling one of the stations corridors, and to move the alien shot out long tentacle-like arms, seized a wall, and then pulled itself rapidly forward. Supposedly to create the effect the crew filmed the tentacles at full stretch and then reeled the arms in like a fishline. The film was then reversed, making it look like the arms shot out from the body, yet when hawks saw the footage he disliked it, claiming it looked just far too weird.

Rumour #3 - Speaking of cuts, Nyby explained he'd been asked by fans for years about a lost scene of pure horror. *They always claim we made a scene of the guys hanging upside down in the greenhouse, but we never did...We did make one close shot of The Thing, when he first came in, before they threw the kerosene on him...He was just too good-looking a guy to use the close-up.*

Rumour #4 - Legend has it when the humans opened said greenhouse door, only Tobey knew the Arness/alien was standing on the other side, so the reaction of horror and shock from the rest of the cast was genuine. Is it true? Who knows?

Rumour #5 - Did Leslie Neilson go for the role of The Thing? The following is from his autobiography, Leslie Nielsen - the naked truth (1993 – Pocket Books).

So I continued answering every casting call I might be right for. Among the parts I almost got was the title role in RKO's science-fiction thriller The Thing. A good friend of mine, a talented young actor named Barry Cooper, was up for the part of the mad scientist and had a copy of the script. "They describe the Thing as 'an intellectual carrot,'" he told me excitedly. "You'd be perfect for that role."

I laughed at his joke. "It's not a roll," I corrected, "it's a carrot." But the idea intrigued me. A carrot? It would be a stretch for me, but I was confident I could do it. About the closest thing to an intellectual carrot I'd ever done was in an Off-Broadway drama in which I'd played a smart cookie. But this was very different.

I prepared for the audition as I had been taught at the Actors Studio. I tried to understand the carrot's motivations, its hope and dreams. What did this carrot want? What was standing in the way of this carrot's getting what it wanted that had to be overcome? I tried to put myself in the carrot's place, to peel away its emotional defences, and by the time I'd finished I'd managed to get to this carrot's roots.

The audition itself was gruelling, but I thought it went very well. A few days later, though, I found out that an actor named James Arness had won the part.

Was Neilson actually up for The Thing? Well, records show Arness was the first actor hired, so it's not likely they interviewed for the role. My suspicions exploded when I read the following...

...*they must have liked my audition because a few weeks later I was invited to audition for the title role in the movie version of the Broadway hit Harvey opposite James Stewart. Harvey was an invisible six-foot-tall rabbit who could be seen only by Stewart. This was another difficult audition. As soon as the producers saw me, I failed it. The part eventually went to a character actor named Harmer Johnson, who apparently got the part by failing to show up for his audition. When the producers looked for him and he wasn't there, they liked what they didn't see. They knew they'd found the right actor.*

In a sense I was glad I didn't get it. Johnson gave such a great performance that he became typecast. A few years later he was nominated for an Academy Award for his sympathetic portrayal of the Invisible Man, but after that there were few parts for him, and he eventually disappeared.

I love Leslie Neilson, but the guy spun the truth and lies together like a spiderweb.

Not a Rumour #1 - As previously mentioned the American Society of Cinematographer (ASC) website has reprinted the George E. Turner article from their 1991 magazine. It reveals some scenes may have been filmed after all.

Film editor Roland Gross told us he was forced to drop a number of scenes... following an early preview screening, to keep the Thing indistinct. These cuts included closeups of the Thing as well as group shots in which Arness appeared with other players. In one cut sequence, the Thing kills two scientists and a sled dog and injures Eduard Franz in the greenhouse. As it stands, the scene is described by the surviving scientist while the investigators react to the off-camera corpses and find the body of the dog stuffed in a cabinet.

Another excised scene showed the Thing hurling a guard into the base's oil pipeline, plugging up the system. In the final cut, it is assumed that the Thing has sabotaged the base's heating system deliberately.

Two months of tests elapsed before Arness went infront of the camera in the approved makeup and costume. By that time Greenway's $10,000 budget had doubled, and the film makers had chosen to go with the man-in-a-tinfoil-suit-look, with gloves designed to resemble thorn-like claws on the fingertips and knuckles. The head makeup, full of well-crafted veins allowing coloured sap to flow through (a strange specification for a black and white film), meant The Thing ended up resembling Boris Karloff's Frankenstein.

But why did they really change the alien from a shape changer to the man-in-a-tinfoil-suit as the script was completed and folks were working on the effects? I believe it's now that the spectre of Howard Hughes rose again.

Having promised to be hands-off, the owner of RKO started firing off memos about the film, and one of the first things he asked about was the alien. Hughes specifically noted he didn't want to see a Frankenstein monster.

After decades of harassment an ill blood between the two men, and now having that same tormentor trying to influence the way he was creating his latest project, to me it seems we have Hawks taking the tiniest amount of revenge on Hughes. He doesn't want a Frankenstein-looking monster, well then...

Make him look like Frankenstein!

Did Hawks ever come right out and say this? Legend has it he did. To me the evidence is there, this was a simple matter of revenge and spite. We got the human-looking Thing because Hawks wanted to piss Howard Hughes off.

For a movie made over 70 years ago we have an astonishing amount of information from behind the scenes. We even know the cast knew about the changes to the creature from the original story to the movie version, and they weren't happy about it. In a Starlog interview Tobey recounted reading the original story as part of his research.

I thought the story was really wonderful...I was impressed by the fact that nobody knew what the 'thing' was. That seems to make for complete terror. If something is threatening you, but you don't know what it is or even that it's a threat, it's twice as scary as seeing a big monster. In fact I've always thought Howard should have shown even less of the creature, because the imagination is so much stronger than reality.

Did the actor speak about his concerns with the crew? Hell no. Tobey finally had his shot and he wasn't going to be stupid and blow it. *I actually liked the story better than the script. It seemed to me much scarier, but I thought it would've been in bad taste to mention it. When you're working with a famous man like Howard Hawks, you don't criticize your vehicle.* He does give us a reason why they did it though. *I guess they felt they needed an entity you could see, and not just a substance in the bloodstream.*

The Forgotten

This could become the king of all trivia questions. Name the actor from The Thing that was in Wizard of Oz, Gilligan's Island, The Twilight Zone, Bewitched, Star Trek, Planet of the Apes, Superman and the Batman TV series?

Fans are aware that Arness played the alien – and for most of the film that was absolutely true, but in its final moments when its body is struck by bolts of electricity, the alien's plant-body begins to shrink. Step in Billy Curtis, an actor with a 50-year career who was also a stunt man that often-replaced child actors (including Shirley Temple) when they needed to do something dangerous.

Curtiss had dwarfism, and he also played the Thing, dressing as the alien when it shrank. There's a great series of photos taken with Curtis and Arness, looking for all the world like the Thing had a Mini-Me. Despite these comical images, Curtiss took his career seriously and was a leading light for all actors to be awarded full membership and voting privileges in the Screen Actors Guild. *At one point, I had my own midget wrestling show*, Curtiss said in a 1968 interview... so maybe he didn't take it all that seriously.

We're not done though. In the same electrocution scene there was a third actor playing the alien. Teddy Mangenes played the Thing between the large form of Arness and the smaller form of Curtis. In an interview Robert Cornthwaite mentioned that during filming he had several body doubles. Some were obviously used for location shoots when the actor wasn't available like Mangenes *who doubled me* and *was the middle Thing*.

The Real Stars

To say there were no stars turns out to be not exactly true. Bob Hope and Bing Crosby were both in the film.

Two of the eleven huskies whose part of the dog sled team in Howard Hawks- 'The Thing' should feel right at home in Hollywood... they were whelped in the movie capital a few years back while their mother was working a Bob Hope-Bing Crosby film, 'The Road to Utopia.' Identical twins, the dogs were named Bob and Bing in honour of the two stars... (The Northern Champion, 26 Oct 1951).

Trivia: There's a shot of the dogs moving through the snow in the film. Whenever you see the teams outside there is no actor with them, instead they are local intuits hired to play the actors.

One of the most famous scenes in the film is when the Thing is attacked by sled dogs, which manage to rip the giant carrots arm off. This is collected and experimented on. Back in the lab the scientists show everyone that the detached arm was still alive. This harkens back to the original stories blood test, so to say the alien was nothing like Campbell's original creature is a little unfair.

Greenway made several versions of the arm, with the prop that comes to life played by a woman hiding under the table, who simply put her hand through a hole and animated the limb from beneath. That's the official story, but behind the scenes things didn't go quite this easily. During an interview with the cast in 1982 a child asked, "how did they tear the arm off the monster?"

James Young, who played Lt. Eddie Dykes, explained: *they brought in bobo the wonder dog...for one shot, and the trainer did nothing for two days except tell stories about how great his damned dog was...He only had to do one trick, that was tearing the Thing's arm off.*

George Fenneman played Dr. Redding and took over the story. *These dogs were supposed to take out after the Thing, bark at it, and tear its arm off. But when the Thing came running out into the snow, they literally put their paws over their eyes and tail between their legs. They eventually put wires on them and prodded them into at least looking up.*

Young expounded: *that was the only time I saw Hawks mad.*

The Filming

The stories of cursed films and the woes and horrors their cast and crews suffered are legendary in Hollywood. We've already explained how movies like Hell's Angels had killed people, and the issues making Apocalypse Now are so legendary that they made a movie just about that insanity (Hearts of Darkness: A Filmmaker's Apocalypse). Well, The Thing had more than its own issues getting onto the Silver Screen.

Before Hawks had even put a frame of film through his camera the movie was in trouble. The Advertiser (13 Jan 1951) reported:

Hollywood Producer Howard Hawks will have to get by without any insurance whatsoever in 'The Thing.' Five major insurance companies have rejected Hawks' plea for $125,000 worth of insurance on the visitor from another planet...Refusals came 'when companies read the script and discovered The Thing has to survive being frozen in a block of ice, hacking by axes, dozens of bullet holes, an attack by a pack of huskies, fire and the effects of 1,600,000 volts of electricity. A full crew of special effects men and make-up experts worked for three months to perfect The Thing, at a cost of some $40,000. Insurance companies estimate it would cost twice that amount to replace it in the event of a slip-up... the paper then explained ... *Hawks will now try to get by...hoping nothing goes wrong.*

The Locations

There was never any chance in the 1950s of a Hollywood crew heading to the South pole to film any outside location shots, so more practical locations were needed. Variety announced that *Winchester Productions will shoot snowstorm sequences for "The Thing" in Montana, instead of Alaska, as originally planned.* Not only would Alaska have provided fantastic vistas that would resemble those found at the Poles, the nearby US army base could provide items those on location would need, such as weather specific vehicles. There had been a long-time agreement between Hollywood and the services, however, Hawks and his team were about to get more bad news.

The script of Winchester Pictures' proposed production The Thing has been reviewed, and it is regretted that we will not be able to extend cooperation as the story revolves around flying saucers and their possible contents.

The Air Force has maintained the position for some time that there are no such objects as flying saucers and does not wish to be identified with any project that could be interpreted as perpetuating the myth of the flying saucer. Also, the Air Force seriously objects to any mention of Air Force personnel and equipment, or pictorial sequences representing Air Force personnel or equipment, being included in the film.

Providing your company plans to proceed on the production without Air Force cooperation, we request every consideration be given to the Air Force objection in the interest of maintaining goodwill and relations. The Air Force has dispatched a wire to the Commander-in-Chief, Alaska Theater stating their objections.

Sincerely,
DONALD E. BARUCH
Chief, Motion Picture Sect. Pictorial Branch

This is an interesting response, and their refusal to be involved with a UFO movie could harken back to what happened to the USAAF in 1947.

The Aliens

On June 26th, 1947, America was shocked by the story of civilian pilot Kenneth Arnold's claims he saw flying saucers, triggering a wave of copycat reports. Flying saucer mania swept the world, and this went into overdrive when, less than two weeks later, an isolated New Mexican rancher called W.W. 'Mac' Brazel reported finding debris from one of these UFOs. Soon the local sheriff and the Air force became involved – with public information officer Walter Haut, on July 8, 1947, issuing a press release stating that a 'flying disc' had landed on a ranch near Roswell. I think that'll do for this occurrence and I cannot really encourage you to look up the incident further. Doing a little research, I discovered a whole world of crazy and paranoia around these incidences. In fact the world went a little crazy for the next few years, and the intensity of this mania was so great we still feel its effects today. Roswell is synonymous with UFO, and an entire industry has grown up around the possibility of a flying saucer crashing in New Mexico.

Cashing in on this craze was The Thing From Another world – the first flying saucer movie containing a man from another planet arriving on earth, triggering a wave of similar films over the next decades.

I should point out the Airforce did relent, indicating they'd indeed supply whatever The Thing production needed if the movie could be *presented as a dream*. Both Hawks and RKO agreed that would never work and decided to move ahead without government support, even though it meant the studio now had to supply everything they needed for the shoot.

The Things that went wrong

Hollywood filming in such a remote region was big news, and the crew headed north to shoot backgrounds. A great resource of what happened next is the regions newspapers and historians, for example the blog 'Montana History Revealed' covered the studios visit to their town.

When the crew travelled to snowier Lewistown in January 1951, they employed local "actors" to use a sled dog team to search for "The Thing" across the hills east of town. Missoula's Johnson Flying Service provided DC-3 planes used in the movie, and the crew modified them to look like military C-47's.

The Hungry Horse News (December 15, 1950) noted: *RKO movie producers out of Hollywood believe the terrain around Cut Bank strongly resembles the North Pole. Result is that now underway near Montana's oil capital is shooting of outdoor scenes for a $1,300,000 production which is called "The Thing."*

The Cut Bank Pioneer Press was following the project closely and mentioned something surprising that may have led to one of the most famous scenes in '51 and The Thing '82. *According to RKO representatives, the army frowned on elaborate treatment of the mysteries of flying saucers, hence the story now calls for destruction of a saucer…* In the film the flying saucer was destroyed in the ice, was that on behalf of some late support by the military to regain their trust?

Another newspaper announced there was even going to be work for some lucky locals…*about 25 Cut Bank area people are to serve as extras, with another 10 as standing for actors. The standings must be of weight, build and colouring similar to the actors they replace in scenes, but need not have facial resemblances.* It also explained the reason why Alaska was dropped for Montana. *Advantages of Cut Bank over the North Pole includes a day's shooting time compared to two hours at the pole at this time of the year.*

Most of the cast and crew were placed on salary as it was expected to be a short shoot and stayed at the Glacier Hotel, which supplied meals for everyone. For 8 weeks they sat around Montana waiting for snow to fall, never understanding that it was never going to happen. If only someone bothered asking the locals.

The crew managed to get out and took some background shots and establishing images – including one with the spaceship buried under the snow. Later Nyby recounted how much this scene annoyed him. *The two fellows who were clearing the area with a tractor snowplough were still in the shot…You can still see them if you look close – or at least I can.*

For everyone else they had to continue waiting as there was still no snow. They sat around playing poker and watched the skies – yet still no snow. Everyone got bored and started playing practical jokes on each other – and still no snow. They listened to the radio and bet on horseraces – and still no snow.

Some began shooting skeet and the practical jokes continued – and soon both collided. In an interview with Cinefantastique, Nyby recalled watching the skeet shooters and *Paul* [Frees] *thought there wasn't anything to this. He took a couple of shots and shot the clay pigeon. And he kept doing it, over and over. So, feeling very confident, he started betting higher on his marksmanship. Then suddenly he couldn't hit a thing. He didn't realize that Klee Greenway, who is one of the country's top shots, was standing behind him shooting the things out of the sky.*

The clock continued to tick by and yet no matter how many muttered little prayers to whichever god they believed in were whispered, the ground remained snow free.

Scouring the US, the producers had decided on Cut Bank as the air force had built a large runway there, making it perfect for their 'North Pole' outpost. The place is large, the landscape flat and runs off to a horizon almost devoid of any hills. The place also received around 2ft of snow a season, enough to be visibly spectacular, but not enough to hinder the crew and production team. This annual snow fall was why everyone was standing around scratching their heads.

With no snow it was time for some old fashion Hollywood trickery. Expanding the onsite team with locals, the Winchester crew started building the large scientific outpost set – but made sure the walls were only 4ft high. This ensured the buildings would look much larger when covered in the snow that was sure to start falling soon. Until it did: *propmen stapled bedsheets stuffed with newspaper around eaves and on roof* to fake the snow.

Now I'm not sure how much of this is real or just a story, but apparently as the crew were building the set a curious local walked up to find out what they were doing.

"Why are you putting all that white stuff on there?"

"So that when it snows, it'll look like… look, don't bother us, go way." Said the crew member a little testily.

"But it doesn't snow here," the local explained.

"Don't be silly. It snows 20 feet a year in Cut Bank. We've got the government reports."
"Right, but it doesn't snow HERE!" they explained.
"What?"
"Oh, I mean it snows, but the wind blows all the snow away every morning."

A quick investigation proved the local was correct, which explains why the government had built an air force base there in the first place. You wouldn't build an installation like that where it could get snowed under for months of the year after all.

After so many days with no snow the decision was made and the cast and crew began packing up and returning to Hollywood, then out to the RKO ranch and began turning southern California into the North Pole. Shipping in cornflakes by the ton that were then coated with flour and paint to look like snow, next the crew then hid the semi-arid California flora behind a huge cyclorama to create the arctic sky and horizon.

Tobey later explained:

We waited six weeks for snow to shoot scenes in Cutbank, Montana...but we never did get very many scenes up there — just a couple of dog sled sequences and shots of the airplane landing and taking off. We came back and worked out in the San Fernando Valley on the hottest day of the year, wearing all that heavy fur clothing. They had to spread photographic solution on the ground to make it look like ice.

This means the majority of outside scenes with the actors in them were filmed in California during summer.

When it came to filming the saucer being accidently blown up by the scientific outpost staff, Don Stewart set up the shot the night before. Unfortunately, he laid the explosive charges and the night proved to be a damp one and all the black powder became wet. Undaunted, Stewart set more charges, stood back, cleared the set and lit the fuse at 11am. When the explosives detonated, everyone within the area dove for cover as a large part of the San Fernando valley was put into orbit.

Instantly the regions telephone system jammed with people calling in the explosion. Why? Dick Kinon was the films script clerk and he claimed he thought: *This was it.* At the time *everyone was atom-bomb conscious, and this thing went up like a real mushroom cloud, just like newsreels of Hiroshima.*

One person unhappy with the explosion was Nyby, who pointed out the fireball rose higher than the background cyclorama backdrop, and watching the film you can see California in the background...and you know what? You can.

Returning to Hollywood after the Californian desert the production moved into an icehouse where they could control the temperature – specifically to keep things as cold as possible. There would be no way to fake the look of the cold on the actors faces, they needed to actually be cold while filming.

The icehouse was situated on Mesquite Street, and here is where the quality of the Winchester film comes through. Rarely would you think the film was not shot in the cold or on a real base. The interiors never really feel like a typical cheap sci-fi set with Styrofoam walls, what they feel like are the demountable buildings such an outpost would be using at the time. In reality these buildings had to be transported a long distance and put together as quickly as possible to give those living in such a hostile environment like Antarctica, shelter.

To begin, by placing the set inside a cold storage room the film immediately added an effect near impossible in an LA summer. Tobey explained:

We'd drink a cup of hot coffee or soup and hold our breath until it was time to speak...This way our breath would show for our first sentence. We worked there for a couple of weeks, and it was about 30°. There was a problem with the cameras freezing up, but the technicians were excellent and had things pretty well covered. Russell Harlan was the cameraman, and he was wonderful. The photography had a semi-documentary look, and that's what we had in mind.

The set looks cold, it looks used and lived in – sure there's windows in some rooms that make zero sense considering how much heat a window loses in that environment, but we can forgive that. Luckily for us a reporter managed a set visit at the time, and over 70 years later we have ourselves a firsthand account of what it was like.

The set, inside an icehouse, was 20-odd degrees cold...Director Howard Hawks wanted the chill air of a nice house to give his players the foggy breaths of frigid climes. Also, real shivers were expected to be more convincing than shakes faked on a comfortable stage. The wardrobe man zipped me into fleece-lined boots, pants, sweater, jacket, helmet — till I looked like a wool-stuffed man from Mars myself. The cold hit me in the face. "We call this pneumonia hall," my guide said.

Pretty Margaret Sheridan, the picture's leading lady, confided that she was wearing red flannels under her Arctic finery...Her eyes were sore, and she thought this was partly from ammonia in the refrigerated air. The make-up man said he was using lots of pancake to tone down the actors' cold-reddened noses.

An arc light was trained on the camera, to keep its mechanical innards from freezing. The camera was treated more considerately, in fact, than the actors. "It is hard to get cameras," the cameraman explained. The building's chief engineer said the weathered, barn-like structure was built originally to store 10,000 tons of ice...It was good to step back into sunny southern California and get those bulky wrappings off.

"Take these," the wardrobe man cautioned, handing me an envelope. It contained anti-cold vitamin pills— a daily ration distributed to all members of the cast.

These were rough conditions to work in, and we're lucky to have this report as the film became famous for its security to try and keep its secrets. The Mail (21st Jul 1951) carried the following report that: 'THE Thing' is the first film since 'Confessions of a Nazi Spy' to be shot behind locked doors... Yet thanks to all the interviews and set visits, somehow the background of the alien got out, and it's pretty clear the culprit was TIME Magazine, which reported in May 1951 that: *The Thing (RKO Radio) is a ferocious vegetable, eight feet tall, delivered on a flying saucer from another world. It bleeds green, howls like an aggravated banshee, multiplies by dropping seeds into the earth. It thinks like Einstein, looks like Frankenstein's monster and, like Dracula, thrives only on a diet of human blood.* Yup, pretty sure Time gave it away.

The Filming

In 1951 movies were still being routinely filmed in 1.37 : 1 – which was the Academy standard at the time. There was no Panavision, wide-vision or cinemascope – so a modern viewer might be taken a little aback by the more squared-off image on the screen that is so common on many classic films. However, it was filmed on quality stock and with some of the best lenses available, so it still looks sharp. I'll give a warning this is for modern prints, older video and even the old laserdisc version, which added a few missing scenes, don't look fantastic. That's more to do I believe with the transfer process as not a lot of effort was given to old 'classics' like this being transferred to video.

The crew only used a single camera, creating the master – without the normal process of using other cameras for close ups and establishing shots. This meant that when it came to editing it made it very hard to match the dialogue from shot to shot. Add to this the chaos of actors talking over the top of each other in the Hawks style, often spoiling one take by making the dialogue indecipherable, meant the editors Butch Gross and Clem Portman began going a little crazy.

Step in Dimitri Tiomkin, who scored the movie and was in fact on set writing the music to ensure it matched what was being filmed. Tiomkin worked on several Hawks projects, and for this one he wrote what is arguably his least melodic score, concentrating on instruments that played in a lower register and with a strange beat. This was specifically to give the film a very edgy, alien tone. As the editors struggled to mix the film their workload increased as the composer asked to "Make the music louder". With a sigh the editors went back to work, mixing music and dialogue and creating a master soundtrack for the film unlike anything else at the time.

This leads us to one feature that was retained from the original story. Campbell had described the sound of the alien as *a savage, mewing scream*, so the filmmakers decided to try and keep that effect. The sound effects department recorded some cat cries, then slowed and distorted these noises to create the haunting off-world howl of The Thing. This bizarre noise was then enhanced by one of the world's strangest musical instruments.

The Theremin

One of the most common musical effects from the early years of sci-fi movies came from the ætherphone/etherphone/thereminophone – better known as the theremin. That strange box with a few metal aerials sticking out that you wave your hands around to create a ghostly electronic wail. This unending tone rising and falling helped create the alien atmosphere of a spaceship or some unearthly creature skulking behind foam rocks.

Invented in October 1919 by the Russian physicist Leon Theremin (Lev Sergeyevich Termen) it was the result of Soviet Union research into proximity sensors. Termen toured the instrument throughout Europe, playing its alien tones to an astonished audience, before selling the rights to manufacture them to RCA.

The theremin was popular in early sci-fi movies and made its first appearance in Russia's 1931 Odna. In Hollywood it appeared in Spellbound, The Red House, The Lost Weekend, Rocketship X-M, the Day the Earth Stood Still and of course The Thing From Another World, where its presence was noted by the press when they finally saw the film.

"The Thing?" No, that's a theremin, the electronic instrument much favoured for movie effects of a dreamy or weird nature. The player is Dr. Samuel Hoffman, chiropodist and onetime Meyer Davis violinist, who practically has the film studio music field all to himself... (Down Beat, 1951).

The Song

As I've mentioned, one issue with researching the film was to differentiate if a reference was about the Grean penned tune (from the last chapter) or the movie. The article specifically mentions the instrument was used in movies, so its most likely referencing Hawks film, but having read so many of these articles I'm not 100% positive as it was printed in a music industry magazine. For example, just a few pages later there's an article about the Red Caps recording their own version of Harris' The Thing. Redbook also noted: ...*the Thing which is the basis of this unusual film is something far more fascinating than "The Thing" which has led the hit parade of songs recently.*

Most articles and interviews that mention the song and the movie point out they had nothing to do with each other, though Collier's magazine created ads to highlight both together, hoping each would help sell the other. Well, let's end this little issue once and for all. RKO knew all about the Grean/Harris song 'The Thing' – it was the top of the charts at the start of 1951 after all, and it most certainly influenced a lot of what they were intending to do. As mentioned, it takes time to prepare and release a film and everything from RKO in the year before the movie's release clearly states the film was called 'The Thing'. This publicity was so effective we still call it The Thing today.

Either feeding off media releases or interviewing those involved in the movie, articles in newspapers all mentioned 'The Thing' was the film they were all looking forward to. This means when dealing with song and film it's been a little confusing trying to work out which was the focus of a certain article or competition as both had the same name in 1950.

However, at some point RKO made the decision to separate the film from the countries #1 song. The first item was to change the movies name – now, I have no direct evidence of this, but it's clear this is what happened. The studio had all their publicity ready to go, posters and other art were commissioned, and advertisements appeared in the worlds magazines and newspapers.

Then the song hit, and as the IMDB website for the movie notes: *Howard Hawks added "from Another World" to the title to avoid confusion with the song called "The Thing" that was popular at the time.*

I may not have direct evidence, but I do have secondary proof of why I feel the movie had begun cashing in on the song's popularity, then trying to move away from it, such as this article in an Australian paper.

But one aspect has the Hawks' organisation worried. Title of the new film The Thing cannot be changed without destroying' the strange storyline. But that is also the name of the batty tune fast sweeping the nation over records, juke boxes, radio and even elaborate television production.

This article clearly occurred during the very time RKO was looking for answers what to do, and several Australian papers carried similar stories, likely because the song was released much later Down Under and was still charting when the movie arrived. leading to some speculation of their own.

Howard Hawk's production commences today at the Ritz Theatre. Made some months before the popular song was written, the film...has no connection to the comic song, but strikes a more serious note (Goulburn Evening Post).

Another paper carried the story, but surmised it might be the other way around. *There's a curious hit-tune popular abroad now called "The Thing." Whether by coincidence or not, Howard Hawks has just given his latest production this very name.*

Clearly this cannot be the case because, as we know Hawks had been working on the film for some time before the song – and we do know the tunes author (Grean) had a habit of writing a ditty to cash in on a new craze like hula-hooping.

It turns out there was also friction growing between RKO and the music company. In the first months of 1951, as the film was starting to roll out and the song continued to rake in huge amounts of cash, newspapers like the Saskatoon Star-Phoenix carried the following story:

There's a lawsuit on the legal horizon between the music company that published 'The Thing' and Howard Hawks, who's producing 'The Thing' for RKO. Profits from commercial tie-ups, not the title, will be at stake...

The Suffolk News-Herald recognised there might be an issue with the public, the movie and the song.

Howard Hawk big science fiction movie, "The Thing," which may have to acquire a new title because of the Phil Harris song hit, was slated to be the first man from another-planet film.

And to finally prove once and for all the tune deserves its place in 'The Thing' lore, and that it clearly had an impact on the 1951 movie.

When the Phil Harris novelty song "The Thing" came out during filming, the RKO publicity department printed up business cards for the cast. "We all got one of those," smiled actor Bob Comthwaite, "except Jim Arness" (Cinefantastique Magazine #13). The card simply stated:

No! I am not THE THING.

RKO had clearly become concerned about their movie being associated with the song and we know they had their marketing ready to go, so they decided instead of changing everything all they had to do was add 'From Another World' to the film's title to avoid confusion. I'm not the only one who was speculating this by the way.

Howard Hawks' The Thing is being treated by RKO in an aura of deep mystery. While the plot is one of those pseudo-scientific melodramas dealing with the arrival of some strange monster from another world, the title might cause it to run the risk of being mistaken for a comedy based on the novelty song that swept the airwaves a few months back. "Boom! Boom!" Remember? (Film Bulletin 1951).

Trivia: After all this, the studios changed the name of the film to 'The Thing from Another World.' If you look at any artwork from this time the film is clearly branded 'THE THING', but underneath, in the smallest type you can imagine, as though it was placed there as an afterthought (which it obviously was), are the words 'from another world'. What's funny is the new title proved to be too long for most exhibitors, who turned around and simply omitted the last three words from their marquees above the front door.

The Screen And The Insanity

Principal photography wrapped on March 3, 1951 and postproduction began. There were some tweaks to be made, for example the bleak footage from Montana had dark clouds added to the empty skies above to really increase the feeling of oppression and atmosphere. The biggest tweak was one that's been forgotten and lost over the years and goes a long way to answering some of the modern criticisms of the film.

The head of the RKO camera effects department was Linwood Dunn, who got to work on the film, creating a series of dissolves between scenes and, using an optical printer he put effects on any scene when the alien was on screen. When the final print was sent to be copied for release it had a note that these scenes should be 'printed down' – making them darker and so hiding the features of the monster. Now that the Thing couldn't be seen properly it made the monster even scarier as the viewers imagination was left to fill in the rest. Sadly, this note was never followed on the subsequent TV and video releases, so every time you see the monster on these versions, it's basically in full light. This explains why so many find it disappointing to watch the movie today and see the-man-in-the tin-foil-suit. It was never supposed to be seen this way.

The next effect created in postproduction was the end of the alien itself. Arness was supposed to walk down the corridor and be hit by lightning, with the next two actors stepping in to replace Arness in the exact spot, from larger to smaller, making it look like the alien was physically shrinking inside the lightning trap.

Electrical expert Kenneth Strickfaden, who worked on movies including Frankenstein, created the practical effect of the electric spark leaping from the trap to the actors, and that's how it was filmed. Things continued to go wrong as the final effect was far below the standard everyone hoped for, so Dunn took a print of the movie and literally scratched, frame by frame, the lightning directly into the film's emulsion. This removed the original image and allowed bright white light to shine through when the film was processed and projected. This created a far brighter lightning effect. Add the sound to the special effect and you now could watch an alien potato monster being electrocuted before your very eyes.

There is one practical effect that I cannot go past, one that, the more you watch the more you realise the entire scenario is pure, unadulterated insanity. If you're reading this book I'm going to assume you know the scene without me even saying it...ok... I'll say it as I'm sure there's someone out there who doesn't know the film that well.

The alien is on the loose. It's already tried to bushwhack the humans in the greenhouse but is now circling the building on the outside. Inside the barracks, the humans prepare for battle, grabbing axes and lugging kerosene buckets to throw on the space turnip. Giger counters scream, warning the alien is close, and when it smashes through the door the soldiers jump into action. One throws a bucket of kerosene directly over The Thing, and from inside the room someone fires a flare gun. Fire erupts across the floor, the beds, the rear wall and the alien, which begins staggering around the tiny room looking for a victim. Someone steps forward and throws a second bucket onto the flaming carrot (I laughed out loud when I made that reference knowing those of you out there who get it...just got it). The alien staggers under the intense blaze...and it's a serious blaze now.

It all then takes a turn when Nikki (Sheridan), who's hiding along one wall behind a thin mattress pulled from one of the sleeping cots, catches the aliens attention. Still on fire, the Thing staggers forward and attacks. From behind someone flings a third bucket of kerosene at the alien...and the actress hiding behind the mattress. Fire simply explodes everywhere, across the alien, the wall, the mattress and everything in between.

A few more arm swings and the creature turns, drops its head, charges forward through a small window and out into the snowy exterior and escapes, its flaming mass disappearing into a snowstorm.

I've done this scene no justice and you have to watch it – check it out on You Tube, you can find it everywhere. The scene is BONKERS and has to go down as one of the most dangerous stunts ever put on film. I have no idea how they escaped seriously injuring or even killing someone during this fire...well, it turns out not everyone involved escaped unharmed.

Tom Steele was a tall stuntman, meaning he was the perfect substitute for Arness. He was tasked with what's considered the longest, most spectacular fire walk ever filmed at the time. The set was built on RKO's Stage 7, where Steele punched his way into the barracks. His suit was created out of a special asbestos material (crazy to hear that today), while his face/helmet was made from a fire-proof plastic. Two tubes ran from his nostrils into a special reservoir on his chest, giving the actor around thirty seconds of air once the fire was ignited. He was then trained like a dancer to get the moves he'd have to make once set on fire right as there was no way he'd be able to see anything once the kerosene was ignited.

The records and interviews are a little unclear how many stuntmen were used in the scene. Nyby always insisted only two because: *The principal actors were in the sequence except for dangerous things like throwing kerosene, where stuntmen were swapped in. The actors carefully rehearsed each motion: then an asbestos-clad stuntman was set alite with 30 seconds of oxygen in his suit...That was the only time we used a two-camera set-up.*

Despite all the choreography and care, apparently two stuntmen received nasty burns filming the scene, and I'm pretty sure you can see these accidents happen if you watch the clip a few times.

The actors also admitted to being either in the shot or standing behind the camera to watch this spectacular stunt. Young mentioned the room was *Hotter than hell*. Cornthwaite agreed that it was *Damned exciting to watch*.

The Hokum and Ballyhoo

This is the time of year to be shopping around for "trick" pictures. The public is less critical of pictures upon occasion, and sometimes ready and willing to accept the unusual—what we in the trade call "hokum." As long as the entertainment qualities are in the subject, it has the chief requisite.

Off hand I would select 'The Thing" and "Destination Moon" if the terms were set up properly and the distributor would go along on a participation policy of sharing in the advertising cost. To get the maximum out of these subjects, prepare yourself really to get the bull by the horns and get every dollar return you can reasonably expect from your area. They are subjects that are intriguing to the public, but without star value. For this reason, they must be "circused" to the hilt; and the time the majority of the public expects a circus or a carnival is right now."

That's how the Motion Picture Herald described the film in 1951. Cinema tickets sales had been falling for years and TV had become a serious threat. Why go to all the effort of heading out and paying your hard-earned cash when you could stay home and be entertained in your own lounge room? Film studios were aware of all this, explaining why so many industry magazines had appeared to train cinema managers how to sell their upcoming pictures.

Excitement was rising as the word was Howard Hawks new film was something different and people were going to want to see it in large numbers. Now rebranded 'The Thing From Another World', RKO knew they had something special and used the Motion Picture Herald to explain how cinemas could sell their picture and increase ticket sales further.

For three months a teaser campaign of unprecedented proportions had brought this picture to the attention of the entire reading public, in 152 publications, for an audience of 1,85,837,000 persons. They'll be waiting for THE THING, and it will get the business...use all kinds of teasers, large and small. Start your local campaign with small teasers, such as have been used in the national campaign to connect the ideas.

Cinemas everywhere began using these ideas to create their own advertising displays, often highlighting the security around the making of the film to help stoke the imaginations of all involved. Please note how often the actual Thing wasn't used to sell the film.

...all requests for information as to the story were refused, the sets at the studio were closed... "The Thing" is best described as an exploitation picture with nostalgic overtones of the serials of yesteryear. By its makeup, the opportunity for the enterprising showman to give it the merchandising works, is large.

In May Variety followed up this information.

RKO is offering 1250 in cash prizes to exhibit in the N. Y. metropolitan area drumming up the best promotions for 'The Thing'.... and all theatres in the territory are eligible to participate.

The Exhibitor newsletter at the same time also carried the story of how cinemas could enhance their sales and what others were doing.

RKO Palace is conducting a contest with The Ohio State Journal to identify "The Thing"... Jerry Baker arranged a unique radio contest over WHAM for "The Thing," with announcer Mort Nusbaum giving a clue each day for contestants invited to write a 15-word essay on what it is for $200 in prizes...

This periodical was full of Thing stuff, and was feeding cinemas tag lines they could use with their local media, such as: *Why Did They All Fear 'The Thing' From Another Planet?"; "A Strange Space Ship Lands With 'The Thing' Near The North Pole"; "A Gripping Tale Of The Invasion Of Earth By 'The Thing' From Another Planet."*

Exhibitors were also given a short synopsis, which the trade mag called an x-ray, to help them sell the film. *Here is a suspenseful, well-told yarn about the invasion of earth by a single thing, and it makes absorbing highly interesting screen fare. The pace is a fast-moving one, and suspense is on high throughout. There are loads of selling angles that can be utilized by active showmen.*

Later in the year the Motion Picture Herald - excuse the pun - heralded exactly how well received RKO's efforts were in advertising the film and some of the idea's cinemas had presented.

The "THING" campaigns are Terrific'. Prize winning campaigns in RKO Theatres contest for the best showmanship displayed in the metropolitan area with "The Thing' have been re-entered in the third quarter for the Quigley Awards. One cinema made "a complete exhibit of all the stunts" and ran a "screaming contest" on stage that we thought was very good. A very scared girl, with a sound truck, did the same thing for street ballyhoo, and even if you couldn't hear her scream, you could see her...but we bet you could hear her for several blocks. Ray Gillespie, assistant manager of the Rialto theatre, Tacoma, froze a very authentic marine monster in a block of ice, as street ballyhoo for "The Thing".

The use of the girl screaming in the truck wasn't the only time a vehicle was used in such a way, with the most interesting advertising for The Thing another mysterious, black truck.

"The Thing" opened first here and in Dayton, O. Stressing the eerie mystery angle, RKO exploitation director Terry Turner whipped up a crescendo of advance interest in "The Thing" with a giant black truck. "The Thing Is Inside" was described in bold green letters on each side...newspapers in advance of the truck's visit, through a contest titled "What Is The Thing?", assured long lines of the curious waiting to inspect the inside of the truck.

Local ballyhoo resulted in 8,000 replies to the newspaper contest and a truck queue of 3,000 persons. Entering the truck, a person walked warily through pitch darkness till a foot hit a switch. In an instant, the interior was suffused in green, then a return to darkness, and when the person came out he had an eerie tale to tell of what he saw. No two persons told the same version of what they saw.

This truck became a large part of the movies initial release. There are images of the vehicle with huge, black words 'The Thing' blazoned across its sides. Some magazines claim the truck just sat out the front of the theatre, while others explained how it opened for visitors to enter and see The Thing for themselves.

To sell the movie the studio next organised press events for the actors.

Saving grace of 'Hal Sawyer Views Hollywood' was a highly interesting sequence in the closing minutes which revealed how a film feature is made...Margaret Sheridan and Ken Tobey, stars of RKO's "the Thing", read some lines from a cold script. For comparison. The finished product was run off after the same scene had received the benefit of Christan Nyby's direction along with studio technicians' polish (Variety).

NOTE: Some cinema displays even leaned into the presence of the song with their displays, having a locked box sitting in their foyer. Sadly many of these images were of such low grade quality they could not be included in this book. However, if you go to the book's facebook page, we will post them there, along with any other images we find in the meantime.

The Reviews

It's important to remember all of this marketing was done with the studio and distributors having one hand tied behind their back. Every fan of the film today knows the iconic image of the Arness/Thing, with his Frankenstein-like makeup and rose-thorny hands looking scary and intimidating. However, that image remained hidden until the 1980s. As previously mentioned, Hawks and the movie's producers liked the idea of keeping the alien hidden as much as possible so that it could remain a surprise, so having an official photo doing the rounds of Arness in the make-up was exactly what they didn't want. These official images were locked away and didn't reappear until well after the films initial release. The fact they exist at all is a minor miracle, though perhaps they were used inhouse to show people like Howard Hughes what the alien looked like. This explains why so many newspaper reviews were so vague, seemingly having agreed to play the game.

There has been a lot of comment about the motion picture. "The Thing." It will be around here before long. I believe in September, so I thought you might like a little preview of this most unusual picture To begin with, It is a scientific horror film...If you like an unusual picture that will keep you on the edge of the seat all the way, be sure and see "The Thing" (Gloucester Mathews Gazette-Journal, 26 July 1951).

A couple of kids around the house have been whipped up for some time by announcements in the newspapers of a movie called "The Thing" (RKO). But I doubt very much if they're going to get to see it (assuming I have something to say about the matter) until they pass their present impressionable ages. I was scared to death for a considerable portion of the running time by this Howard Hawks production, although two of my companions at the viewing claimed they'd been charmed throughout. "The Thing" falls, I guess, into the category of science fiction, and it would seem to me that if the category continues to be as well treated as this there's going to be a bright motion-picture future for the stuff...the director, is in for some high compliments for keeping the tension of the audience at a keen, awed pitch and for the convincing detail that keeps one's inclination to disbelief suspended until the lights go on...your nerves have had quite a jolt. This comes close to being a horror masterpiece for my money... (Hollis Alpert, Saturday Review).

The following review was penned by the infamous Louella Parsons. Her most famous role was making Citizen Kane arguably the world's favourite movie as she was the driving force behind ridiculing and blacklisting the film across the US. Partly she did this for her boss, newspaper mogul William Randolph Hearst, but also because she'd asked Orson Welles to his face if the rumours were true the movie was based on Hearst. Orson flat out lied to her that it wasn't, and she took that as a personal betrayal. It would seem a decade later Parsons and RKO had made up because her review of '51 was more than glowing.

This is the dog-gonedest "Thing" to hit the entertainment world since King Kong. "The Thing" is the most original picture of many a year. Now "The Thing." Words fail me. In the movie, they describe "The Thing" as "an intellectualized carrot." Can you understand that? No? Then you're right. Nobody can understand it. Hear this now. "The Thing" is rampaging around the North Pole. You first glimpse it when its baleful eyes glare at you from a solid hunk of ice. But is it vegetable, animal, or mineral? That is the question needling our Air Force, which is trying to trap it, and our scientists, who are trying to analyse it.

They pursue it with dogs, men, flame throwers, and bombs, and they manage to pull off its arm. It looks like a human arm, but it has no blood, and it has fangs for fingers. Are you getting scared? Broooooother!! You ain't seen nothing yet! For the dead arm, brought back to our air base at the Pole, starts to grow. And that is only the beginning.

You've never heard of anyone in the cast before, but they are all fine, doubtlessly due to Howard Hawks' masterly direction. Hawks has a masterpiece, of a kind, in this mad opus. As for Edward Lasker. who produced it, he just has millions and millions heading his way.

"The Thing" is out of this world—and thank heaven for that!

Now there were critics, and to be fair I think these reviews had the same issues many fans have. There was plenty of suspense and the film built all the way up to the final death scene when a lumbering silver suited giant came clomping down the hallway. Yes, I'm saying it here, the ending was weak. Manny Farber reviewed the film for The Nation, pointing out The Thing: *is a slick item thriftily combining a heavy science story with a pure adventure yarn for better than ordinary entertainment...Despite its indulgence in the cliché of the Mad Scientist—a vaguely Russian-type "Nobel Prize winner"—and the final let down when the Thing turns out to be merely the familiar Frankenstein monster...the film almost convinces you that its imaginative predictions may someday all come true.*

The film was a hit, and its rising popularity meant there were places where the movie began causing serious issues.

RATED-X

All across the world 'The Thing' was drawing people back to their local theatre. Thanks to the RKO media blitz the film was being talked about weeks before it arrived in England, building up a great sense of anticipation. In London *such was the movies popularity, the police had to be called in to control weekend crowds outside the cinema* (Kinematograph Weekly – or KW).

Reading all these articles and newspapers, I wouldn't say the movie was the Star Wars of its day – it never did that kind of money or ticket sales - but it was most certainly the ALIEN. It was a great movie made by skilled craftsmen's that sci-fi fans loved and the general public appreciated. It did strong sales and is still a film many of us talk about today with affection...despite being over SEVENTY years old.

Overseas campaigns began later as film prints cost a lot of money, so once the movie had done the rounds of the US, copies were then free to send overseas – a practice that was still occurring for some films up until cinemas recently went digital.

A year later the British industry newspaper KW began alerting their local cinemas about the film – calling it: *An infallible money-spinner for popular and industrial halls, despite its 'X' certificate.* It also reported that in Germany the 'Das Ting' *campaign...created quite a stir in Buckeburg. From waste materials a grotesque 8 ft. replica of The Thing" had been placed in the foyer.*

The newspaper then recorded how the film was going as it crossed the UK, and how it was *still packing in filmgoers. Playing four theatres on the Southan Morris circuit at Newcastle. Stoke, Tunstall and Burslem...at the Theatre Royal, Sunderland, is so good that the management held it over for a second week...* and then announced the film had broken *records at the London Pavilion.*

The British cinema industry had recently created a new way of categorising their films. For example horror films would carry 'H', but one of the first films to receive the new adult 'X' certificate was The Thing, which the KW believed was just the 'thing' to put new life into jaded box-offices.

KW explained what they thought of the film. *The Picture, sheer baloney, is so artfully encased in persuasive and convincing scientific data that interest is fully held and terrific suspense created, while stage is set for the 'Frankenstein-like thrills'.*

England's censors have a history of cutting films. For myself, I recall visiting London in the late 90s and getting excited to buy the letterbox version of James Cameron's The Abyss (a film not released in Australia). I then carried said video all the way home, only to find out yes, the movie was in the letterbox format but when I popped the cassette in the video player I discovered it had been cut...

...I'll say that again. The British censorship board censored THE ABYSS!

In the 50's several English cinemas refused to show any 'X' rated film, and The Thing found itself shunned. You can bet everything changed though when the serious money started to flow through the few cinemas that did carry the film. One cinema that had screened the movie was The Odeon, that announced: *The 'X' certificate has been commonly associated in the public mind either with horror or sex, which this organisation considered generally unsuitable to the family trade upon which so many of its theatres rely.*

Yet in the UK it didn't seem to matter. The films small release and an audience that had a long-time love of science fiction meant things went so well it smashed records. The Hawks biography notes: *In London, it shocked the trade by breaking the twenty-one-year-old box-office mark in its first week at the London Pavilion.*

The Thing was also dominating the US having created *an effective campaign and intense local ballyhoo in particular cities kept the film between second and fourth place at the box-office nationally for five weeks running between mid-April and mid-May. It was the number-two film for the entire month of May…and enjoyed particularly outstanding runs at such prestigious theatres as the Criterion in New York and the Pantages in Los Angeles.*

The film ended *as RKO's sixth-biggest earner of 1951 and forty-seventh overall, moderately ahead of the other alien-invader classic of the year, The Day the Earth Stood Still.*

Looking back on the film today it's amazing to think many of these reviews, even the glowing ones, came with a stern warning. Just like in the UK, there was a growing fear how such intense films would effect children. Harrison's Magazine reported the film was: *on the whole, an effective and imaginative thriller that should more than satisfy those who enjoy weird, horror-like tales…"* Though the magazine did leave the reader with a warning "Some of the scenes may prove to be too horrific for young children.

Even Bosley Growther, writing for the New York Times issued a warning.

Adults and children can have a lot of old-fashioned movie fun at "The Thing," but parents should understand their children and think twice before letting them see this film if their emotions are not properly conditioned.

The Grail magazine highlighted the rise in popularity of the sci-fi genre, but also ended with a warning.

At present, the cycle is one of "science-fiction", which is enjoying a corresponding boom in book and magazine publication at the moment… On the other hand, Howard Hawks epic, "The Thing from Another World" is so far from being a realistic piece of fantasy that it seems intended for a rather subtle piece of satire on the trend…There is, it seems to me, little attempt to convince the audience that the story is even possible, let alone probable, in contrast to "Rocketship Moon" which gives the impression of historical fact. Both are, however, in their respective ways, good entertainment, and "The Thing" has some rather amusing moments, even though some of them are not, in all probability, intentional. The latter is not, however, recommended for family viewing—the horror, for one thing, gets a little too horrible at times.

This new expectation of reality and taking such films seriously leads us to one of the strangest accusations made against the production company.

The Betrayal

With all the money spent on trying to design a Thing that matched the original story, the script had the scientists kill the creature but soon realize it has invaded several of their number, rapidly taking control not only of their bodies but their minds and personalities as well. In Campbell's version it was the scientific community working collaboratively with the military that wins the day.

Hawks changed all that. It was his favoured military, specifically against the wishes and intentions of the scientists, that defeat the creature. Did Hawks have an issue with science? He reduced Carrington to a mad scientist and the rest of the scientific team fall away into background characters as the film progressed. Carrington was reduced to a mad scientist and the rest fell away into background characters. You could even argue that when Carrington notices the severed hand moving and mentions "it's alive," he's mirroring the greatest mad scientist in film history, Dr Frankenstein.

In The Chicago Tribune, 1951, Mae Tinee covered this exact issue:

Looks as tho Frankenstein will have to crawl back into the laboratory. That once popular monster is now outmoded by more modern devices than the mad scientists of yore concocted. Actually, it's the same basic principle, embellished by present day devices such as seismographs, Geiger counters, and flying disks, to say nothing of voracious visitors from other planets. However, two old stand-bys, the slightest unbalanced scientist and the good old vampire legend, are still with us...

In 1951 it was clear that Hawks had created a more modern Frankenstein, yet there were those who were disappointed with what Winchester films had produced. Some were hoping a new age of science fiction was on the horizon, one that treated the subject with a maturity that Astounding magazine had become famous for thanks to its long serving editor, John. W. Campbell Jr.

Some critics knew the strength of Campbell's 'Who Goes There' – it had become the gold standard in many ways for this new wave of sci-fi after all – and were disappointed with the result of this big budget film made by one of Hollywood's greatest directors. Gone was one of the most unique aliens ever put to paper, the shape-shifting three eyed, tentacle haired spaceman. You can understand their disappointment after getting instead a 7ft vampire vegetable that wasn't even in Antarctica anymore.

Despite these issues, what Hawks and his writers had done was create something new, a movie that didn't need its key character. Not until JAWS in 1978 would the cinema produce a film filled with such paranoia and fear that it created a generation-wide terror. The difference, in 1951 people weren't refusing to enter the Arctic lest they come face to face with a cello playing killer carrot. Instead, kids in the 50s were making sure there wasn't a Thing hidden under their bed. It was the thought that behind any door, stalking down any corridor, a hidden monster could be waiting to grab you. This was something new – a real horror movie that contained serious jump scares. Even Tobey had to admit: ... *I know most of us in the cast didn't realize we were making a classic. I thought it was well made. I saw it at the premiere in Pasadena, when Hawks brought his family. I sat in the balcony, and almost jumped out of it when the 'thing' was on the other side of the door and suddenly appeared* (Starlog #62).

It could be argued, just like JAWS, what The THING did initiate was the coming wave of big budget Science Fiction films that would become a Hollywood staple for decades. This phenomenon was even noticed by Australia's national broadcaster, ABC.

Quick to spot a trend in public taste, Hollywood producers have embarked on a spate of science-fiction stories. They have noticed that...Howard Hawks' The Thing are coining money wherever they are shown. It's odd that although the popular scientific field has had countless devotees for years among the reading public, movie-makers have not previously exploited it to any extent... Now... the big movie companies are all competing to make films about scientific, or pseudo-scientific subjects...like The Thing, which introduces screen audiences to life from another planet in a truly nightmarish way... No one can say that Hollywood isn't taking its science-fiction dramas, interplanetary thrillers and atomic fantasies seriously.

That's not to say there was nothing in 1952. RKO re-released King Kong, then the flood began with The Beast from 20,000 fathoms (1953) – a film routinely agreed to have helped inspire Godzilla. There was also one of the most popular films of all time (and directed by another Hollywood sci-fi heavyweight) George Pal's War of the Worlds. Next was THEM! (1954), This Island Earth (1955) and the influential Forbidden Planet (1956).

After a few good decades sci-fi began to wane, then came 1977. Star Wars didn't have the biggest budget, but the money was enough to ensure what was on the screen was quality. What followed were big, budgeted sequels – and films like ALIEN and today's wave of MARVEL movies. These films created some of the most important moments in the history of Hollywood. No matter what you think, Ripley waved the banner for empowered women for years and you have to agree films like Captain America Winter Soldier were far more than the BIF, POW, BAM of earlier superhero fare...and films like Black Panther have become a true moment for a section of humanity that have been woefully under-represented.

A bit of a stretch? Again, think of how Hawks presented his lead female – a character not even in the original story. Nikki Nicholson was tough, smart, quick-witted, held her own (if not dominated the men thanks to that weird chair/rope scene), who actually came up with the way to destroy the creature. It's a shame we would have to wait until Ripley killed the Xenomorph that we'd have another woman heading a Hollywood sci-fi movie.

As for Hawks being a science hater? Well, the director answered this very question in an interview with a fellow director and film historian. Peter Bogdanovich asked if he'd deliberately put in an anti-science stance, and Hawks explained: *Oh, no, its just worked out that way. You see we had to make it plausible – why they let the thing live. In order to make it plausible we turned them into heavies – it had to be an honest sort of dedication on their part...*

It's very possible RKO itself was aware of the coming anti-science criticism. In one of the many ads for the film I found in magazines from the time was of a scientist sitting at his work bench. Looking over his shoulder at the reader he announced: *As a Scientist, I say we must destroy it or it will destroy us.*

To be fair there were supporters of the film who felt its scientific outlook was of great value. Gavin Souter in The Sunday Herald recognised the film was *a mixture of science fiction and traditional horror films, which may be the first of a new film species, is now breaking box office records...* and that Hawks was *responsible for infusing this new "scientific" blood into the anaemic body of horror films...By adroitly making use of Geiger counters, atomic energy, jet flights and other developments with which the daily newspaper has familiarised the public, Hawks has made the presence of this visitor from outer space credible and frightening.*

The Dispatch newspaper led with the headline 'High School student Finds "The Thing" scary'. Its staff had been invited to a preview, and there was a competition prize of: *a two month pass to the student who wrote the best essay after seeing the picture.* The reviewer then asked a scientific question I had not read anywhere else. When discussing the attempts to shoot and burn the creature with no results, they asked: *How would you kill living vegetable matter? That is the problem confronting this small group of men. Upon them rests the responsibility of finding the ley to the universe from being smarter than they or ridding the world of a monster that endangers lives.* The reviewer then ends with support for Hawks movie. *The finger points at you. What would you do? Come and see how science copes with such an adversary...*

...and people did.

The Trivia

- RKO got into the spirit of its upcoming movie release by presenting the staff who visited the studio commissary an unidentifiable meal called THE THING for sixty cents. *The Thing... It's a meat loaf* (Photoplay 1951).

- For such a famous horror movie, the death count in The Thing is two (and maybe a few dogs). The latest Disney movie has more deaths in it than that.
- In 2001 The Thing from Another World was selected for preservation in the U.S. National Film Registry. Now Howard Hawks officially has ten films on this prestigious list, Scarface, Twentieth Century, Bringing Up Baby, Only Angels Have Wings, His Girl Friday, Sergeant York, Ball of Fire, The Big Sleep, Red River, Rio Bravo…well, I think we can make that eleven as we know he directed The Thing as well.
- The film also garnered some serious fans. In 1983 Starburst Magazine (SB) #74 interview the two men ruling horror at the time, George Romero and Stephen King.

SB: You two love scaring people, right? So come clean now…what was the first movie to really scare the pants off you?

KING: The creature From the Black Lagoon. Oh Boy, I was terrified by the idea of him being walled up inside. That was terrible.

ROMERO: The original Frankenstein, which I saw as a kid on a re-issue with, I guess. Bride of Frankenstein. The scene with the tramp, that shook me up. But the first to knock me out was… er… The Thing.

The Chair

For a movie made in the 50s there was a very, very strange scene in the film that rarely gets mentioned. When Captain Hendry arrives in Antarctica and starts flirting with Nikki Nicholson, a woman he's clearly known for some time – she's happy to talk to him, but only after certain precautions have been taken.

Cut to the next scene where Hendry is sitting in a chair and Nikki is tying him in place. She explains this is for her own safety as he cannot get any handsy ideas, but the fetishism of the act is dripping from the scene. Was this particular perversion something Hawks or Nyby was into? Was it innocent or was it hiding something darker?

There's another scene with Bacall tying up Bogart in The Big Sleep (1946), so it's not the only time Hawks filmed this, and it's not like this hasn't happened before. Most cinephiles know Quentin Tarantino will shoot his female leads feet every chance he gets.

It's pretty clear Hawks has a thing for doors. Special shots of a character doing something through a door fill his movies. On the website Zekefilm.com, Robert Hornak writes an entire column about how Hawks uses doors in the western Rio Bravo, and then there's the numerous times people get shot through doors in The

Big Sleep. The list just goes on and on, and in The Thing, Hawks uses some doozy door shots, especially to enhance the terror of the film. When the men open the door to the greenhouse and the alien is literally standing right there and takes a swing at them...and of course there's the famous fire scene where the creature crash through a door and attacks the soldiers.

If something appears once or twice, well that could be a coincidence, but when it shows up time and again, that's a fetish.

In 'Figuring the Fetish', Elizabeth Cowie explores fetish imagery in art, and recorded how Hawks "uses objects circulated and exchanged" that often "will signify not a public erotocism but a private sexuality".

As I keep pointing out, when it comes to The Thing, nothing is ever what it seems.

PART THREE
This Isn't Dog, It Just Looks Like Dog

The Remakes

Now I was originally going to place this film in the previous chapter as it was created to cash in on the success of The Thing 51. What stopped me was the following 1953 Imagination Magazine #7 article by none other than Forrest J. Ackerman (the man behind the Famous Monsters Magazine), which also reveals The Thing wasn't the only movie to go through a few name changes, and sent me down a rabbithole of potential remakes many fans may not be aware of.

IT CAME FROM OUTER SPACE (as it's currently being called — I couldn't hazard a guess as to what it's liable to be named 10 minutes from now. I believe it began as "The Meteor", and has since been known as "Ground Zero," "Atomic Monster," "The Invaders from Outer Space" and "The Strangers from Outer Space".) At any rate, Ray [Bradbury] originally did a 28,000 word screen treatment composed of elements of "Who Goes There?" (the good ones omitted from the cinema adaptation, The Thing) and the denouement of the at-this-writing unreleased WAR OF THE WORLDS…At last report, it was still about 80% o.r.b (Original Ray Bradbury).

Bradbury's treatment about shapeshifting aliens was given to screenwriter Harry Essex to complete, and for years Essex claimed sole credit for the film, with Bradbury receiving only a story credit. In an interview with Tom Weaver (who would participate in a commentary track on the movies DVD), Essex said Ray never did a treatment; he did a three-page short story. Apparently, Weaver confronted the screenwriter with evidence Bradbury had written a treatment over 100 pages long, yet Essex continued to hold true to his story, adding: He tried to write a screenplay…and it was just no good.

However, I'd like to point out when Bradbury was interviewed years later by Donn Albright, he explained Essex was very kind about it and very generous and he told the story often over the years, giving me credit for much that went into the screenplay.

Now Bradbury was a class act and had a good-natured funny streak, which I cover in my first book HORROR, after he caught E.C. Comics 'borrowing' his stories. Well, it could be true and Essex had relented, or this could be Bradbury moving on from the issue as he was no longer bothered.

For his part Essex stuck to his story and continued to claim that Bradbury only did a three-page short story, nothing more. Not even when Weaver confronted him with evidence, instead, he claimed he was stumped that Bradbury's part had been overemphasised – though he did eventually admit he understood why people were curious as Bradbury was a famous writer and had brought a lot of credit to the film.

This is the story a lot of resources carry about the movie the two men wrote. Some in the media really give Essex no credit for his work, pointing out his career never went far after this movie, possibly because he'd taken credit for Bradbury's work. This is ridiculous as Essex's next film was a true monster of a movie, The Creature from the Black Lagoon. He also wrote a script for John Wayne called The Sons of Katie Elder...so not really a failure then.

My point is that other than Ackerman's article, no one, not Essex or anyone else connected to 'It Came from Outer Space' thanked John W. Campbell Jr., whose story was the basis of the movie in the first place.

The Unofficial Sequel – something has survived in the ice.

Let's see if you agree. At a small American Navy weather station, a USAAF flight with scientists appears from Antarctica and crashes. The plane was carrying a few captured penguins and prehistoric trees. Soon sentient botanical creatures, described as 'undernourished cactuses' start making their way through the island, killing for food.

1966's The Navy vs. the Night Monsters was not officially based on The Thing from Another World but a 1959 novel by Murray Leinster called The Monster from Earth's End. This was a very cheaply made movie that the king of b-grade films, Roger Corman, apparently helped produce. It's a flick that Ed Wood could have been proud of as its full of ham, cheese and just about every stock footage shot the director could get his hands on. Honestly, the only parts that really harken back to The Thing '51 is that it starts with an interesting narration about Antarctica, the monsters are plant-based...oh, and fire...trust me, if you watch it, you'll see it.

NOTE: The most interesting thing about this film? When the cast and crew discovered the film would be called The Navy vs. the Night Monsters they threaten to quit en masse.

The Doctor

Friday 6:30 pm 8 September 1978.
Scene: A young Phil is sitting in the rarely used loungeroom of the house. Here is the good sofa, 70s brown of course, and his parents' massive stereo system with all their 50s, 60s and 70s records stacked up in the wooden stereo shelves. In one corner is the family's original TV – a giant 36in black and white set sitting in its own purpose-built cabinet. Shunned and ostracised into the loungeroom

after being replaced by the new colour TV- and with only two channels, one commercial and one public - no one is going to interrupt. Young Phil loved these Friday nights. Older than his brothers and sisters, he was starting to forge his own identity and rituals in life. One of these was sitting in front of the unused black and white TV by himself and watching Dr Who on ABC 3. Dinner was a glass of milk and a pile of Vegemite sandwiches...

...and on this night, I began watching an episode I'd never seen before called the 'Seeds of Doom.'

Scene: Two men digging through snow in Antarctica uncover something in the ice. When they take this organic pod back to their camp, an image of the discovery somehow reaches the Doctor (working with the British army group, UNIT), who recognises it and immediately sets off for the camp. In Antarctica the pod has burst open and infected one of the scientists. The alien is a plant-based organism called a Krynoid, meanwhile the infection is spreading, and all too soon the first victim is wandering around the base, killing anyone who gets in his way.

The usual paranoia and Hijinx ensue – with one group looking to catch the pod/alien and take it back to civilization, where a rare plant collector has bribed them to capture a living specimen. The story has the usual Dr. Who tropes. Cheapo sets, isolated miniatures, too many deaths due to tripping over and being unable to outrun something slower than a 10ft snail. a terrible monster suit which is little more than a garbage bag with dead foliage glued over it. Side note: the monster from this episode was actually a suit used in an older story (The Claws of Axos) that was just painted a different colour.

And of course, when the mad botanist capture's the Doctor and Sarah Jane he begins playing some weird electronic music he'd specifically written for his plants.

'Timeless adventures: how Doctor Who conquered TV' by Brian J. Roob claims the first two episodes from Seeds of Doom *are a pretty shameless remake of The Thing from Another World*... and I'd argue so was the end when they need to administer a blood test. It's clear the storyline is based on 'Who Goes there', and the 'Doctor Who In Vision' magazine #13, agreed.

The story is a sort of Thing spending The Day of the Triffids watching the Quatermass Xperiment to a musical accompaniment by the Phantom of the Opera'. The first two episodes borrowed heavily from the 1951 science fiction film The Thing (remade in 1982), right down to the Antarctic setting (although the original had an Arctic location) and the vegetable nature of the alien.

Now perhaps because of the influence of the earlier horror film this is not your usual Dr Who episode. The Doctor doesn't arrive by TARDIS in Antarctica, he goes there with government approval. It's also by far the most action-packed doctor you are ever going to see. He gets into numerous fist fights, snatches weapons, which he carries around for some time as though ready to blast someone. There is even one scene where I thought he broke a man's neck (instead it must have been some Gallifreyan neck nerve pinch). It's also not really the Doctor who saves the day, but the soldiers of UNIT…and finally, keeping a tradition that will hold for all versions of The Thing, the episode was deemed so violent it brought the ire of the infamous Mary Waterhouse, who was on a crusade at the time to purify the media for all innocents.

NOTE: UK TV fans recognised these episodes were also very similar to another property, and have been vocal it was just a rip-off. We're not talking the Thing by the way, but a 1965 episode of the Avengers called the MAN-EATER OF SURREY GREEN. In the episode, a telepathic space-vegetable claims to be from the Moon. Oddly, many of the elements from the Dr Who episode that don't match up with Campbell's original story are very similar to those from the Avengers. Well, there could be a reason for that – the author of The Seeds of Doom, Robert Banks Stewart had earlier worked on The Avengers.

Having gone through both series though, I do believe they are more like the 1951 movie than originally believed. Instead of a group of scientists, in the Dr Who episode it's a group of politicians and botanists who are trying to collect and protect the alien from the soldiers and scientists who realise its danger and are trying to exterminate it. The show even has soldiers attacking the alien plants and the head botanist, who'd sided with the Krynoid and had been trying to protect it…

…and we're not done. Most everyone involved in the 'Seeds of Doom' were involved in an earlier storyline, based around the Loch Ness Monster.

The 'Terror of the Zygons' was released in 1975 and was about a race of shape-shifting aliens that had crash landed on earth centuries ago. Living in their submerged spaceship, they'd been tinkering with a creature they brought with them called the Skarasen, which they augmented with their technology and released as the Loch Ness monster. This begins attacking remote outposts of humans (on oil rigs), bringing the interest of UNIT and the Doctor. Clearly a lot of this matches up with Campbell's original tale and the 1951 movie, and when you add both together we have almost the entire story.

One last Dr Who reference. In the 2010 video game the Blood of the Cybermen, the Doctor is investigating an attack at The Geological Survey Outpost at Zebra Bay. As the Doctor and his companion Amy step out of the TARDIS and into the frozen waste land of the north:

AMY: *Doctor, did you ever see The Thing?*

DR: *The Carpenter Kurt Russell Thing or the Howard Hawks Thing-y with the walking carrot?*

It would seem the Doctors been familiar with Campbell's creature for a long time.

The Train

In 1972 a Spanish made horror film was put up for an award at an international festival of horror, and though it didn't win best picture, it scored the prize for Best Story at the Sitges Film Festival.

At first the film sounds like it would be terrible. Small budget, ageing actors, yet though it sounds like it would be a dog, 'Pánico en el Transiberiano' (Panic on the Trans-Siberian) is most certainly no mutt of a film. Known as the Horror Express in English, the reason why we're looking at this odd film is simple – it's a remake of The Thing.

Let's see if this reminds you of anything?

In 1906 a British anthropologist called Saxton has discovered in the wilds of Siberia/China the frozen remains of an ancient creature. He hypothosizes the creature is the missing link between apes and modern humans, and so the block of ice is collected, boxed and moved to Peking. Here man and specimen are placed on the Trans-Siberian Express to Moscow, then on to London. At the station Saxton bumps into a long-time rival/friend from the Geological Society, Dr Welles.

When the train departs both men, as well as a handful of other scientists, a police detective and several soldiers and civilians depart for Moscow. One man is left to guard the luggage cart, but screws around with the box with the frozen fossil in it – allowing the definitely-not-dead creature inside to free itself and start killing everyone on the train.

In a confrontation it admits to being an alien made of pure energy that can transfer itself from creature to creature. It had been left behind in the prehistoric past when its crew sailed home, and has been surviving on "protozoan, fish, vertebrates". Turns out the alien can transfer information, such as memories and intelligence, from a victim through its eyes, somehow burning them out in the process and leaving the brain smooth.

Trapped inside a train moving through Siberia with a murderous, seemingly shape-shifting alien killing everyone – creating paranoia and fear as no one can be sure where its hiding or who the creature is at the time. Sound familiar?

Though the film was an Italian production, the producer was not. Bernard Gordon was a Hollywood veteran who wrote classics such as Circus World, Battle of the Bulge, 55 Days at Peking, Invasion of the Triffids, Earth vs the Flying Saucers and the 1964 version of The Thin Red Line. Sadly, in 1951 the West was concerned with the creeping spread of communism in the world, and part of the US Government became concerned with Hollywood coming under the influence of the Red Scare. This led to the formation of HUAC – the House Un-American Activities Committee that began looking into the possibility there were communists in the nation. Though the committee's anti-communist investigations are often confused with McCarthyism, there is a difference as Senator Joseph McCarthy actually had no direct involvement with HUAC. Again, I went into all this in my earlier book HORROR as these hearings all but ended Horror and Crime comics for decades.

This government sanctioned witch hunt into Hollywood led directly to the famous blacklist, where several movie employees – almost all writers – were banned from working in the industry. Several were even sent to jail for not co-operating with HUAC.

Born of Jewish Russian immigrants, Gordon lived in New York before moving to LA to work in pictures. Here he became involved in several political causes, and for a short time joined the Communist Party – as did many people at the time it should be noted as the communists really were one of the only organisations fighting for the rights of the poor. It was his party membership that led to HUAC subpoenaing the writer to testify before them as someone had named Gorden as a communist. Though they called him, Gordon never officially testified before the committee – but the subpoena proved enough for all the Hollywood studios to officially backlist him...

...officially. Like so many others that had been shunned by Hollywood, the industry still needed their best writers producing, so unofficially most were offered work under the table – using pseudonyms to disguise their real names. For example, Gordon often wrote as Raymond T. Marcus.

In later years Gordon's work was recognised, and his name returned to many of the movies he wrote during this time, yet the writer would prove he could neither forgive nor forget. When the Academy of Motion Picture Arts and Sciences looked to give their Lifetime Achievement Award to Elia Kazan, Gordon vocally fought against this as the man had cooperated with HUAC during the blacklist era.

This leads us to Horror Express. Though only listed as a producer, Gordon most likely wrote the movie that contains many scenes reminiscent of The Thing '51 and the book. It starts in the frozen wastes of the north, has an alien stuck in a block of ice, has a bunch of soldiers and scientists trapped in a confined space using their skills to try and find then defeat the creature, which seems to be able to hide in plain sight. The creature is also able to reanimate corpses as telepathically controlled servants to do its biding, so paranoia grows as you can never tell who is under its control and who is still in the fight.

To uncover the creature, instead of investigating everyone's blood to find out who might be the Thing, the scientists discover the creature doesn't like bright light and its eyes glow blood red, meaning the humans can test and find the hiding creature. In some form, so many of these elements can be found in The Thing '51 and the original Who Goes There?

There are very few reviews, though Famous Monsters #112 called it *the horror from another world*, clearly associating the movie to the Hawks film. Science fiction movies by Philip Strick (1976) also leaned into the similarities: *twenty years after The Thing, has yet another alien carved out from the ground and permitted to loosen up a little...*

Nearly a decade later Andy Mohammed wrote about the movies video release. *You say you've seen all the movies worth watching? Rent old B-grade horrors.* After a quick review, Mohammed admitted: *Now, "Express" really isn't as bad as it sounds. There's plenty of suspense, and some quality acting is supplied by Telly Savalas. So if the idea of an alien-controlled primate running loose on a Russian train appeals to you, rent "The Horror Express."*

The lack of reviews makes it hard to know for sure, but it would seem it wasn't until you could rent the video that people started really associating the movie with The Thing – or more precisely Campbell's original story 'Who Goes There?'

The Amazing Stories Magazine (1985 #1) had a review section written by Biard Searles, who asked the question: *have you noticed in the last five years or so the tendency to take old B-movie horror themes and redo them with great seriousness?... Iceman is the prehistoric thingie revived {Trog, Horror Express, etc.).*

VideoHound's horror show (1998) also noticed the similarities. *Horror Express... Imagine The Thing on the Trans-Siberian.* Cult science fiction films (1995) also recognised *the movie as a whole has the claustrophobic feeling you find in classics like The Thing From Another World...*

Starburst Magazine's Horror Obscura section (December 2015) was more critical. *The story is loosely adapted from John W. Campbell, Jr's Who Goes There? – albeit uncredited... It arguably makes a better fist of the material than the version produced by Howard Hawks for RKO in the fifties.* Their point is instead of a vegetable, at least *Horror Express...make the transference of the alien lifeform into a human...*

Note: Horror Express was later re-edited into a 2021 episode of Creepshow: Night of the living Late Show, where the main character of the story invents a way of putting himself into, then interacting within classic films like Horror Express.

What's old is new again

And like ouroboros swallowing its own tail, our story comes full circle. The storyline of Horror Express is somewhat familiar to a short story by the master of horror, Steven King. The Crate is the tale of a box from an 1834 Arctic expedition that has been discovered under the stairs (of course) by a janitor at the zoology department of Horlicks University. Staff at the university open the crate to discover something of a missing link inside, still alive and hungry. It attacks and starts munching its way through the nearby personnel. The creature looks like a Tasmanian devil *that appeared to have not four but six legs and the flat bullet head of a young lynx.*

This story would appear within comics and horror anthologies, but most famously was adapted into an episode of the 1982 film CREEPSHOW, which changed the creature to more of a missing link– just like in Horror Express. In one of those weird little coincidences that seems to occur around The Thing franchise, one of the characters in the story, Wilma Northrup, was played by Adrienne Barbeau…but we'll be getting back to her soon! The Crate is a nod to both Who Goes There? and the 1950 song The Thing.

Trivia: Crates addressed to the Holicks University have been spotted by eagle eyed fans of The Walking Dead and in other horrors, such as Jason Goes to Hell.

The Parody

Between you and me, I'm a little upset that the world's longest running parody comic, MAD, never did a spoof about The Thing in any of its forms. That's not to say The Thing never appeared in the magazine, though.

> When the Thing
> Starts slob-ber-ing
> In some cheap double feature,
> He shows real ability
> Actin' supernatur'lly!

In 1964, 'Mannie Get your Ghoul' appeared in MAD magazine #85. Written and drawn by Frank Jacobs and Jack Rickard, this was a spoof of a Broadway musical starring old movie monsters. *This was a satire on the Broadway musical & Hollywood film, ANNIE GET YOUR GUN. One of the songs was "Doin' What Comes Natur'ly". Mad redid this song into a take-off entitled "Actin' Supernatur'ly".*

The comic starts with the musical's authors sitting around a piano tinkling away, singing their song about old time monsters. One of the writers then opens an advertising folder and holds up an image of The Thing from Another World, making sure you don't, miss the reference with which Thing he was singing about. Over the next few pages, more parodies of songs sung by all the Universal Monsters, who are then joined by Hollywood's most famous horror faces like Vincent Price and Peter Lorre. Together they create a chorus line of actors and monsters warbling away.

Then to the tune of 'That Girl That I Marry' they sing:

> The 'Thing' that I bury
> Will have to be
> A real Transylvanian monstrosity –
> The 'Thing' for which I crave

Will have two bloodshot eyes
Staring up from the grave!

So, if this appeared in MAD, why are we about to talk about an issue of Famous Monsters magazine that came out a year later I hear you ask? I'm glad you're so involved in our conversation here. The quote that began this little article was from a letter that appeared in Famous Monsters #37 titled 'Monster, Hang your heads in shame'.

My favourite magazines...I read regularly, are FM & MW, Mad Magazine and U.S. News & World Report. Sometime ago in Mad (#85, March '64) an article was run under the name of "Mannie Get Your Ghoul"...I almost dropped dead when I saw this tome in the form of a poem in your letter department, where a reader of Waban, Mass., claimed the work to be his! This was just too much; some people, it seems, will do anything to have their name published. An apology to both you & Mad would be in order.

An eagle-eyed reader had noticed that the songs in the MAD mag were reprinted a year later in the letter column of Famous Monsters by some fan claiming they'd been the author.

Famous Monsters response I think serves to be highlighted to end this section on remakes: *What this boy did is a very bad thing. It is called plagiarism...It has been demonstrated time & again that no one can hope to get away with pretending another person's work is their own— there are too many alert readers to trip them up. In this case, a swarm of irate filmonster fans descended on the offender like hornets...*

Mad may not have ever done a full parody, but that doesn't mean there wasn't one. Warren Publishing made its bones with Famous Monsters and adult style comics such as Vampirella, Creepy and Eerie. In the late 70s they decided to try a Sci-fi title, releasing 1984 in 1978... I guess they thought 1984 sounded future-y.

Now there were a lot – and I do mean a lot of problems with 1984. Racists, sexist, juvenile...I am warning you just in case anyone out there is a completist and may think of trying to grab an issue of 1984 #5 for their Thing collection.

This issue contains the parody Rex Havoc and the Ass-Kickers of the Fantastic, featuring in the 'Spud from Another World! or Who Grows There?' This was the second of the ongoing Havoc tales and is a clear parody of The Thing '51. Penned by Jim Stenstrum, with art by Abel Laxamana, the story is a familiar one - an alien found in a block of ice. This one's still alive because it managed to stick a straw out of the ice before being completely frozen so it could still breathe. Of course, the alien later escapes, kills a bunch of humans and when its finally visible it's a cross between the hulk, Frankenstein, and a giant carrot with shark teeth. What's great (and likely to ensure they didn't get sued for plagiarism), all the characters from the film have been renamed with the actor who played them. For example,

Dr. Carrington was changed to 'Dr Cornthwaite', while 'Hendry' became 'Tobey'.

Beware, Science Fiction Chronicle #22 noted: *DreamWorks is also bringing the comic book character to the screen...In it, the dull-witted Rex leads a "crack" team of adventurers on missions to take down monsters such as the Spud from Another World...*

We could well have another Thing movie in our future if this project ever gets off the ground and they use the storylines from the series.

Note: When Warren reprinted the Rex Havoc stories a few years later, the one-story missing was the 'Spud from Another World!' This could be because Warren found itself in serious trouble when it got caught publishing stories based on the work of authors like Harlan Ellison. If you recall with Ray Bradbury and EC – there are ways of dealing with this situation. Bradbury played nice and got paid, Ellison went the other way and sued. To be fair, he'd already said no to Warren using his stories and they did so anyway, so it's not like he wasn't justified. Still, there are rumours it was this lawsuit that eventually sent Warren into receivership.

The Comic

Gold Key Comics first began publishing stories in 1962, and became popular for printing licensed material, especially film, Disney and TV properties such as Star Trek, Hanna Barbera, and the Twilight Zone. The company also had some success with its own titles like Turok, Son of Stone and Magnus, Robot Fighter. I'm trying hard to not say they concentrated on the more juvenile market of primary school age readers because that's clearly not true. The company released horror titles after all like Boris Karloff's Tales of Mystery and The Occult Files of Dr. Spektor.

This brings us to 1975 when one of their inhouse imprints, Whitman, wanted to cash in on the larger magazine style comic format that was hot at the time. Starstream was an anthology series sold at .79c an issue – a high price when most comics were around 25c. There were only four issues, and they contained a mix of original and tales based on famous sci-fi stories from important authors, including Campbell.

Starstream #1 included arguably the first real adaptation of 'Who Goes There?'. Yes, the Thing '51 was loosely based on Campbell's story, but major elements were missing. Well, those were back in this comic. Adapted by Arnold Drake and with art by Jack Abel, the story begins with an interesting image, a handful of scientists looking down on a spaceship, and it takes a moment to realise the point-of-view is from deep within the ice looking up. It's clever images like that which really show the power of the comic medium. Great news, we finally get the three-eyed alien described in the original story. They also use the blood test and there's some half decent science in the comic as they try to figure out what's going on – there's also a fair amount of stupid (one character sleeps on the block of ice containing the alien as they carry it back to their camp on the flatbed of a truck...outside...IN ANTARCTICA). Still, it's not a bad version and you can find the pages hosted on several webpages if you do a search.

The Alien

Ok folks, I was sitting here looking through my notes and working out how I was going to add the influences of the Thing on ALIEN when a little thought snuck into my head. ALIEN IS THE THING.

Now, bear with me. An outpost of humanity surrounded by a cold, hostile environment discover a crashed, partially buried spaceship. When they investigate, they discover the previous occupants dead in a gruesome manner (the space cowboy), and further searches uncover an alien life, which they bring back onboard their ship. The creature then begins to alter its form and hide, and every time the humans encounter the creature again it's completely changed shape...

...Yup, ALIEN is another remake of The Thing. Want more?

Both creatures are survivalist, doing what they evolved to do – it's not about conquest per say or resources, its far more primal. Both use a host to survive and incubate, both burst out of a body, both creatures are outnumbered and need to remain hidden and stealthy to survive, then pick off their victims one at a time. Both take on aspects of their host – the Thing completely, the xenomorph takes on the body characteristics of a human or whatever it hatches out of. Even the heroes – both are not in command, but as time goes by they start taking charge of the situation.

If you need more proof, well, let's look at a little history. O'Bannon and Carpenter met at the University of Southern California and collaborated on the directors first film, Dark Star, which O'Bannon also played a roll in. They both then collaborated on a film called 'They Bite' (later renamed the Drone), which contained nasty little insect creatures capable of imitating anything. In 'John Carpenter, The Prince of Darkness' (Gilles Boulenger, 2003) the director admitted that film *was patently ripped off from John W. Campbell's story Who Goes There?*

Also, if we go all the way back to chapter three, we know that a certain Daniel O'Bannon had complained bitterly about how little the Hawks film had to do with Campbell's tale... so, O'Bannon was clearly a life-long fan who had a habit of remaking the story.

Conclusion, ALIEN is a Thing remake.

Star Wars

Just kidding.

PART FOUR
John Carpenter's THE THING

He sits there in a red chair, looking if not regal, then comfortable in what he's talking about, the mastery of his craft. "I love this movie."
Turner Classic Movies is a great channel, especially when they began hosting monthly guest programmers. This day the host, film historian Robert Osbourn sits opposite the director John Carpenter, who's presenting a selection of his favourite classic movies. Today's choice, 'The Thing From Another World'.
Osborn leans forward and probes Carpenter about his love of the movie and to explain why he'd made such a choice.
JC: I didn't see it in its first release, I saw it in its rerelease because I was too young...
RO: Hhmm...
JC: It scared me...It really scared me; and then I saw it later in film school and I began to appreciate some of the Hawksian elements that I could see in it. The... dialogue and the characters dealing with each other in the exchange of cigarettes and props, and I realized the kind of influence that Howard Hawks had over the Thing. In addition to just being a science fiction film, it is another expression of his kind of group adventure idea that he's done in so many films.
If you're reading this, you're almost certainly a fan of John Carpenter's The Thing. Is there anything new to say about the 1982 film? Well, I'll give it a go.
Now, what I'm not going to do - partly because we just don't have the space, but mostly because it's unnecessary - is go over the mountains of information that's so readily available to fans of The Thing '82. My reasoning, if you're reading this book then you own one of the numerous DVD/Blu Rays that have been released of the film. You've either watched (or now have the chance to watch) all the commentaries and special features that these excellent disks contain - so why rehash them?
Mostly what I wanted to do here was collect some of the reactions to the movie and see if we can uncover a few unusual nuggets of information, you may not know...so let's just see where this will lead us. And now for a little psychology. Every time you read one of the subheadings in this chapter, play the Thing theme in your head.

The New Hitchcock

...in the opening of Halloween, the remarkable use of colour in the numerous night scenes, finally that of the cinemascope which allows it to create a greater

intensity. His films where anguish is distilled with a minimum of effects and a great economy of means are above all extraordinary pieces of suspense which lead him a little like Hitchcock to play with the viewer's nerves as well invited to participate emotionally in the fiction told by the filmmaker.

This is how La Revue du Cinema in 1984 was talking about John Carpenter and his monster independent hit. 1978's Halloween had more than one critic talking about the young director possibly being the new Hitchcock and a true master of suspense...so, you know, there was no pressure.

At the start of the eighties Carpenter was on a roll. Halloween had exploded across the planet like the arterial blood from a stab wound you never saw in the film (seriously, there's so little blood in the movie, it's remarkable). The simple premise of an uncaring murderer in a mask killing teenagers in a quiet leafy suburb surprised everyone.

Halloween began a remarkable string of films for the director and his investors. Next came The Fog (1980), followed by Escape from New York (1981) – movies that cost very little and made millions. Meanwhile Halloween was still making money and there was growing pressure for a sequel. Carpenter wrote and produced Halloween II, a film he never had his heart in, yet it still managed to do very well at the box office. This led to another sequel that Carpenter and his team produced, Halloween III – a movie routinely hated by many fans as it didn't contain the mask wearing, carving knife carrying Michael Myers.

Why didn't Carpenter direct the sequels? Well it turns out 1981/82 were very busy years for the director. Fangoria magazine wrote an article about this new wave of horror and interviewed Carpenter about his work and his favourite movies.

My favourite films have always been escapist in nature, and horror movies are a great way to escape. Often, the more bizarre the content the better.

And when they asked him about his success inspiring a wave of copycats jumping on the bandwagon, the director answered: *The same thing happened in the 50's, the same thing happened in the 60's, it's part of the Hollywood syndrome.*

Talking about copycats, sequels and remakes, the magazine asked what was coming up next for the horror director. There were a few things he had cooking...

...sources at Paramount tell us that plans are afoot for a collaborative film to be directed by John Carpenter, David Cronenberg and Walter Hill. The film is planned as a three-segment anthology, with each director responsible for a one 30-40 minute segment.

I think we all missed out when nothing came of this movie – but in my research I discovered this was a common occurrence at the time. Film after film was announced in the early 80s that Carpenter was to direct... *Without a Trace... El Diablo*, a sequel to *Escape from New York*, and Steven king's *Firestarter*. None of these were made, though the most infamous was a western Carpenter continually talked about called El Diablo (not sure how it was supposed to be a sequel to *Escape*), which was eventually filmed as a TV movie in 1990. It took me a while to find out why the western he signed to make with EMI was dropped, finally finding the answer in a Carpenter Starlog interview.

Poor El Diablo...I made a development deal for it in 1979, when I was in a very different career position than I am now. I like to keep to my word and not suddenly try to renegotiate a deal, but I don't want to go back and collaborate with EMI. I want to make it my own film — I don't want John Travolta playing the lead in my Western. It's a very difficult situation. I don't want to be a jerk and start pulling fancy stuff. I'll do the movie for the same fee I agreed to, money isn't the issue — it's the control.

DID YOU KNOW? The director was a serious fan of westerns, and in 1991 he had another script filmed for a TV movie called Blood River. Again, this was from another old script he'd written for none other than John Wayne, who died before it could be filmed. It makes sense Wayne and Carpenter, who wrote and directed like Howard Hawks, almost worked together. When the classic director taught a class on filmmaking in the 70s the future director was in the audience. Carpenter even talked about this in the TCM studios.

Howard Hawks is my favourite director for a number of different reasons, and this came during my time at films school. I began to study him, and the way he makes movies. His narrative style, his invisible camerawork. Essentially for the most part not calling attention to itself like a lot of other directors. But his dealings with characters and their interactions...the away they exchange props with each other. The men and women relationship. The split between his adventure films and his comedies. I know this is a man, a master in charge of his cinematic vision. And he worked within the Hollywood system, which I admire enormously. So, he wasn't somebody who struck out on his own as an independent... I just love his films.

Back to that Fangoria interview from 1981. The magazine ended their Carpenter conversation with some speculation after all these failed films: *...we wouldn't be surprised if some totally different project surfaces in the next couple of months.*

Well, funnily enough...

*...*in July 1981 Starlog #48 hit the shelves and reported everyone would have to wait at least a year for Halloween II until Carpenter...*completes his most ambitious film yet, a new version of The Thing for Universal which he hopes to begin this August or September.*

The article has some interesting information, and we'll get back to that later, but I just wanted to share its end, and how bittersweet it is for us fans who know what was about to occur.

As his previous pictures have proven, Carpenter usually delivers far more than he promises. With a new film for release and two more in production his career is certainly in high gear. But unlike some other acclaimed directors who unfortunately take their reviews too seriously and become self-indulgent in their work, John Carpenter tries to use his unprecedented success as a shield with which to protect himself from peaking too soon. However, he's learning that's not always easy to do.

Yup, Carpenter was about to learn exactly how hard that was to do.

The Refashioning

I'd like to clear something up before we move on. We all know the 2011 film is a prequel, but was the '82 film a remake? People have been debating this for years, but during an interview I think Carpenter gave the perfect answer to what his film was.

Remakes and sequels are probably the hardest films to make...because it's built in that they're not going to work. I'm reminded of Philip Kaufman's remake of Invasion of the Body Snatchers. When I saw it I thought: 'Why did he do this?' The original was so much better and showed so much less. In terms of remaking The Thing I had it easy, because I wasn't trying to remake it. The producers are wondering what to call it— maybe a 'refashioning?' However you want to say it, it comes down to the fact that it's an entirely different movie in tone and style. Once it's released, that won't be an issue anymore (Starlog #60).

The Thing '82 was a 'refashioning' with very little in common with the '51 version. The director also gave a reason for separating both films, while keeping a few tips-of-the-hat to the original.

There are a couple of obvious 'homages' to Hawks, like the flying saucer buried in the ice and the block of ice out of which the 'thing' emerges, but I don't know if the two pictures can even be compared. The original was made a long time ago, before there were movies about monsters from outer space. I remember seeing it as a little kid, and I just went out of my chair. Today I think a lot of people are amused by the monster and its description as being an 'intellectual carrot,' and there's a lot about the film that's dated, but it's still terrific. I wouldn't try to do mine like the original because it had too many unique elements to it. I'm not so presumptuous as to think I'm going to imitate Hawks in any way. I wouldn't dare, because I admire him so much as a director.

Well there's something about the Thing we're always talking about, imitation.

The Origins

I think there's something weird is going on with The Thing '82. It's nothing bad, and honestly I almost did not catch it myself, but there seems to be a little revision of history happening about the making of the film. If we look at Phil Edward's review for Escape From New York, he was so happy with what he'd seen from the director, he wrote:

So what's disappointing about Escape From New York? I liked the film a lot. It demonstrates Carpenter's growing ability to handle increasingly bigger budgets and bigger casts. Like the Fog it shows that the director is in control of complicated effects sequences.

Edward's then did a little speculating. *It bodes well for Carpenter's next film, a remake of Hawks' The Thing. From all reports Billy Lancaster's script is tough, hard and terrifying. I can't wait for that one.*

So far so good. The issue comes when we try and work out just who came up with the idea for remaking the film, and for that we start in an unusual place...ALIEN.

There was a most extraordinary note at the start of EMPIRE magazines special edition review of the history of Ridley Scott's 1979 film.

The legacy of Alien is unprecedented, its reach is so much greater than 2001: A Space Odyssey or Star Wars. Not only through the sequels and prequels set within its own universe, but via the set-up of a grouchy crew picked off one by one by an elusive alien presence, which can be seen in The Thing (1982), Lifeforce (1985) and Predator (1987). The influence of Scott's space-noir aesthetic can be felt as far afield as The Terminator (1984), Event Horizon (1997), The Matrix (1999) and Pitch Black (2000). The cyberpunk and dystopian genres owe the film a huge debt. Horror owes it a huge debt. Comics, novels, toys, video games, clothing lines, artwork and the flattery of endless parodies: Alien has spread like a contagion through pop culture.

We know today EMPIRE began this article with a false premise – it wasn't Alien that influenced The Thing, it was 'Who Goes There?' that influenced Alien – and by starting at that point influenced all those films EMPIRE had just listed.

This reference again takes us all the way back to the broken relationship of two former friends. John Carpenter and the author of Alien, Dan O'Bannon had begun their careers working on projects we've seen were 'inspired' by their love of the Thing '51. They'd been so influenced by it they were working parts of the story into their various projects. This is an important fact to keep in mind as we go forward.

The Script

In the late 1970s there were rumours Hollywood was looking to remake The Thing from Another World. Scripts were commissioned, directors were approached, but little seemed to be coming of this work as no one seemed right to help steer the remake. In 1978 The House of Hammer #19, announced: *Producers David Foster and Lawrence Turman are re-working Howard Hawks 1951 The Thing...Let's hope they adhere more strongly to the (superior) initial concept.* While all too easy to make fun of today, it was a great movie in its day. Let's hope it remains so.

One script produced at the time was by William F. Nolan, whose most famous work was Logans Run (the novel series and the TV pilot). Nolan also later wrote the introduction to the Campbell reprint in 2009 to cash in on growing interest with The Thing prequel.

Very little happened with the Nolan script, and another soon appeared by one of the hottest young properties in Hollywood, a man with a cheaply made horror film that had everyone talking.

Tobe Hooper's Texas Chainsaw Massacre caught everyone by surprise, and the director had arrived at Universal with the studio keen for him to do work for them. The Thing was offered, and Hooper immediately dismissed the idea the producers had come up with as he wasn't a fan of the whole internal paranoia storyline. Instead, he and Kim Henkel came up with a script similar to Moby Dick – about a captain battling with a large creature without any shape-shifting ability. No one thought this was a good idea, so Hooper was out and the search continued.

Just a few years later Famous Monsters #164 announced Carpenter was: *to remake THE THING FROM ANOTHER WORLD*. When the magazine asked if he meant the 1951 movie or the original Campbell story, Carpenter explained: *Oh, the story – definitely the story. I intend to base my movie on the written work...*

NOTE: A Carpenter interview in 2014 with the website Vulture confirms a lot of this, adding a little more about the earlier script by Hooper and Henkel. *All sorts of drafts were written before I came along. One was underwater ... they were just trying to make it work.*

An underwater THING – the mind boggles.

The Revision part one

Most sources on the film explain that for Carpenter, this was work-for-hire, a job that the studio had on their books and approached him to direct. Carpenter agreed because he loved the story so much. A 1981 Starburst interview with the director explains why this became the prevalent belief.

Well, about two years ago now, the producers — Universal own The Thing — bought the RKO rights to the film, and David Foster and Larry Turman asked me if I'd like to make it. I re-read the short story by John W. Campbell Jnr ... I agreed to do The Thing, if I didn't have to write it. I didn't feel I could do that, just as I'd never try the male camaraderie thing the way Hawks did it ... you know what I'm saying? So, we hired William Lancaster. He's Burt Lancaster's son and a tremendous writer. He wrote The Bad News Bears...

This suggests Carpenter had just been a work-for-hire director and he was part of the conversation in hiring Lancaster to write the script. In 2015, Total Film and SFX released a special magazine on 80s Movies, and the article 'E.T vs The Thing' noted:

Burgers sizzle, milkshakes slurp. The year is 1975 and John Carpenter is sitting in a Big Boy restaurant in Hollywood with Stuart Cohen, a TV producer at Universal. Over lunch they talk movies and Carpenter pitches an idea for a remake of Christian Nyby/Howard Hawks' B-movie classic The Thing From Another World.
"Let's go back and do it right," Carpenter tells his friend.
Cohen pauses mid burger-munch... "How?"

If this is true, Carpenter had been the one to suggest doing a new version of The Thing in 1975 – years before he was attached to the film in any serious way. This explains so much that would occur in his work over the next few years. Anyone who knows the first Halloween film made in 1978 are aware that playing on the TV that night was The Thing '51 – and there's more evidence of Carpenter's early connection to The Thing if we go forward just a few years. What's the final line in his 1980 film 'The Fog'? *To the ships at sea who can hear my voice, look across the water, into the darkness. Look for the fog.*

How similar is that to the final line of The Thing '51 "Watch the Skies"? Were these little nods to his greatest influences, or perhaps they're in-jokes for his fans for what was coming next? At the very least it suggests Carpenter knew what dream project he had coming up.

Note: The 2015 article also quoted Spielberg, whose warm and cuddly, family friendly E.T. is often pointed out as destroying The Thing at the box office in 1982. Well, something you may not know is Spielberg admitted he'd actually been thinking about making a horror film about aliens terrorising an isolated house. Spielberg, however, decided to go the other way. *It went against my grain as a storyteller...I saw I was doing nothing more than harking back to the old days of Earth vs The Flying Saucers, Invaders from Mars and War of the Worlds.*

Can you imagine if E.T. had been a Jaws-like horror and the film being unfavourably compared to Carpenter's superior made Thing? Another possibility, a brutal E.T may have whet-the-appetite of the public for a more mature horror alien film and helped The Thing at the box office, and a successful Thing would have given Carpenter's career a totally different trajectory. Oh, what if....?

Before 1980 we have different versions of how Carpenter became attached to The Thing, and the picture's origins doesn't become clearer after 1980 either. Fangoria asked: *two years ago, the Hollywood trade paper Variety carried a small item saying that producer Wilbur Stark was to remake The Thing...Who, we wondered, is Wilbur Stark?*

Let's get this one out of the way. The rights to many RKO films were held over the years by several people and studios, and at some point Stark bought a package of titles from Wall Street investors. Universal later bought these film properties from Stark, explaining how RKO's The Thing from Another World became a Universal property.

Producer David Foster next explained *"About six years ago, my wife and I attended a party...and met Stuart Cohen.... Sometime in the course of the party, he said to me, 'I really like to go on to features: If I were to come up with an idea, can I talk to you?'...A couple of weeks later...he came in with a copy of the John Campbell's story 'Who Goes there?'*

The pair began working on how they could get the rights. Stark happily stepped aside for an Executive producer credit. Then: *Foster first spoke to Carpenter about The Thing almost three years ago* (1979) ...however...

Starlog Magazine #61 (1982) carried an interview with Cohen, and his story is a little different. He admitted already knowing Carpenter before ever speaking to those other possible directors, recalling: *John and I first talked about this project close to six years ago...* that would be 1975-6 – a full three years before David Foster recalled Cohen first talking to Carpenter about directing and about the same time as Foster and Cohen first met.

We were sitting in Bob's Big Boy Restaurant on Vine Street in Hollywood. We agreed it would be a wonderful idea to make a movie that was more faithful to the story. We thought that to just remake it wouldn't do the picture or ourselves justice, because we liked it so much...John wasn't well known either at that time. He was just finishing Assault On Precinct 13 and hadn't made Halloween yet.

This is when Cohen claims he went to his fellow producers, and they began building the film package – and he recalled the result was: *there was still no great interest in John as the director. Ned suggested it be assigned to the very promising director/writer team of Tobe Hooper and Kim Henkel (The Texas Chainsaw Massacre), who'd just been brought on the lot by William Friedkin for a development deal of their own.*

Cohen wasn't comfortable with cutting his friend out, but *John was tied up then with Warner Bros, as a writer and producer.* So, the team – without Carpenter – began looking for a scriptwriter.

If you check out the great website monsterlegacy.net, they have a fantastic history of the filming of The Thing, and when it came to this sequence reported: *At this point in time, Bill Lancaster began working on the script — quickly joined by Carpenter after the release of Escape from New York.*

This of course gives a different story to the Starburst article mentioned earlier, where Carpenter suggested he'd been part of hiring Lancaster.

So again, lets clear this up.

The Writer

In the early 80s John Carpenter was one of the hottest new directors in Hollywood, so any move he made obviously brought tremendous interest. This spotlight also fell on anyone associated with his projects, giving us a different view of how The Thing was made.

Thanks to the rise of the horror industry in the 80s, along with a prevalent fan-based magazine industry we have an unusual resource for this film. What's interesting is that we can move through these interviews and articles, almost in real time – or maybe like a reverse Benjamin Button. We know what's going to happen – we know the result of everyone's work and the reactions it garnishes. What soon appeared in my research was this, spreading through all these questions and answers is an interesting, almost tragic story by itself – one that ends in real triumph.

Bill Lancaster was Hollywood royalty. The son of Burt Lancaster, Bill had his first script filmed just a few years earlier, which had a lot of eyebrows raising when he was chosen to script The Thing '82. 'The Bad News Bears' was a comedy about a kid's baseball team being managed by an angry older man – perfectly played by Walter Matthau. How did the author of a comedy sports film become the writer for what's considered one of the most important horror/sci-fi films ever made?

Sadly, Bill Lancaster died in 1997, and records show he was involved in very few films after The Thing. Luckily, Starlog Magazine (#48) interviewed Bill and we have this record. When Bill was asked why he was chosen to write the movie in 1982, he laughed: *To tell you the truth, I don't know...I think most writers who are relatively capable should be able to work in different genres. I feel that I can, but who knows?* Perhaps in response to some of the reviews and questions that were already filtering out he pondered: *"Maybe I've screwed it all up."* Audiences will be able to judge that for themselves when the movie opens on July 30th, but Carpenter himself has already praised Lancaster's work as being *"the most horrific script I've ever read."*

So, what were the mechanics of him being picked? Well, Lancaster's answers give us a different view to how the film was made and what was happening behind the scenes.

From his Los Angeles home, the 33-year-old...recalls the "curious" process by which he received this unlikely assignment. The producers, Larry Turman and David Foster, had the project at Universal with their co-producer, Stuart Cohen. In 1977 Cohen thought I might be right for it. I'd also been speaking to Turman about a few other things, so they had me in to see the original movie as a courtesy. We all agreed it was great, but I didn't want to remake it because it was too good to try and imitate. I'm not sure how Larry, David and Stuart saw the project, or even if they all saw it the same way, but I felt they wanted to stick closely to the movie. I hadn't read the short story at that point (SM#58).

The producers at this stage had the script written by William F. Nolan, but for some reason they were looking to go another way. This is when they began searching for a new writer.

Then in August 1979, my name was brought up again. This time John Carpenter was involved in developing it, so I met with him. This was just prior to his finishing *The Fog*, which he was then looping and scoring. I'd read the short story by then and was very intrigued with it. On the basis of that I told him I'd like to do the story but not re-do the movie. I think John had felt the same way from the beginning. In essence I was begging for the job, because I really wanted to do it.

Straight from the Lancaster's mouth so to speak. Before he was offered the job Bill had been interviewed by the director. Lancaster admitted he wanted to move the storyline away from the 1951 movie and align it more with the original 'Who Goes There?'. This required a lot of creative thinking as there was never a lot to that story, being only a novelette. Lancaster even admitted to having trouble as *It's a very interior story and can get a little confusing.*

For anyone who has read the original, you'd be aware there could be an issue when converting it into a modern horror film as: *There's very little action in it — it's mostly talk.* Lancaster explained: *Our problem was to try to turn it into physical action as well as verbal action, and to clarify the weirdness of this monster as much as we could.* Oddly, the 1982 film has become well known for its lack of action and dialogue. It's one of the most minimalist films ever made, with long sweeping shots of people thinking about stuff – often with their back to an open door and with the scene ending in a fade out. This of course helps build the intense paranoia and atmosphere the movie has become famous for.

Back to Lancaster.

As a kid growing up in the 1950s I was a freak for all the horror and science-fiction movies, he explained. *Nowadays I rarely get the chance to watch prime time television, but on Friday and Saturday nights I still stay up until 5 a.m. to see those absurd 50s SF pictures. I especially remember seeing Them, The Creature From The Black Lagoon, all the early Hammer films, and the crazy Japanese monster movies. I also ate up Roger Corman's Vincent Price/Edgar Allan Poe films. I've always loved eerie movies like Psycho, and William Castle's Straight-Jacket scared the shit out of me. Unfortunately, I was a little too young to see The Thing when it first came out, but I saw it about five years later and liked it a lot.*

Lancaster next described how working on the film's script was a team effort.

I didn't know who the heck John was...Then I realized I was working with the big cult hero director. I was impressed with him right away. He's a very nice, low key, straightforward, totally unpretentious guy. We hit it off, and the groove seemed to be pretty good.

During the next few months: *John and I met about six times and kicked ideas around. I came up with an approach of how I thought we should tell it, and he had his own thoughts. It's good to work with someone like John, who is himself a writer, because he understands a writer's problems. It's also helpful to have someone off whom you can bounce ideas. He encouraged the way I wanted to approach the script.*

After their meetings Lancaster got to work. He *wrote the first 40 pages. They were well received, and I finished the rest of it some months later. John was abreast of what I was doing from the beginning to the end, and for the most part he gave his blessings to it. I don't think it was that much of a surprise to him, although he may have been surprised by the execution of it since he wasn't physically writing it with me.*

One of the biggest changes from the original story came with the cast. *Who Goes there had around thirty people working the outpost*, but Lancaster had some different ideas about that. *Thirty-seven seemed a little excessive*, he explained, as it was *very difficult to deal with that many people. It would have been harder for the audience to identify the characters, and for each of them to register a personality and a difference.*

The next change would be to the actual structure of the story. Who Goes There? begins with a flashback, with McReady recounting how the creature was discovered in the ice. *The opening of the story is pretty conventional*, Lancaster explained, *so I never wanted to do that. The conventional way would have been to show that something had crashed and the men heard it and went to search for it, but that would have been a great deal like Hawks' movie. I thought it would be far more interesting to blast the film open in mid-story.*

Next to go was the finale. *The story ends on a rather dull note."* How? *Since we're doing an action/adventure/thriller/monster movie, the audience deserves to see this confrontation. They've sort of been promised it, so we went back to the conventions of the horror movies in that sense.*

Another issue, a novelette with over thirty people meant there could never have been a whole lot of character development. Lancaster immediately changed all that for the filmmakers with these brief introductions in his script.

MACREADY
35. Helicopter pilot. Likes chess. Hates the cold. The pay is good.
GARRY
46. The station manager. Stiff. Ex-army officer. Wears handgun.

CHILDS
33. Six-four. Two-fifty. Black. A mechanic. Can be jolly. But don't mess
BLAIR
50. Sensitive. Intelligent. Unassuming. An assistant biologist.
DR. COPPER
45. Professional. A decent man. A good doctor.
PALMER
27. Second string chopper pilot. Crack mechanic. Long hair. Slight sixties acid damaged
NAULS
22. The cook. Bright. Black. Irreverent. But kind-hearted. Roller skates
NORRIS
44. Stocky. Rugged looking. A geophysicist. An incipient heart condition
BENNINGS
38. A meteorologist. Dutiful. An old pro.
CLARK
24. The dog handler. Likes it here. Good at his job.
SANCHEZ
21. The radio operator. Hates it here. Lousy at his job.

Lancaster explained his thinking.

The characters were pretty one-dimensional in the story...I think the character of MacReady that we came up with is sort of neat. It's 1982, so what the heck are these guys doing there? They must be pretty weird to begin with. I wanted it to be an ensemble piece with one character who would emerge as the 'hero,' rather than have a Doc Savage-type of superhero. MacReady isn't the all-American hero, but when the chips are down he'll come up. He's semi-cynical and boozes a lot, so I thought he would be an interesting character to pit against the Thing.

When the magazine pointed out there were some similarities between MacReady and the last hero Carpenter had in a film, Snake Plisskin, Lancaster conceded the point. *Maybe that's true...although Kurt isn't playing him the same way. There are distinctions, but I know what you mean. He's kind of an anti-hero type of person.*

The scriptwriter didn't let it lay there, though.

John didn't want the character to be played the same way he's delineated in the story. He's a fan of Humphrey Bogart and that type of hardboiled cynicism, so he may have had an influence on me. In fact he used to tease me constantly by saying: 'MacReady is really you, isn't he, Lancaster?' Actually he isn't. There are slight elements of me in him, but I don't spend my time drinking tequila in the snow wearing a sombrero. I suppose John is a strong enough director in his storytelling style that he would naturally have an influence on the material.

MacReady was a composite of Humphrey Bogart, Lancaster and Carpenter... who knew?

The Broads

In the original story there were no women, but as we have seen Howard Hawks changed that when he filmed The Thing '51. Hawks liked having a strong woman in his movies that often took on the men at their own game. Fast talking, intelligent and ready for action, they became known as the Hawksian women.

Many have pointed out the character of Nikki Nicholson, played by Margaret Sheridan, was just a token female role in '51, perhaps created for a little unnecessary sexual attention to help sell the movie as something more than just the usual sci-fi/horror fare of the day. To me this thinking is unfair – as we noted, Sheridan held her own against the male actors in the film and her character was the one who came up with the idea to kill the alien by just cooking it.

Some may not be aware, but there were women in The Thing '82 as well. One to provide some humour and the other who helped create a real scare. If we turn to the Lancaster script, it records a lost scene.

Bleary-eyed, MacReady is in the process of blowing up some strange inflatable object. As he puffs away, he still keeps an eye on the Norwegian video tapes. His balloon begins to take shape. It blossoms into a life-size replica of a full-breasted woman. Something on the tape catches his eye. He rewinds, then starts it forward again.

Starlog pointed out one: *...of Lancaster's additions is an inflatable rubber doll in the shape of a voluptuous woman, which not only serves to further humanize MacReady's character but also provides a humorous scare amidst the mounting suspense.*

Lancaster admitted: *I thought that was kind of cute...because there are no broads in this movie. I think it works well, since it's not just a grace note. We also make use of it towards the end.*

Leading us to that "humorous scare"? Let's go back to the script to when the survivors are looking to blow up the compound and leave nowhere for the alien to hide.

> *Nauls kicks over a chair. A naked, fleshy object bounds high into the air. Nauls thrusts out his torch, catching the breasts of the inflatable woman. She pops and is sucked out through the hole in the roof.*
> *Nauls tries to catch his breath.*
> NAULS
> *Goddamn white women.*

"Broads...?" That's what Lancaster had called women. Though it's easy to just blow this off as a term of the day, I'll point out Starlog also picked up on this odd turn in the conversation and followed up with the script writer on this.

SM: *The absence of women marks a return to a key component of the collective paranoia featured in Campbell's story. However, Lancaster justifies their exclusion with a seemingly sexist prejudice.*

Lancaster: *In reality there usually aren't any women in these kinds of situations. I remember thinking as a kid that the obligatory love scenes in horror movies interrupted the action. It seemed more honest to have a group of just men in that situation. It may be a commercial gamble, but Kurt Russell is a handsome guy so maybe the girls in the audience will fall in love with him. Women have taken a different role in 1982 than they did in 1951, so perhaps we should have put in one or two, but they would have seemed gratuitous to me.*

In 2011 The Atlantic published an article By Noah Berlatsky 'What 'The Thing' Loses by Adding Women' as a reaction to the prequel film released that year with its female characters. I think it missed the point when talking about the 1982 film, as the article concentrates on how it was about men being men, and the homosexual undertones as a result of this, especially with the men constantly inspecting each other to ensure they weren't the Thing.

Was this the case? I have no idea – but I would point out that in the early 80s, women in horror were there to show their boobs, be murdered or be saved. All three would have changed the entire flow of '82 and made it into something far less, something I think many commentators miss when discussing the sexist nature of the film. A woman in peril would have unified the men, and a woman killed would have turned the film into a revenge story or at the very worst, an alien slasher film. Gone would be the paranoia between characters and the fight to ensure the alien doesn't make it to the rest of the world.

NOTE: Women have also taken a larger role in 2022 at the South Pole than they had in 1982 and 1951. Records show today at least 1/3 of those working on Antarctica are women.

This was one hell of an extensive interview with Lancaster in Starlog, and one possible reason could have been because Carpenter had severely restricted media access to parts of the movie to try and keep its secrets. To me this meant when those with an interest in the film, such as sci-fi magazines, had the opportunity to question anyone involved, they asked as much as they could to try and garnish some insight. Fans were keen and they wanted to know what the film was going to be like.

Before we move on, I did mention there were two female rolls in the '82 film, and I know many of you already guessed this one. For a film that's eminently quotable, we visit one scene with a great line that everyone seems to love – MacCready playing chess. The actress Adrienne Barbeau not only appeared in Carpenter's films like Escape from New York and had a roll in the Creepshow episode featuring the Thing clone, the Crate, she also played the voice of the Chess computer in '82. I contacted her about this cameo and got the following back from Barbeau's assistant.

Thank you for reaching out. Adrienne sends her apologies because she has absolutely no recollection of recording the lines for the film, and didn't even know she had voiced it...

DID YOU KNOW? Just like Hitchcock, Carpenter also likes to have a cameo in his films. In The Thing he (and most of the producers) play the Norwegians on the video found at their destroyed camp. Not the figures standing around the spaceship mind you, they were local Inuit's, but the one's standing around the frozen ice block.

The Effects

Since films like ALIEN, the Godfather and the Wild Bunch, a gritty streak of realism and violence had entered Hollywood. The Thing was about to take that to a whole new level, partly thanks to the brutal script Bill Lancaster handed in.

Basically I just wrote with no holds barred, he admitted, *but in certain sequences I left the details out. Then we would go over the script to make things practical.*

Why leave those details out? The answer was simple.

We have Rob Bottin doing the make-up effects, Roy Arbogast doing the mechanical effects, and Michael Ploog doing the storyboards and illustrations. We sat around together and bullshitted a lot. At one point I told them: 'Look, gang, you don't necessarily have to stick to the specific exposition of the special effects in the script. You guys are crazier than I am, so think of something weirder'.

With such a creative team working on the film it was clever to get their input as much as possible, and may explain why the effects in the film were of such an incredibly high standard. People usually do their best work when they're emotionally invested.

They would decide what was feasible. Then we'd all put our ideas together in the script, so they'd be there for the different departments to see. Some of the effects were just too difficult, but for some of the others we'd come up with a more interesting concept.

We wanted to use everybody's input, especially people like Bottin, Arbogast and Ploog, who have been coming up with this weird stuff all their lives. Lancaster explained.

Sometimes I'd come up with an idea and they'd say: 'Screw the writer — he's nuts. How can we do this? But occasionally they'd suggest something and I'd say: 'How the hell do you think you can do that? They'd say: 'Watch us' — and they'd do it.

One name you may have recognised in Lancaster's list of those involved in creating the effects of the film was Mike Ploog, who I was lucky enough to have a few online chats with. Lancaster highlighted the work of the veteran comic and movie artists and his work on the film. *He's a superb illustrator... To help the rest of us visualize our ideas he'd sketch them out in sequence, and John could steer him in other directions. He was a very helpful person to have on a movie like this, which is filled with effects.*

Ploog was a fantastic artist who began his career with various animation studios like Hanna Barbera, working on cartoons like Batman, Motor-mouse and Auto-cat, Wacky Races and Scooby-Doo. This led to Ploog moving to Marvel Comics, helping draw or create horror titles in the 1970s like Ghost Rider, Man-Thing, the Monster of Frankenstein, Planet of the Apes and Werewolf by Night …or as the Little Shop of Horrors press kit noted about his work, *anything with hair on it.*

Ploog eventually left comics and returned to Hollywood, helping design creatures and landscapes for classic animated films from Bakshi Productions like Wizards and Lord of the Rings. He also did designs and storyboards for Superman II, Young Sherlock Holmes and Jim Henson productions such as Little Shop of Horrors, Dark Crystal and Labyrinth.

The Thing is the only real horror/monster-type picture that Ploog has ever been involved with. For it, he worked closely with director Carpenter and special make-up effects whiz-kid Rob Bottin to come up with the look of the 'Thing' itself. There were many meetings and discussions, and many more drawings that were done to finally create the special creature.

I'm convinced, says Ploog, "this isn't going to be a monster movie, it's going to be a nightmare movie! I mean, this thing is really weird! It really does look like someone's horrible dream." He chuckles and points at a drawing near the desk of something that resembles an anguished human head growing out of a lump of fettuccini, on two legs. *"that's something we never used, but it's along the same lines as what we did use."* Ploog and the crew affectionately refer to the drawing as 'The car wreck." Whatever they call it, it is indeed weird (Fangoria #18).

The Lost – or 'I don't know what the hell's in there, but it's weird and pissed off...'

Before Ploog began creating critters there was an artist attached to one of the earlier versions of the script that did some seriously freaky stuff. Dale Kuipers spent most of his life in Wisconsin, creating art and helping to build some of the effects for the states famous haunted houses that pop up at Halloween. This is a long way from Hollywood – but his time in Tinseltown made him a local celebrity and I did find a little exposé on Kuipers by a local TV station in 1996 (you can watch it on YouTube). A reporter visited him at his studio and Kuiper talks about being a young kid at school and being asked to draw a bluebird. Instead, he drew a pterodactyl. The interview is the usual fluff piece about a talented artist explaining his art, but it's worth watching because at one point there's a brief image of some monster sketches on a page – and they look like Thing images to me.

Note: They were.

Kuiper was hired to do effects for an odd little spoof movie with Ringo Starr called Caveman. Later he helped create effects on The Howling (sculpting werewolf hands) and he may have helped design and build two aliens from Star Wars - Hammerhead and Walrus Man. The rumour is he did so secretly because he'd not been approved by the make-up artists' union. One last thing about the interview, there's a line Kuiper said that I found worth repeating. When asked about modern horror films he explained: *I detest slasher films. A monster movie is trying to catch a sense of wonder using your sense of make-believe.... While a slasher film...is trying to make you into a monster.*

Larry Turman and David Foster were attached to Caveman and suggested Kuiper could help them on The Thing. He was flown to LA to meet the director and recalled: *I sketched a concept in Carpenter's office right before his eyes ...John was really excited by it* ...and was hired to continue designing for the film.

Kuiper got to work. *John asked for a creature that wouldn't swim, fly, crawl or walk...I saw it as being able to generate pseudopods from a concentrated, pod-like base. The appendages could instantaneously assume the shape of anything from a tentacle to a lobster claw. In some ways it would be almost arachnid-like, except that its body base would have a fiery nucleus.* The artist later mused: *I guess it was never my place to tamper with the story or screenplay, but I did want to share my ideas with the producers.* Well, we have Kuipers suggestions as the letter he wrote recently surfaced.

The thing (our Thing) is an incredible organism. Its life blood is a yellowish multi-viscous slime. Within each cell of this slime exists genetic codes for instant generation of nearly any physical body, appendages, or parts needed for survival and full defence, the strength behind these appendages will instantly become equal to any situation they face. This self-same lifeblood can be disintegrated to powder by will of the thing after each physical addition has served its purpose. Its eyes are not eyes in the classic physical sense. They function (instead) like solar collectors, taking in and polarizing for instant use any, and all radiant energy in any given environment. Gravity is a non-existent physical factor for The Thing...

through hundreds of projection tubes located over the entire surface of its helmet-like 'body-head' it can shoot fastening ribbons to any available surface, solidifying, disintegrating and re-shooting in a split second.*

Now a little speculation. There's one painting by Kuipers showing the dog-thing attack in the kennel. "It can shoot fastening ribbons to any available surface..." ...is the attack on the dogs in the kennel a remnant of Kuipers work? Let's have a look at the script.

                  INT. KENNEL - NIGHT
  Barks. Growls. More frenetic pacing. The din escalating.
     Three dogs start to close in on the stranger.
                They attack.

         THE SHADOW OF THE NEW DOG

   against the kennel wall. The shadow suddenly lurches
        upward, seeming larger. The kennel roars.
 The light finds a mass of dogs in a wild melee in the corner.
  Barking mixed with hissing, a gurgling, a screeching.
  Dogs being hurled about and then charging back into the
             fray with a vengeance.
 The flashlight illuminates parts of some "thing." A dog.
 But not quite. Impossible to tell. It struggles powerfully.

So, the script had nothing about tendrils of goop wrapping around the dogs, but Kuipers work does. The one person who might be able to clear this up was Mike Ploog, who drew the storyboards for this sequence. Did he work off Dale's information or art? I asked and found out Mike was on holiday, but his assistant sent him the question and I got back the following answer.

Hello there. Mike said that as far as he can remember, and very unfortunately, none of Dale's art was used. He remembers Dale as one heck of a nice man. (Mike finished his work on the THING and moved on to SUPERGIRL fairly quickly. THING on Friday, SUPERGIRL on Monday, so he was quickly moved on from all things... THE THING). They had called Mike and asked if he could do some more production work but he had already moved to SUPERGIRL. He said that at the beginning of THE THING it was literally him working in an office by himself, and then very quickly others started arriving. Rob was among the first.

To me this just means Ploog doesn't recall using Kuipers art for anything he worked on. I just find it an odd coincidence that Kuipers earlier art for this scene contains exactly the image of shooting tendrils of goop that we see in the film. Ploog said something similar in an earlier interview.

To be absolutely honest, you cannot say one particular thing was your idea. It's something that's born out of an enormous amount of discussion. you can come up with a brilliant idea, but unless it has a certain degree of practicality or a certain degree of cinematic believability, your idea is useless. It takes a marriage of minds.

One reason Kuipers didn't return was the film had moved away from his original idea for the creature. He designed an alien that sat on the head of a victim, cracking open the skull and entering the brain to access memories and create a perfect duplicate. It could then generate whatever it needed, arachnid-like arms, whatever, to protect itself. Kuipers idea was the alien would be vulnerable at this point as it was merely creating an illusion and no one could see the truth. It: *would be an extra-terrestrial Lon Chaney, Sr. producing a thousand faces of fear to demoralize and decimate all defences...the creature was highly stylized, as unique as Giger's Alien.* It's important to note Kuiper had also moved the creature away from a man in a suit and got so far as building a maquette of the creature.

Sadly, the artist was then injured when he was thrown into a store window by a drunk motorcyclist, so needing to keep moving forward Carpenter turned to Bottin. *At that time, I didn't know if I wanted to do it or not...it was going to be a big studio picture, Pretty scary,* Bottin explained in his interview for Cinefantastique. When asked about the work Kuipers had completed, Bottin admitted:

I'm a big fan of Dales work, he'd come up with something that was a lot better than ALIEN's facehugger, but it was basically a big bug... It was a very good bug, and it was really neat, but it wouldn't be spooky enough. I told John, 'look I don't want to compete with a movie like ALIEN because it was very good, and I also believe the audience has great expectations about what a monster from outer space would be. When it turns out to be a guy in a suit – or a guy in a bug costume – it just isn't going to cut it now because people want to see more.

Bottin began sketching, and Carpenter liked what he saw so much he offered him the gig. At Bottin's request, Kuipers was offered a job as a designer sculptor, but he declined, because he felt Bottin's ideas were too far removed from his own. At that point, according to Bottin, 'Dale just dropped out of sight, and that's too bad because I really could've used him.'

I got to ask Thing producer Stuart Cohen about the artist.

Dale Kuipers was a very nice man, a gentle man seemingly unsuited to the rigors of monstermaking. When he left Los Angeles after our first series of discussions he left believing everything was settled - he would begin sculpting, and that John was doing "cartwheels" over the designs. John was in fact becoming increasingly uncomfortable with Dale's mechanical puppet design, and the fact the designer had no plans to relocate to Los Angeles for the duration. He would commute from Michigan when necessary, leaving Roy Arbogast to run the day to day effects shop. This was a big problem for us, and we were trying to figure out what to do when the matter resolved itself in the most unfortunate way possible - with Dale's accident. We had to move on to a new designer immediately...

That was it for Kuiper. He'd work on a few more movies and TV shows before heading back to Wisconsin. His Thing work is cool, and it can be seen in a few places – but I think dumping it was the right call. A bug's a bug and we have plenty of those movies, but there is only one Thing. As for the kennel scene, the fact that he drew exactly what was filmed before anyone else had joined the production team indicates that part of his work did indeed survive to the silverscreen. This all happened a long time ago during a truly chaotic shoot, memories fade...and yes it's only a small matter, but not I dare say to Dale, who's work deserves to be remembered.

The Transformation

In 1981, Carpenter was asked about the upcoming effects in his film.

We're still in the planning stages, really, but at this point in time there are a number of scenes, a number of 'transformations,' you could call them...the movie will have a certain weirdness that will, I hope, go beyond the story. We've got Rob Bottin doing the effects, and he's got some really unbelievable ideas...Rob's ideas really go pretty far in that direction.

In the 1982 Fangoria interview, Bottin admitted something weird had been happening when he was awarded the job to design all the creatures.

I was under so much pressure to come up with something that nobody could imagine, that I started having dreams about myself sitting at my work table with all my tools in front of me, trying to come up with ideas. In the dream I would finally build something, or sculpt something, and it would look really good, so I'd take it to John the next morning.

It's hard to believe today, but when Bottin first started showing his designs and ideas: *John wasn't too enthusiastic about what I had in mind for the Thing...he said it was too weird...I just told him, whatever you have in mind, John...*

The director then asked Rob to sketch some of his ideas, but Bottin admitted with all the work he had to do, there just wasn't time. Though some sources indicate he was already working on the film, it seems it was now Carpenter suggested maybe Bottin could work with someone like comic book artist, Mike Ploog...who if you recall explained he was working on the film before Bottin and maybe that's why Carpenter recommended him?

The long, arduous makeup process began with concept sketches and storyboards; artists Mike Ploog and Mentor Huebner were key figures. Ploog. in particular, was instrumental in defining the look of the film, story-boarding many of the effects scenes, and nearly all of the live-action photography.

These comments prove we owe Mike Ploog all the thanks we can bestow on him for much of Thing '82. Yet, like Kuiper, there's one artist that seems to have been somewhat forgotten. Mentor Huebner was a storyboard artist who'd worked on over 200 films – including some true classics like Forbidden Planet, North by Northwest, Ben-Hur, Planet of the Apes and Blade Runner. His presence on The Thing should have been a big deal, yet you really need to search to find any mention of him.

One report claims it was Huebner who first sketched the chicken-dog – the hairless dog-thing first seen in the kennel - and storyboards still exist showing Huebner's work on the kennel scene. They're highly detailed and Carpenter looks to have followed them very closely. In one of these the dog-thing is shooting tendrils of goop at the other dogs, so again we have evidence that someone other than Kuiper had worked on this particular effect... yet, I again come back to the point that Kuiper had worked and painted the exact same scene earlier, so its likely Huebner worked from Kuipers idea.

Eyeballs

In December 1982. Time Magazine's cover announced their Man of the Year was in fact the Machine of the Year - the personal Computer. It could be argued this heralded the coming of a modern Hollywood, one fuelled by so many computer effects that literally anything today is possible. I'd argue this has proven to be somewhat false and the speed that computer effects have evolved has proven to be their Achilles heel. Think of how an effect looks great one year, then often ridiculed just a few years later.

You know what's never been ridiculed? The Thing's effects. Indeed, they're still heralded today as iconic and the film itself is routinely mentioned as being the very peak of practical effect movies. I guess if you make it look real, it will always look real.

There's been a lot of interviews with Rob Bottin over the years, but one I thought was interesting (on YouTube) gives a snapshot of their meetings on designing the Thing. *John gave me the boundaries that it is imitating, you know it only imitates its host at the moment that it's with it, so in other word if it takes over you know it looks like you, but then when it freaks out...who knows what it looks like, so it could do anything.*

This video is great because it gives a lot of closeup shots of the models – something Carpenter fought to protect as he didn't want images of his monster hitting magazines out of context or in a way that would make them look silly. Ploog also indicated the bizarre nature of the alien they were designing.

You should've seen some of the ideas we came up with for the Thing. They're the most absurd looking monsters you've ever seen. We went through our 'dead-baby' phase, but that was way too gross.

So, we got no weird baby-things running around, but some of their joking struck a chord. In a TV interview Bottin explained: *I would just say a joke out of black humour like 'you know the guy's stomach rips open and turns into a big mouth. You know, and he bites this guy's arms off,' and John would start laughing... 'you know that's not a bad idea.'*

Lancaster agreed... *out of the five or six big sequences, I had written something I thought was pretty bizarre, and I didn't know how they could do it... But then Bottin and Ploog got this look in their eyes and said 'oh, you think that's strange, Lancaster? Watch this! Right then, it was like a game of 'can you top this?' Looking at where they'd taken my idea. I had to ask, 'is that really possible?' Bottin said 'Sure.'"*

The artists themselves needed some inspiration to get going, so Bottin and Ploog reached back to their childhoods and the E.C. horror comics from the 1950s they all loved.

"Rob and I had the same idea," Ploog recalled. "We wanted it to have the 'old pulp' look as much as possible. One of the first things we came up with was the head stretching off the table and the tentacles coming out. that's right off the cover of an old pulp magazine... and we didn't inhibit ourselves with the practicality of it... you can't come up with something great and different if you're concerned with how you're going to have to do it. You go ahead and come up with something ludicrous, and then sit there and say, 'well, we can't do that, can we...can we make it work? And then you pull it back. You depend on people like Rob and his crew to eventually figure it out. That's much more effective than creating something built around what somebody already knows how to do. You don't come up with anything innovative if you do that.*

Well, there's words to live by.

The crew were obviously striving for something new, and they occasionally had trouble passing on what they were thinking with each other. The following from Ploog explains just why movies rely on conceptual artists. *We just ad-libbed it...It's a matter of listening to the things people are saying, and taking an impression of what they're giving you. You know what they mean, but they might not be able to say it, yet. Suddenly you draw it, and they say, 'That's it!'* ...and just like the Thing-baby, Ploog admitted not every idea was worthwhile.

Rob was always saying. 'Make it a big mouth'...So you'd say, 'A big mouth is horrible. It sounds good, but it's horrible. You have to have more than just a mouth.'

Well, put some eyeballs on it.' You can't just put eyeballs on a mouth!' Well, you go back and start playing with it, toying with it. pushing it and pulling it around, and then it becomes something.

One scene that was all Ploog's was the death of Outpost #31s manager Garry, whose face gets absorbed into Blair-Things hand.

Sometimes between the line's of the script, there's a huge space...If you don't fill it, nobody fills it. So, you throw something in. It's just like my comic days—you never read a writer's script because writers are the worst people in the world at filling in the gaps of the story. Everyone loved what the crew was doing, with only the occasional suggestion to change a small part of a creature like make an arm longer or relocate a stray eyeball.

The Thing

Did you know The Thing was on set for real?

Much like a method actor and screenwriter, I became The Thing in my mind, reasoned out my behaviour and pitched it to Carpenter right on the spot...

Having decided that the alien could take on any form, new thinking was needed to make sure their creature didn't fall back into a giant bug or a man-in-a-suit. Bottin decided to do this by thinking of himself as The Thing and from there working out what reaction he'd have to a situation. This led to the creation of arguably the most famous scene in the film, and Bottin passed on his conversation with the director about this during a 2007 interview with the Rue Morgue magazine.

In the beginning of the story we see my spaceship crash-land on Earth. But where did I just come from and why does the story refer to me as 'The Thing?' What if I crash-landed on Earth because I barely escaped another planet where the life forms there discovered me, attacked me, and sent me packing? And what if before that I was on yet another planet where a completely different life form discovered me, attacked me, and sent me fleeing into outer space, again?

Carpenter: *"Okay, but where's this going?"*

I continued: "Rather than simply living inside each different life form on each different planet, what if I had literally imitated each one's physical appearance? Like a fugitive on the run fleeing from one planet to the next, desperately trying to blend in by shape-shifting, disguising myself as each life form I encountered, hoping to go undetected, just to exist, to be left alone."

Carpenter; *"I'm liking this, but what's the point?"*

I asked John to hear me out: "Okay, here's the best part; If I'm The Thing and I know my survival is dependent on successfully hiding, blending in with those around me by way of shape-shifting-imitation capabilities. I'm obviously a paranoid creature who's very afraid of being discovered. But when I am discovered - taken by surprise, attacked, my advantage is I can physically recall any aspect of any previous life form I've imitated, utilizing its most appropriate physical defence mechanism to protect myself. And if any part of me is destroyed when attacked by those I've imitated, the rest of me will survive because each part of me is an individual whole. I'm not an alien-bug, nor alien-animal, nor alien-vegetable. I'm all those THINGS - and more! That's why they call me THE THING"

Carpenter was becoming interested: *"That's a wild concept, Rob. But it sure sounds complicated. So how would you show all that shot by shot? Can you give me an example?"* That's when I riffed the most famous scene in the movie, the perfect example of my imagination at play, which has always been my strength. Still pretending to be The Thing, I tell Carpenter, *"While hiding among the men, they know I imitated the dog in the kennel and therefore can probably imitate any one of them. Now paranoid themselves, they start turning on each other, the level of fear escalating to an unbearable fever pitch.*

But unfortunately, I've imitated perfectly the cellular composition of a man who has a heart condition, and as the men begin to fight, suspecting anyone might be The Thing, I suffer a heart attack. But this might be good because if I appear dead, they'll leave me alone! But wait. They're not leaving me alone! What is this?!? THEY'RE HURTING ME! Attacking me - shocking me with a defibrillator! I can't take this anymore! Without missing a beat, I transform my physiognomy into the most readily available physical means of attack: ripping my flesh open, shape-shifting, transforming my human rib cage into a set of gaping jaws - I spread them wide - the man attacking me falls inside my giant stomach-mouth, and I bite his arms clean off! But now I must escape! I chew up the man's arms - shape-shifting my intestines into a separate creature, an inhuman abomination designed to send fear into my attackers. I spit that up onto that air duct to create a distraction! Since every part of me is an individual whole and any small part of me can survive, I stretch my neck until my head slides down to the floor, separating from the rest of my body! Once my head is on the floor the men won't see me! Since I don't have legs, I send my tongue lashing out, pulling myself into the shadows and hide there under the cover of darkness!"

Carpenter's jaw dropped, he started laughing hysterically, pointed at me and roared, *"You're The Thing Rob - you are The Thing!!! What happens next? What the hell are the men doing?"*

I go on: *"While the men are distracted, watching MacReady blast The Thing abomination hanging from the air duct with his flame-thrower, my decapitated head sprouts spider-legs, then I look up from the floor to see if the men are watching! The coast is clear so I make a run for it! I must survive! I almost make it out the door, but I'm spotted! The men see me!"*

Carpenter: *"What the hell is someone going to say after they've seen something like this, Rob?"* When screenwriter Bill Lancaster saw the Norris sequence for the first time, the crescendo being the spider-head, escaping, he turned to John with an utter took of wide-eyed shock and said, *"You've got to be fucking kidding!"* John thought Lancaster's reaction was so funny; he clamped his hands on Bill's Shoulders and said, *"That line's going in the script!"* The rest is history.

Well, that's new to me. The Norris-thing was a decoy, distracting the humans while the Thing in head form escaped.

The One Scene

For an almost seamless practical film there's one part that hasn't aged well. Originally there was a large sequence of stop motion action for the alien, and there's surviving photos from these scenes. Cundey (the cinematographer) noted: *Stop-motion at the time was still very stuttery and so, they decided to eliminate what had been designed in the storyboards and keep it down to one shot.*

The stop-motion was done by Oscar winning Randall William Cook, who worked on The Lord of the Rings trilogy and Ghostbusters. Carpenter explained: *It was some great stuff...The creature comes up out of the floorboards and you see these tentacles. The problem is that everything we'd done was live-action* [and] *it just didn't fit. It just looked like a different movie and that was troublesome. So we just used the bare minimum.*

Today all that's left from this sequence is when the Thing-tentacles come out of the floor and snatch the explosive's detonator.

The Cast

In 1981 Fangoria interviewed Carpenter about the cast for his next film.

...we're looking for an ensemble of 12 men who will work right together. We've seen some pretty good actors, so far. No one to announce yet. Fangoria followed up, asking if there would be any famous faces in the crowd? *No names...that's not something I'm looking to do on this film. Perhaps some familiar faces, though.*

In almost every interview you read the same comments over and over, the producers and Carpenter talking about never intending to have a big star in the film – yet this may not have been entirely true. As Carpenter was wrapping up his work on The Fog he gave an interview to British journalists, who were surprised he was remaking an old movie.

The director explained: *I'd like to shoot it with a big star, shoot it in the Arctic and really go for it ... But I'm not really answering your question: Why re-do The Thing? Well, it just seems like the right thing to do. There's certain elements in the* set-up of people stuck in the Arctic that appeals to me... I like people in isolation... Anyway, I think The Thing is the king of the monster movies and it'd be fun to try it... The Thing is the greatest title of them all.

The search for 12 men could very easily have given us a different film. One fantastic resource for this is a small booklet by producer Stuart Cohen called 'The Making of The Thing'. Oh, how it could have been so different.

For such a big budget film the casting call brought forward a lot of names for the various roles, and some are truly astounding. For Blair, Halloween's Donald Pleasence was considered, yet Cohen recalled *my notes from the time reflect a concern he might have been too identifiable.*

Other possible actors in the running for parts? For the semi-comedic Palmer, up-and-coming comedians like Jay Leno, Gary Shandling and the voice of Roger Rabbit, Charles Fleischer were looked at. The most surprising suggestion came from Rob Bottin... himself. Apparently, the FX supervisor pushed hard for a shot at Palmer, but the wise decision was made he'd be far too busy with the effects, many of which would happen while he was in front of the camera if he got the role. David Clennon was eventually selected, and he later thanked Lancaster for his work. *He created these characters and gave them dialogue. I think that's why I wanted to do the film because I sensed on my first reading that the way these 12 men interacted, he had sort of elevated the form.*

The actor was a natural for the stoner Palmer...seriously...a natural. The big spliff was my idea. And in another scene, I was smoking from a little pot pipe. I had a little folding wooden pot pipe that I owned and used in real life, so I was using that on the set.

Peter Maloney won the role as Bennings, who later recalled his audition in New York. *I went up there with a whole bunch of other guys... John led us in improvisation. We teamed up, turned the tables over, and threw things back and forth across the room, pretending that we were at war with this monster, which was, of course, not there. That's a fun audition.*

Before Richard Masur was elected as the president of the Screen Actors Guild, he headed to his audition for the role of Gary. However, something changed because after reading the script *I said, 'The thing that I'm most attracted to is the dog handler.' [John] said, 'Really?' I said, 'Yeah, I love this character. I just think he's so misanthropic. He doesn't seem to want to be with anybody, but the dogs.'* He said, 'Well, it's yours, if you want it.' And that was it.

Joel Poliso played the biologist Fuchs and recounted to halloweenlove.com: *I got an audition through my agent for a remake of the 1951 Sci-Fi Classic, The Thing (From Another World). Having watched that movie on TV a dozen times while growing up (it scared the bejesus out of me, especially that scene where the dogs attacked the Thing in the snow and he was throwing them around like stuffed animals), I was completely stoked for the reading...It turned out that John...had actually seen me act in a student film...and he remembered me from a particular moment in the film.* However, we really connected through an abrasive remark I made to him about his not ever having directed in the theatre and, God Bless him, he smiled at my brashness. Lawrence was appalled at my choice of language and I'm sure just wanted me to leave, but I am convinced that my moment of cockiness won me the part.

Poliso then decided he needed to understand his characters motivation by enrolling in a biology class. *We dissected a frog and I just got into it.* He'd also explained the background of a famous unused scene and photo.

Originally, he had me killed on the set indoors...I've got a great picture of me hanging from the door with a shovel in my chest. He took a look at it and went, 'No, no — this isn't a slasher movie.' And so, he devised [this new death].

For Childs they looked at numerous African American actors. Ernie Hudson, Isaac Hayes and Carl Weathers, but Keith David scored the roll, and later recounted seeing Childs as: *the strong, silent type. He was a man a few words, he didn't say a whole lot. But when he did, it counted. I just took him as being* [someone] *who observes and notices everything at least twice.*

For Gary, Lee Van Cleef and Jerry Orbach were considered. Thomas G. Waites was hired for Windows, who originally was called Sanchez because Lancaster asked for a Hispanic character in his script. Carpenter was happy to find the best actor for the role, and the not-at-all-Hispanic Waites later explained how the character got his name. Waites felt Windows wanted: *to be in the movie business and be a movie star. And movie stars wear sunglasses. I picked up a pair of green sunglasses in Venice* [California]. *I was wearing them* [when] *I came into rehearsal, I kept them on, I read the character, and I went up to John on the break. I said, 'John, from now, I want everyone to call me Windows.' He looked down at the floor, and he looked up at the ceiling and took a long drag on the cigarette and put the cigarette out. You could see him thinking it through and he went, 'Alright, everyone! From now on, Tommy wants everyone to call him Windows, okay?'"*

Apparently, this did not go over well with some of the cast, who complained about the name change and the fact he would be wearing sunglasses through the entire shoot. *John said, 'Okay!' And Bill Lancaster, who was with us there during those weeks, said, 'Okay!'*, so that was it, he was now Windows.

The Great American Curmudgeon

Not all the cast were happy. Walter Brimley infamously hated being in the film, and in Starlog #141 explained: *I thought The Thing stunk. The instant* [Carpenter] *said, 'Action,' I knew I was in deep water.* Well, fans have made a lot of fun of Brimley over the years, partly because of his apparent lack of respect…however… let's have a look at the full interview this quote was taken from shall we.

Both [the offers to make] *The Thing and Remo Williams came at Christmas time and I didn't have a nickel, otherwise I would have passed on them,"* Brimley claims. *"I thought The Thing stunk. The instant* [director John Carpenter] *said, 'Action,' I knew I was in deep water. The Thing was misrepresented to me. It was supposed to have been these guys who – lets talk about Cocoon. Lets not talk about The Thing. Hey, lets move on.*

The article reveals what Brimley said was bad but did not really carry the darker context of just the quote by itself. This happens again as a picture in the same article carried the following quote: *The Thing really did put Brimley in knots. "I have a place right where my rib cage comes together,"* he explains. *"If there's no knot there, I feel I'm involved in something pretty good.*

Again, that line sounds bad but it's not entirely accurate. What Brimley actually said was: *I have a place right where my rib cage comes together, my solar plexus. If there's no knot, then at least I feel that I'm involved in something pretty good. Most of the time that's a good meter, at least for me. I can't explain it other than that, really. It's just a feeling.*

Yes, he could have been talking about his time on The Thing, but the last line and the fact he'd very specifically said he didn't want to talk about the movie, to me this suggests the actor was moving on and was just talking about how he knew if he was in a good or bad film by his gut. I'd also like to point out the class of the man. He clearly felt betrayed, that the movie they were making wasn't the one he'd signed on for, and yet instead of unloading on everyone involved he just explained why he was disappointed and then refused to say anymore.

By the way, his outlook later changed. Talking in 2016 to LA Weekly Brimley admitted Carpenter was: *a wonderful man. Everything he did put us in the right frame of mind. He understood what a director is supposed to do, and that's his gift. He didn't say very much, which I think is the best way to be.* He then admitted: *I didn't go to the premiere. I didn't see it in a theatre. I finally saw the movie in my home, and I thought it was really good.*

NOTE: Now here we find a potential link between The Thing '82 and '51. Brimley *was born in Salt Lake City, Utah and raised in California. Following a tour of duty during the Korean War, he found employment as everything from a wrangler and blacksmith to a ranch hand. He even served as Howard Hughes' bodyguard…"*

Brimley was the bodyguard to the guy who owned RKO in the 50's while they were making The Thing from Another World. Could Brimley have been on set when Hughes made one of his visits to the studio?

Famously, Kurt Russel was the very last actor to be hired, but he was a long way from being the first choice for Mac. In the 80's Brian Dennehy seemed to be in every second movie and TV show and was in the running for the lead, but he wanted the role of Copper. Apparently, the role was his, but Carpenter went another way, meaning Dennehy missed out completely. Other actors up for Mac? Names like Christopher Walken, Jeff Bridges and Nick Nolte are often noted, but there's one I was shocked by.

If anyone knows Breaker Morant and watched Jack Thompsons spirited defence of the three accused Australian soldiers at their court martial during the Boer war, you'll know he was more than capable of playing Mac. Interestingly, The Sydney Morning Herald in 2005 carried a revision of the actor's life called 'Jack's back', and noted:

*Breaker Morant made Thompson's name. Nominated for an Academy Award, the film won him Best Supporting Actor at Cannes, after which it was generally thought he would waltz into Hollywood. But that didn't happen. He turned down the lead in John Carpenter's remake of The Thing (it ended up going to Kurt Russell)...*well, it turns out this story is only partially true. Again, I went straight to the source. Stuart Cohen wrote me:

Jack Thompson was NOT offered THE THING. His agent represented to us he was dying to do the role and was willing to fly him in at his expense so he could meet John. Carpenter met with him (at Tail O' The Cock on Ventura Blvd, recently immortalized in LICORICE PIZZA) and found the actor less enthused - something about " playing second fiddle to a monster" - and we needed someone who would go all in...

The Controversy

When the comedian Franklyn Ajaye (Car Wash, and I know him as 'Spider Mike' in Convoy) read for the part of Nauls, instead of giving a performance he spoke out against the stereotypical dialogue written for the character. Apparently, this didn't go across very well with the movie's producers, however, Lancaster then later worked with the actors to make sure he wasn't using such language in the film.

This wasn't the only time the picture was linked with racism either. Now I'm not the smartest egg in the dozen, but this one left me scratching my head. The 2010 book 'Black Space - Imagining Race in Science Fiction Film' by Adilifu Nama has brought some serious allegations against the movie.

The Thing is deeply inscribed with the paranoid logic of racial eugenics – that just below the surface of white racial appearance may lurk the 'impure' and dangerous black racial 'other' and, as a result, 'experts' are required to test and measure 'bad' black blood and to locate its carriers.

"Now I'm not racist, but..."

I'm a big believer that you need to be wary when someone tries to explain themselves by claiming they aren't what they're about to talk about...so be warned, I'm kinda going to do just that.

The result is a film that symbolically calls most into question the black characters' human authenticity and indulges in the notion that blacks cannot be trusted.

Now I have to point this out right now, racism is not something you can generalise, its personal, private. We generally know racism when we see it – but you can never discount if an individual feels they're being discriminated against or seeing something they feel is being discriminatory. You cannot simply dismiss these claims as silly or oversensitive... however, just because they see discrimination doesn't mean that was ever the intention of the filmmaker, and personally, I'm having trouble seeing racism in this movie.

Given that two of the remaining subjects who are suspected of being a Thing are black, the scene is highly charged with racial symbolism concerning the eugenics movement, what has a long record of couching non white races as physically abnormal, mongrel, and alien.

Why did T. K. Carter think everyone was racist according to Carpenter? Maybe there were incidences, maybe something was said? Maybe he too was aware that the role could come across as a stereotype? Only Carter can tell us if and why and what he was feeling, and I did ask, but received no response from the actor. I also could find no specific claim by Carter against the film...not saying there wasn't one, just I couldn't find one...

...ok, there's one, but not by Carter.

Of the nine men stationed at the isolated research base, the two black characters... have been the most at odds with the white protagonist... When MacReady is forced to break into the camp after being purposefully locked out, Childs and Nauls are shown backing MacReady into a corner, where he delivers the racially inflected indictment "You little sweethearts were about to have yourselves a little lynching party."

Here's my issue with the argument the Thing was racist. EVERYONE was at odds with MacReady. Not a single one of them backed his play after Nauls had cut him free, and it's not one of the black actors he shoots when they try and rush him, it's Clark, whose been arguing against Mac the entire time. There's also constant bickering amongst other actors... 'Windows, where were you?'... is Palmers constant attack on Windows racially motivated against a Mexican?

I'd also point out from those nine characters the two African Americans were NEVER identified as the Thing and both made it to the final scenes...and one even survives the film (possibly). As for Nauls, he just disappears but we can assume he was killed. Further, after they find the blood stores have been sabotaged, Mac tells the three men who had access to the blood to move aside and be tied up as potential Things...and again these were not Nauls and Childs. I don't understand the claim of racism against the film with this evidence.

OK, yes, Mac claiming everyone was waiting to lynch him sounds racist as hell...but what single word gets across this situation? You guys were going to bushwhack me...you guys were going to ambush me? Have yourselves a hanging? Yes, the word invokes heavy racial imagery, but was it racist or simply naïve? At the end of the day its just a word that conveys instantly Mac's feelings and I just don't think Lancaster had any racist intentions when he penned the line.

As for that one thing I do believe is racist. Did You know there's an odd difference between the original DVD commentary and the later Blu-ray? On the commentary track Carpenter noted there had been some racial tension between T.K. Carter and some of the cast. The later Blu Ray was altered to remove this claim. Was this to hide racism? Did Carter hear that part of the commentary and send a message it wasn't true, so they removed it? I could uncover no information about this at all – just a lot of fan comments about it being removed... so at this point I have to say this feels like someone's trying to hide something here, so yes, that would be a racist move.

There was another racial incident, but that I'll leave for later. As for the argument the film is racist because of the purity and impurity of blood, well...

The blood test

We cannot ignore the elephant in the room. I'll admit I was totally unaware of the link between the Thing and the 80's AIDS scare until I began my research. As I explored the charge the movie was about the HIV scare, I was more than a little dubious, but it turns out there's most certainly a link between the two.

After explaining about the use of the actual word 'THING' and how it could be related to *a trans* point of encounter where meaning is in transition*...the Cambridge Companion to Queer Studies (2020) explains: *The Thing illustrates how the paranoid fantasies of the early AIDS crisis were linked with emerging discourses of medicalized transphobia. Although it contains no representations of persons with AIDS or transgender identities, The Thing nonetheless formally animates the sexual politics of the early Reagan era.... The film's original tagline "Man is the warmest place to hide," eerily points to the shared logics of infiltration and passing that would define the transphobic and AIDS-phobic imaginary of the Reagan era.*

Even the book admits: *Although reading of the plots as a cautionary AIDS tale are often dismissed as too pat, Carpenter was highly aware of the first stages of the epidemic, which broke into the US news-cycle only eight weeks before he began filming. While it is not a conscious comment on AIDS, The Thing is nonetheless a cultural mirror reflecting the nationalist horrors of its historic moment.*

Yes, the movie can be considered "a cultural mirror" because I'm thinking that right now. The fear of the monster hidden in our own blood…how could it not? But was that Carpenter's intention?

The first widely read report on AIDS was by Lawrence K. Altman and appeared in the New York Times on July 3rd, 1981. Under the title 'RARE CANCER SEEN IN 41 HOMOSEXUALS', this proves AIDS was entering the public conscious before the film came out, yet I'll argue its clear this was never on the mind of the filmmakers as this time frame simply doesn't work. Yes, the filming began a month later, but as we know this movie was heavily storyboarded and scripted well before this date. I doubt Carpenter added a massive plot point like this while on location.

However, was it on the mind of the public when they went to see the film? Could the growing epidemic partly explain the failure of The Thing at the box office? Many of the reviews at the time highlighted the blood test and thumbs being cut and blood being spilt – and by 1982 the audience were aware there was a disease killing predominantly gay men. Is it possible many stayed away from the film as they were a little freaked out about this new blood virus – especially as it was carrying names like 'Gay-Virus' and 'GRID' (Gay Related Immune Deficiency)? Its hard to say it wasn't a factor for some.

Just like the claims of racism though, I think it's clear this was never an issue the film makers were tapping into – but if that's what the LGBTQ community feels was the case, well you have to understand the pressure they were under – especially in the early 80's. To me, personally, it seems clear. Earlier interviews mention that everyone wanted to return to the original Campbell novelette , especially the blood test in the story – so this theme was on the books well before the news of AIDS hit the public's imagination, and a lot of other commentators out there have also made this conclusion. Even the author of the article admits *…The Thing is nonetheless a cultural mirror reflecting the nationalist horrors of its historic moment.*

The Thing simply isn't about AIDS – though I'll admit only Carpenter could ever tell us if he leaned into the horror of the blood test a lot more thanks to what he was hearing in the news? That most certainly is possible. Kurt Russel from an interview on the set mentioned something similar.

John's film isn't at all relevant to today's political climate, but it is relevant to the human condition. People today are experiencing a certain level of paranoia in their lives. It's being stoked by the headlines in the news. They're wondering whether this stranger on the street is going to be the one who'll rob them or kill them.

What's clear is that the movie and the news of AIDS came out at the same time – and with the world becoming increasingly paranoid about who could have this mysterious blood ailment – its possible 1982 adult audiences simply felt no need to be confronted with a horror like this and stayed away. And if you think that's a stretch, (as of writing this in 2022), what if a movie was released today about an alien that could atomise itself, you breathed it in and it decimated the human population, especially the oldest and the youngest of our society...and this led to a worldwide toilet paper shortage. Any interest in seeing that?

The Rehearsals

Rare for a movie, and almost unheard of in horror, Carpenter gathered his cast for two weeks of rehearsals. He had a large ensemble and was aware the film would succeed if all the men could portray a group who really did know each other. There'd be numerous scenes in parkas or just in the dark, so the audience needed to believe these guys knew each other well. Though Carpenter later admitted he'd never rehearse a film again, there's no doubt this time helped as every character had a strong sense of not only who they were, but their relationships with the others. Richard Masur (Clark) agreed.

John said — a couple of times — that the worst mistake he made was having rehearsals. We knew what we wanted to accomplish with these characters... Ultimately, [rehearsals] *really did contribute to the feeling of the film.*

In 2016 Simon Abrams for the LA Weekly interviewed several of the cast and crew, and their answers explored this time on set. This included Carpenter, who explained why he chose to rehearse.

The biggest thing when you work with actors is helping them to know what they're doing and who they are. Richard Dysart, who played the doc, said, "Well, I'm a Russian spy. I've been up at the North Pole." It didn't mean a damn thing for his performance, but I thought that was interesting.

Masur explained what the actors faced their first day. *Picture this: We're sitting around a bunch of tables put together in an almost pitch-black sound stage. There's a pool of light where the table is. It's a whole sound stage with nothing in it but this pool of light. It was a really eerie setup. It was very John.*

For many this was their first movie, so rehearsal proved to be highly educational. Keith David pointed out how his character Childs was: *the strong, silent type, so I had a one-line response to most things, like "Oh, hell no!" or "What, are you kiddin'?" I learned a lot just by watching guys like Kurt Russell and Donald Moffat...I learned so much about digesting information and not showing everything you're thinking just from watching...Masur also pulled me aside and said, "Listen,* man, *you're doing fine, but you don't need to project as much in this movie." [Laughs] So I had to learn how to pull it back. That was my very first lesson in movie acting.*

Masur also commented on working with David: *[we] ...started talking about how our characters felt about each other. That's how we knew we didn't like each other. Like in the scene where Childs pulls a gun on my character and I pull a knife on him... I wanted it to be a buck knife, so I got one at a survivalist store... you could flick the knife open with your thumb...and cut my hand several times.* Apparently Masur severely cut his thumb and had to get stitches.

Because they had time, the cast got to think about the process of being taken over by the alien. Carpenter explained: *The big question that kept coming to me was: If you were a Thing, would you know? I think Kurt Russell started that one. I said, "I think you would." But he kept asking that question, so I don't think that answer was sufficient.*

David Clennon (Palmer) later complained they did this maybe a little too much.

We wasted hours and hours of rehearsal time discussing fucking metaphysics! Some of the actors were obsessed with this question: When you become the Thing — when the alien takes over your mind and body — do you know that you've become the Thing? Or do you just go on thinking that you are your old self? I couldn't see the point of solving that silly riddle. What difference was it going to make in anybody's performance? The story's point was that every creature looked, sounded and smelled exactly the way it did before the alien took it over.

One achievement from the rehearsals was a tightening of the script. David recalled in an interview with Rue Morgue: *...Masur [Clark], Charles Hallahan [Norris] and Kurt Russell happened to be real science fiction buffs, so all the holes that were becoming apparent in the script, we started to address...The one thing that makes science fiction phony is the inconsistencies, so if The Thing is supposed to do this, then it wouldn't do that, and if it's supposed to be like that, then this wouldn't be true.*

DID YOU KNOW? This wasn't the only time Russel had input on the script. When Carpenter was told by an interviewer about loving MacReady's iconic final line that ended the movie, the director agreed. *I know. Hey, and he wrote it, too... he came up with it when we were sitting there in the snow!*

The Town

...in the small border town of Hyder, one proves one's mettle...At the Glacier Inn, you can get yourself Hyderized with Everclear, 190-proof corn liquor— free if you can down it in one gulp, the cost of staking everyone in the house to a drink if you can't.

I think I've mentioned this isn't a comprehensive 'making of' for the '82 film. Sorry, I just don't have the space and honestly there's very little I can add as these matters have been comprehensively covered thanks to the various DVD/Blu Ray special features and commentary tracks. What I've tried to cover is the stuff you don't get through those usual channels.

For example, we never really got a snapshot of what was happening with the cast and crew when not on set. In one interview the director recalled: *We were in a rough- and-tumble mining town,"* remembers Carpenter. *"Saturday nights were rough. Here were these Hollywood guys, actors and technicians, hungrily and drunkenly pawing at each other for the very few women."*

We do have some unique sources for this as several reporters were invited on set, such as OMNI Magazine's Johnathan Rosenbaum.

...I was flying...to watch one of the final days of exterior location shooting on John Carpenter's The Thing...somewhere in the vicinity of the Arctic Circle and budgeted at $11.5 million...to get to this spot, I had to fly from New York City to Seattle for a night's stopover, continue on Alaskan Airlines up to Ketchikan, and then proceed in a private, amphibian, four-seater plane...which eventually docked in Hyder. From there, it was another hour up a twisting, one-way mountain road to the ultra scenic location — an Air Force compound where Carpenter, his all-male cast, and his crew had set up camp.

One reason for the success of the movie was likely the camaraderie of the cast and crew. These were tough conditions and, after rehearsals and finding themselves isolated in a small Alaskan country town during winter, well I'm sure everyone got to find out who's who (see what I did there?). The movie spent no time establishing relationships amongst the characters because they simply acted like they'd been together for some time and are seemingly comfortable and familiar with each other - exactly what you'd see with people isolated in Antarctica.

Right across the border from Hyder is the town of Stewart... where I'm staying along with a goodly portion of the cast and crew. A town of about 2,500 inhabitants...

Carpenter later explained: *I stayed in a nice old hotel in Stewart. But the crew had to stay on a harbor barge. Luckily, I didn't have to put up with that...* Masur noted that barge turned out to be: *on Portland Canal, which is the longest fjord in North America. Stewart has the highest snowfall in all of North America ... like 96 feet of snow on average. At the end of this canal were a couple of big residential barges that had 30 rooms apiece and were typically used for mining crews. But we were there in December... We were the idiots who came up to shoot a movie.*

David recalled: *It was about 20 below zero. We had our long johns on, so we were never uncomfortable. What you didn't do was walk out of the hotel with your bare hands and touch a car-door handle. You would freeze to it immediately. Because it got dark so soon, the sun wouldn't come up until 9 a.m., and it would set at 3 p.m.*

The Omni reporter mentioned Hyderized, but it was Masur who explained what that meant...*alcohol in Canada has always been more expensive than alcohol in the U.S., and much more controlled in terms of when you can buy it. So two miles from Stewart is a little [Alaskan] town called Hyder which, at the time, had a permanent population of 15 people. There were seven bars in Hyder. Hunters, fisherman, miners and residents of Stewart would go...because it was much cheaper to drink there.*

...In Hyder, there was a bar called the Hyder Inn with a 50-60 feet giant tree... that ran the length of the entire room. That tree was the bar. Kurt asked me, after my first day on the set, "You just got here, right?" I said, "Yeah." He said, "So you haven't been Hyderized yet." I said, "No, I don't know what that is." He said, "We're gonna get off the bus at Hyder, go to the Hyder Inn and then we'll walk back." So I said, "It's fuckin' freezing out here, Kurt." He said, "We're dressed for it, don't worry about it." We wore our costumes back and forth, because why not?

So we got into the Hyder Inn...Kurt says to the bartender, "My friend here needs to get Hyderized." The guy brings this little 4 oz. juice glass, and he fills it with white liquid. You have to blow it back in one shot and then turn it over on the bar. Then the bartender rubs the glass around on the bar, picks the glass up and lights it on fire. The glass explodes instantly because it was full of pure grain alcohol. Your head explodes after the booze hits your stomach. You're shit-faced drunk almost immediately, especially if you've been working all day and haven't eaten in several hours.

Kurt and I walked back. It was a brilliantly clear night. You could see a gazillion stars. It was unbelievably cold, but I didn't feel the cold, 'cause I was loaded. Kurt didn't have anything to drink; I think he was colder than I was. We just shot the shit all two miles back to Stewart. It was great.

What Rosenbaum did uncover during his visit was a miserable director.

"I prefer working on a soundstage," Carpenter admits, standing outside the compound exterior, a facade lined with glittering icicles, under a string of eerie blue lights. He also confesses that he misses some of the challenges inherent in low-budget shooting, where there's less of a "tyranny of money," and it's clear that effects work isn't his favourite part of filmmaking. 'I didn't like it on Dark Star, when I had sixty thousand dollars, and this is just as difficult...I'm not enjoying myself on this location; it's probably the hardest shoot I ever had- But so far the results have been really astonishing. They open the film up."

One reason why Carpenter was likely unhappy? The dangers they faced seemingly every day. In Boulenger's biography Carpenter recounted one incident when things could have become fatal.

...the locals didn't appreciate our drooling over the local girls. Plus some of the miners had never seen a black man before. One of them pulled a gun on T. K. Carter. He was quickly hustled out of the bar. After one of these Saturday nights we decided to go up to the glacier and shoot on Sunday. Even the helicopter pilots were hung over.

Was this the racial incident Carter had been concerned about now missing from the Blu-ray commentary?

Snowstorms and drunk gun-toting locals weren't the only danger. Joel Polis (Fuchs) recounted: *The cast was flown from the desert dryness of Los Angeles into Vancouver... Due to the threat of bad weather, our short plane flight to Stewart, B.C, where we were to be housed during the shoot was cancelled, and we were bundled onto a greyhound type bus to begin a six hour ride up and over the mountains to Stewart....In the darkened bus we had all fallen asleep, when suddenly, we were shocked into consciousness by a scream ... "SLIDE!" The driver had momentarily lost control of the bus on the snow and ice, and the back of the bus slid to the left toward the mountain. He countered by turning to the right and the bus slid again, this time toward the unprotected edge of the road and a precipitous 500 foot embankment. In seconds he wrangled the bus back into his control and stopped the vehicle. We were dangerously close to the exposed edge of the mountain!*

Everyone had almost died.

The Location

The team had busy days as no one wanted to stay on location longer than necessary. Filming on a glacier is obviously dangerous, so time on location was limited. Between the travel up and down the glacier and getting through as many shots as possible, no one seemed to be taking it easy. This meant either through planning or necessity, companion or different angled shots were often filmed on a set or in a more favourable snowy location such as Stewart. Though almost seamless, it's possible to see a few of these shots. For example, as the dog-thing first arrives at Outpost #31 there's a shot of it running across the ice with the helicopter behind. In the foreground is a blue oil drum in the bottom left-hand corner. Next shot is the dog entering the camp and there's the drum in the right-hand corner showing a movement through space, except this drum's covered in logos. The first was shot at the icefields and the second in Stewart.

Academy award nominated cinematographer Dean Cundy proved to be a great source of information, and his explanations reveal how similar their problems were to the '51 film.

One of our first thoughts was to build the sets inside a big icehouse...but we couldn't find one large enough. Then we decided to refrigerate the stages on the

Universal lot. We had a couple of experts figure out the humidity to temperature ratios, and we brought in as many huge portable air conditioners as the studio had. We sealed off the stages and built huge humidifiers and misters to add moisture to the air. We refrigerated the stages down to about 40 degrees. That was very interesting, because we were shooting during a big hot spell. We went into these very cold and wet stages wearing heavy expeditionary clothing and during breaks we stepped outside, where it was 90 degrees. Everybody else working on the lot wondered who these strange people were walking around in down jackets.

Cohen added more to the filming on locations.

A special plastic encasing with hand warmers inside was built for the sound equipment, so we could record production sound. We also spent about $75,000 just to wardrobe the crew to keep them warm. We built the set as a real structure, so there was always some place people could go to get out of the cold. Even so, everybody came down with colds. All in all, though, we were lucky with the weather. It wasn't as bad as we'd expected.

The Look

One person whose work was made that much harder because of the location was Cundy, who'd worked with Carpenter on Halloween, Escape and The Fog.

We went up to Stewart, British Columbia...From there we went up a 27-mile dirt road to a little hill overlooking a huge glacier, where we built the exterior set of the Antarctic research camp...That was quite an amazing experience, because Stewart is considered to be the snowfall capital of North America. The temperature generally ranged around zero, so we were all outfitted with heavy expeditionary clothing.

Clothing wasn't the problem for the camera crew though.

The guys in the various departments contacted people who had worked under those conditions, to pick their brains for any problems we might encounter. We were pretty well prepared, but there were times when it became really difficult to work because of the weather. One of our biggest problems was that the lubrication in the camera lenses would get very thick, so it would take forever to pull focus on an actor as he walked from one spot to another. They'd had the same issue back in '51.

Now Rob Bottin fairly gets the lion's share of praise for much of the movie's effects, but Cundy also deserves credit. When it came to shooting '82 Cundy made suggestions with set construction and lighting to help improve the film and increase options for the camera.

I suggested putting ceilings on all the sets and bringing the pipes into the frame line, to increase the claustrophobia," he explains. *"Lloyd was delighted with that because he likes to put ceilings on sets, but cameramen don't because they like to* put lights up there. Since I've shot mostly on real locations, I'm used to working with ceilings."

I think we can all agree, the claustrophobic sense of the film is one of its defining characteristics, with the sets really helping sell the idea that these men were isolated, confined and in the hostile Antarctic environment. *I suggested using practical lights to make it look realistic, so we lit whole scenes with just the flares the actors carried around...During our original discussions we wanted to shoot in black and white. However, major studios are very reluctant to do that — especially Universal—because they look to colour as part of the potential TV sale. Instead I suggested we take the colour out of everything as much as possible...We ended up using the colour selectively, with the 'thing' being probably the most colourful object in the entire movie. We painted the inside of the Arctic station in shades of grey, and even tested the paint colours to get one that was extremely neutral. We also repainted the props grey. Even the wardrobe was coordinated to be in sombre colours of dark blue, grey and brown... Whenever we wanted to give colour to a sequence, I did it with lights. For example, the lights the men used to get from building to building in a storm were blue, so the lights that came through the windows to the interiors at night were blue.*

Cundy also puts an end to the idea this film was all old-school effects. New technologies were being tested on the set.

Rob and I wanted to change the speed of the camera while it's rolling, so that an object could be made to move quickly and then slow down and then move quickly again...We called a few people about it, but they said it couldn't be done. Finally Bill Edwards, the head of Universal's camera department, heard about what we wanted to do and called up the head of Panavision, who became very intrigued. So they've built an attachment for us that goes on their Panastar variable speed camera. We've been testing it, but it's very tricky to use without a lot of computer control...We've done a couple of shots with it, which I think will appear in the film, but we haven't been able yet to take it to the point we were hoping to.

The Dog

One actor that doesn't get talked about much is the dog from the film's opening sequence. Jed was a Vancouver Island wolf-Alaskan Malamute hybrid, explaining why he's often talked about as a wolf-dog. Born in 1977 and bought by Gary Winkler (the Fonz's second cousin), Jed was trained by Clint Rowe and there's no doubting he gave a remarkable performance considering The Thing was his first onscreen performance.

Masur was the actor who played the dog handler Clark, and he later explained his relationship with Jed in the same 2016 LA Weekly article.

*There was a little room off to the side in the sound stage. During the rehearsal period... Rowe brought Jed the wolf-dog in to get him used to the sound and smell of people. He was a young dog, so he was very jumpy. I worked with Jed and Clint for an hour on the first day of rehearsals and every day after that. It worked out very well during shooting, too. Jed would come and stand next to me, and he wouldn't do that thing that dogs do where they look back at their handlers. If you watch the scenes between us, he's never looking at my hand for a treat. He's just there with me; he's making his own choices. That's what makes his performance so spooky...*and boy, was Jed spooky.

DID YOU KNOW? The Shape himself, Michael Myers appeared in the film? It's all in the little details that made The Thing great. In the scene where Jed walks up to an open door and stares, on the far wall is the silhouette of someone from Outpost #31. The dog-thing then moves into the room and the shadow turns and faces the door. The scene then fades, and we assume the alien has just taken a new victim. To ensure nobody could work out which character it was, none of the actors played the silhouette, thus leaving it a total mystery. The shadow belonged to Kurt Russel's long time personal stuntman Dick Warlock, who played the Shape in Halloween II.

After The Thing Jed appeared in The Journey of Natty Gann (1985), White Fang (1991) and White Fang 2: Myth of the White Wolf (1994). Jed's career is reminiscent of The Thing '51, when two of those dogs, Bob and Bing, also became Hollywood veterans. White Fang caused some trouble when the Disney movie followed the original Jack London 1906 novel and filmed a wolf attack. Immediately Pat Tucker, a biologist for the National Wildlife Federation, explained her concerns to Entertainment weekly:

The wolves in the movie are very scary... When I go out to schools, the first thing kids ask is, 'Will wolves hurt me?' The movie reinforces that stereotype. Disney quickly agreed to run a disclaimer reminding audiences: *There has never been a documented case of a healthy wolf or pack of wolves attacking a human in North America.*

As for Jed, he remained with his trainer until dying in 1995. Buried in Gary Winkler's animal sanctuary in Bellingham, Washington, like all celebrity deaths his was reported in The Times. *Friends of Jed, the husky who starred in "The Journey of Natty Gann," "The Thing" and "White Fang," took out a full-page ad in Variety to commemorate his death. "Running at the head of the pack,"* it said. *"Good luck on your next journey."*

The Interview – Is John the new Orson?

One of the strangest documents we can track today is the video record of The Thing – and with this in mind, lets visit 1982. There's Men at Work on the Radio and a Big Mac comes in a huge Styrofoam container. It's the 9th of June and a very young David Letterman is sitting at his desk giving that famous toothy grin he has. After reading an extended biography from one of his little blue que cards, Letterman stares into the camera and smiles: *Welcome John Carpenter.*

Canned music plays and a tall man in one of the ugliest sweaters imaginable – sky blue with peach diamond checks, walks out, shakes the hosts hand then takes a seat. Dave starts by asking about the recent success of Halloween, and if you watch carefully, there's a sneaky little moment when Carpenter smiles – something he rarely does in interviews as he seems to hate doing them…but we'll get to that.

You know civilians all the time hear claims about motion pictures that made more money, did more money one week…more money in a half an hour, but this one is the most successful independent production in history. Give us an idea what that means.

Carpenter looks at Dave and answers: *The movie cost 300 thousand dollars to make and it made 70 million.*

Three hundred thousand? Dave says incredulously. *You can pretty much do that in your basement… three hundred thousand?* The number seems to have got caught in his brain and just keeps looping about.

Yeah, Carpenter says with a typical Carpenter look. *Cheap film, right? Cheap, and seventy million dollars worldwide to date, yeah?*

Good heavens. Now, do you get a lot of that?

No, not a lot of it… now, a little bit… and right there, for the briefest instance – so quick it could be considered a micro expression - John Carpenter smiles to himself at the thought of how much money he'd made from Halloween.

Dave quickly moves the conversation on. *You preferred doing an independent film I would guess, huh?*

Well, I just started making the studio films with big studios with Universal and I kind of like it…it's fun.

They treating you well? Because I read that you mentioned it that sometimes a motion picture company…would be kind of not the most fun to work with?

Carpenter ponders this for a moment. *I was worried when I went in because I thought maybe they'd take away control of the movie from me. I think that's what every director wants, his control of his film. They were wonderful, and so far things are going…*

Letterman cuts the directors answer off. *Oh…Really…now the thing which we're going to see some footage of. This is pretty bizarre stuff here…*

Carpenter nods, *We tried to make the king of the monster movies…*

Like so many of these interviews, the actual video the studio audience saw is missing, but what we can hear is their reaction….and Carpenter's reaction to their reaction.

The video cuts back and Dave is sitting behind his desk, a look of utter shock on his face and he's almost uncomfortable.

As for Carpenter, he almost looks like he's yawning, like this was just another day at the office.

The crowd seems to have been shocked and horrified, and also to have genuinely enjoyed what they saw by the noise and their nervous laughter.

As the giggles start to peter out Dave asks, *so then, it's the story of a boy and his dog?*

This indicates they'd watched the sequence inside the dog kennel. And then comes the line that I'm pretty sure Carpenter would later regret, or at the very least look back on and sigh at what should have been.

…you kind of know a film is good by the noise the audience makes.

Carpenter agrees with Letterman. *Pretty much. In this kind of film, if the audience is winging it on I know I'm alright.*

Sadly, it would be the reaction of so many that would end the studio career of Carpenter and deny us, his fans, possibly a body of incredible films. And it gets a little worse.

When this film was completed, do you just put it in theatres, or do you screen it and test the reaction of the audience?

Part of making a film for me is when I finished my first cut, I show it to an audience and see their reaction. I'll go back and change things and then show it again. The audience is a big part of the film.

Grinning, perhaps recalling what he'd just seen, Dave asks, *what is the reaction you're after in this particular film?*

Well, Carpenter explains, *it's much the same as getting on a roller coaster. There's a big build-up to the first time you go over the edge and when you do there's no stopping it.*

Dave points out his band leader. *I noticed Paul looked away and people were gasping. That's a favourable response as far as you're concerned?*

The director leans in. *Honestly, in this kind of film you're dealing with something that the whole audience knows isn't real at all. You know that there's no such thing as a monster from outer space, least we haven't seen one in the paper, and I want the audience to believe it. Yeah, when they see this film, oh my lord, look at that, that's real.*

Dave then asks the weirdest question, perhaps because there were already whispers getting out about The Thing and people's concerns about its horrific nature, and having just seen some of it for himself now had a personal understanding. *Would you send your eight-year-old child to see this film?*

The director waits a beat before answering. *I would evaluate my eight-year-old and I would ask myself is the eight-year-old impressionable and could they realize this is a fantasy film? It's really not very harmful...* Carpenter then gets serious, as though he understands this is his chance to alleviate some fears and make sure people understand what the film is like. *...but it's frightening, yeah, and if I thought so, sure.* Then something of a wistful look comes over the director's face. *If I was an eight-year-old kid, I'd want to see this movie immediately ... It wouldn't matter what my parents said, I'd go right out and see it.*

Dave then says something we, the fans of the film, wished had happened.

I would imagine kids will be lining up around the equator to see this one...

The two then chat about how some of the effects were created, with Dave pointing out: *we had a gentleman on, John Dykstra, a couple months ago. He said that the problem with doing special effects of any kind is once you've done them in a film, people get to be blasé about them. So, you have to keep topping yourself. Is this the first time ever for some of these effects?*

Carpenter then prophesies something that has proven to be absolutely true. *I don't think you'll ever see effects like this in a movie... I know there hasn't been a monster movie like this where the monster constantly changes form. It never looks like any one thing, it's constantly in motion and it's pretty hard to pull off...but I think we've done all right.*

Midway through 1982, the entire world seemed to be at Carpenters feet. He's made the most successful independent film ever, and his most recent movie Escape from New York had made money and been well reviewed. And now a big Hollywood studio had given him just about anything he wanted to make his magnum opus. He was doing so well the inevitable comparison between Carpenter and other great directors were beginning, and Dave next pointed this out.

People talk about you and compare you to Hitchcock. Is that a legitimate comparison?

I'm very flattered by that. I really am. I think I'm more influenced by a director Howard Hawks... he did the first version of the Thing from Another World... I admire his work a lot...

I think they're both wrong. The director Carpenter should be compared to is none other than Orson Welles – and let me explain why. Orson had done everything his own way. He took every opportunity he was given and made the most of it. He used fame from one media and transferred it to another, where success would follow. He then used all of this to receive (and arguably made his personal greatest mistake) the most outrageous Hollywood contract. He had all the power, and he used this to make one single, astonishing film that is even today considered one of the most important films ever made.

Not only is Citizen Kane considered the greatest movie of all time for using new camera techniques and special effects, when it was released it was attacked by critics, failed at the box office and never truly found its audience until years later. Welles himself would never again have that kind of control in a studio, and would be shunned and have to fight for everything he made after Kane. Certainly, he made some fun films, but nothing could ever be compared to his first studio movie.

Now consider what was about to happen to Carpenter. His film would be torn apart by critics, would be considered a failure at the box office. He would be fired from his next studio film and never achieve such control again. Sure, he made great movies after The Thing, but nothing would come close to this astonishing film that is still considered by many the greatest monster movie ever made. Certainly Carpenter could film suspense like Hitchcock and action and comedy like Hawks, but his career most certainly is closest to Orson Welles.

The Reviews – or Fuck Roger Ebert

My creative life changed over one film, which is an interesting thing to reflect on now.... The Thing really was a movie that I was extremely proud of and I thought was extremely good, but it was hated by everybody, fans, audiences, critics. The vehemence of the hatred stunned me, It took me a long time to come to grips with it and say, 'What was that about?' I've kind of got it in perspective now that I'm older, but when you're young and you go through these things, they can be pretty powerful experiences. It's always easy looking from the outside and saying 'Aw, the hell with that.' Well, guess what? I think every director probably gets his heart broken someplace along the line and then recovers, and I think that's the sign of somebody surviving it, escaping from it somehow. You can't let it destroy you.
- John Carpenter, Sci Fi Entertainment

Were the reviews as bad as everyone makes out? Yes…yes, they were.

All fans of The Thing are aware that when the film was released, it amassed some of the most venomous reviews of any movie. Not bad, I mean some were serious attacks, bordering on abusive, as though the very existence of this film was an affront to the history of cinema. Think I'm exaggerating?

The opening of John Carpenter's monster movie, The Thing, is very beautiful and very odd. And Carpenter builds the sequence – prolongs our curiosity about this innocent-seeming dog with repeated close-ups of its melancholy face as it lies under Ping -Pong tables or slinks into corners at the American compound…The very blandness of the shots is ominous.

Well, that's not so bad? This was the start of the New York Magazines review of the film by David Denby. It's all downhill from here…

...that's about all there is of mystery, beauty, and fun in The Thing. This movie is more disgusting than frightening, and mostly it is just boring....

Now Carpenter has talked a lot about how reviewers and the public treated him after 1982...and honestly, he's got every reason to be pissed. Denby ends his review by getting bizarrely and inappropriately personal. The Thing is about as impersonal as a movie can be. Maybe the monster took over the directors and the crew too. What the hell? Its ok to like or not like a film – but getting snarky with the crew who were just doing their jobs?

Well Mr Denby, let's see what he said about something other than the Thing... like his very next review.

Don't FILMAKERS EVER GET TIRED OF living off the film noir detective genre of the forties? The futuristic Blade Runner is still of a Humphrey Bogart movie... Blade Runner is all visuals and no story...The movie is full of gadgets – space cars and video scanners and the like – so kids may find it amusing, like some overcomplicated new toy, but it's still a terribly dull movie.

What's the saying, hung on your own petard? Zero for two Mr Denby.

Richard Freedman of The Courier (26 Aug 1982) wrote about both The Thing and Blade Runner and thought little of each...*the characters are so characterless they can only be distinguished by whether they wear beards or not. When they don their parkas to venture into the...cold, there's no telling them apart.* Not once did the reviewer stop to think that was entirely the point. That to produce the paranoia the film is known for today, the facelessness of all the men in scenes like that, hinting that any one of them could have been infected, was entirely the point of the film maker and one of the movies greatest strengths. Freedman's criticisms perhaps reveal what was happening in the world's film review columns...they didn't get it.

Even Carpenter's long time business partner and close friend, Debra Hill, couldn't help but talk about the failure of the film. While explaining why Halloween III – Season of the Witch failed, Hill noted why she believed the Thing crashed to Starburst Magazine (#72).

I think Alien ruined it for us all. When the monster came out of John Hurt's chest, audiences just went crazy and demanded more of that sort of thing. I think the ultimate in that sort of stuff is John's The Thing . . . And yet it wasn't a success. Why not if audiences wanted those visceral type of effects?

John and I are very, very close but I think that the picture was just too excessive. It became more Rob Bottin's picture than John's. And speaking as a movie-goer and not a friend of John's. I would have liked to have known more about the characters. As I didn't know them I didn't feel anything for them as each of them encountered the Thing. It didn't register emotionally. John disobeyed all the rules of suspense that he'd handled so very well in Halloween. In Halloween we spent the first 30 minutes of the film getting to know these girls so the audience would care when they got killed. And in the end Jamie Lee beats out the Shape and wins, whereas in The Thing Kurt Russell and the other guys are just sitting there looking at each other and saying, well, it's either you or me . . . There was no sense of relief at the end.

The producer then admitted to something long speculated by many fans.

SB: I understand he shot more background material on the characters but cut it out.

DH: Yeah, he did. I don't know why he cut it but I never saw what he cut, I only saw the finished movie. I visited him on the set a few times but that was as far as my involvement with The Thing went because I was shooting something else. But I do know he cut some stuff and also rewrote and reshot some scenes, but I don't know why he made that decision.

SB: I think the film is underrated. I like it.

DH: Well, you would, you're a writer for Starburst magazine! That's a real minority group, don't you think?

Today Hill might be surprised at how many of us there are who do believe exactly this. I do understand her thinking though, at the time many Sci-fi/horror fans had turned on the film. Indeed, Starburst's own John Brosnan simply unloaded on the movie during his review.

It was a tough week. First Poltergeist which blew my socks off, and then The Thing. The Thing almost blew my dinner all over fellow reviewer Alan Jorges who had the misfortune to be sitting next to me. I mean, this movie is sick! Lots of fun. Yes, and full of shock-horror moments that you won't forget in a hurry (some of the nightmarish imagery seemed to burn itself onto my retinas — I could see it for hours afterwards every time I shut my eyes! But basically it is sick. It goes about as far as it's possible to go with explicit gore effects — in fact it probably goes too far... The Thing certainly does have pace but that's about all apart from gore and shocks. It certainly doesn't have any sense of coherence... There seemed to be so many bits and pieces of Thing on the loose I couldn't figure out just how many monsters there were...As the film progressed there seemed to be so many monsters on the loose I expected there would be a surprise ending in which everyone turned out to be the alien and that the last real human had gone in reel two . . .Admittedly it's technically very impressive, and has a genuine nightmare quality to it...

The reason why the reviewer was so venomous might have something to do with what he said next.

I'm sorry folks but I have to say it— Things just ain't what they used to be. I don't want to brag but a friend and I handled the problem of a shape-changing monster much more logically than Carpenter...in an outline we wrote a couple of years ago. Called Shaper...

Brosnan handed in his script treatment, it was accepted and then the entire venture collapsed when a similar film was announced in Hollywood. Could the disappointment of not getting his own version of this story filmed somehow colour his review of The Thing? Actually its very likely as we shall return to Mr Brosnan in a short time.

Even in the magazine's letter page fans were venting. Paul Dellinger wrote *The characterisations ...the cast* (of the original '51 film) *added to the original. The Thing are lacking in the new version...* so no, not all Starburst fans and writers had supported the movie.

As for Roger Ebert, well he simply hated the film, and his entire review is readily available for everyone to read at rogerebert.com. However, we'll look at the review that he did with his TV partner Gene Siskel, as it not only has most of the points he wrote in the article, it has Siskel's response.

Siskel: our next film the Thing has already caused a lot of talk before it opened. About two weeks ago something very unusual happened to me, I began getting postcards at my newspaper office from readers telling me that John Carpenter's new movie, I guess they'd seen it in the preview, was one of the most disgusting films ever made. Well, those postcard writers certainly were right about one thing. The movie the Thing does contain a lot of repellent special effects...

Ebert: I would call this the barf bag movie of July. I have some problems with it. One of them is, I think the characters, they're not made into three-dimensional people, their function is to walk down the corridor and be jumped on. The other thing is plausibility, once they figure out that this thing can turn into one of them, they ought to institute a watertight buddy system, and instead they have all kinds of loopholes. People walk out into the snow, come back with a grin on their face, so that the story is totally implausible.

Siskel's review, however, is far more balanced: *...later there's a terrific blood test where they try and check out who was human who was not. I wish this movie were less ugly than it is, because in terms of storytelling and suspense, and that subtext of suspicion of one's fellow man, this is actually a very well-made movie. But at regular intervals, no doubt about it, does gross one out, so a mixed review for the Thing for me.*

Ebert was far less kind: *the movie just basically is an excuse for this very gruesome and repellent creature to gross us out. It is the most nauseating thing I've ever seen on a movie screen.*

If you watch the video, Siskel's face shows genuine shock and displeasure when his partner says this last line, and he even calls Ebert on it.

I think that's quite a statement... for me it isn't about those characters as individual people. I think that's why they can be interchangeable, I think that it's about how a society, this little group here...they think something's going wrong, you're not in the group, you're out...just like that line "move away to one side". It's a very chilling thing and I think if you read the movie in that way, and the implausibility's, and at your level means very little, and so you sit there wishing... and I do wish... that it were a lot cleaner.

Ebert insisted on the last word: *I've got news for you, and that is that 99% of the people going to see this movie are there to see the monsters...very few of them are going to read it as your kind of allegory.*

Fuck Roger Ebert as that's pretty much exactly what most of us took from the film. I prefer the paranoia and background story to the gore. It's my favourite part, personally. Was Eberts' attack personal? In a way I think it was. The year before, Fangoria #15 ran an article covering Siskel and Ebert's apparent war on horror movies. The article noted the critic had something interesting to say about Carpenter when asked about the new trend in horror.

If these movies are able to give a start to directors who may go on to do something better, then that's good. For example, Halloween, which is a very good movie, which was one of my top ten movies of the year, has launched the career of John Carpenter, who I think is a very talented director. Two things. Clearly Ebert had backed the director as a man to watch and to move on to bigger and better projects – so not liking The Thing, perhaps he was personally disappointed he wasn't seeing what he'd hoped.

"...May go on to do something better, then that's good." You cannot tell me with a comment like this that Ebert did not have a bias. A film he considered one of the best of the year was of such a poorly thought of genre that he hoped Carpenter would grow out of making similar films in the future. Instead, in 1982 he got the mother-of-all horror films and I believe was disappointed in some one he thought of as better than that.

DID YOU KNOW? Carpenter had a combative relationship with several critics well before The Thing was released, and he laughed about it during one interview. When asked about why they were bothering with another Halloween sequel:

There's also another reason we're doing it — [movie reviewer] dinosaur Reed claims he'll turn in his press card if there's a Halloween III. I think that's probably the best reason in the world for doing it. I'm even thinking of writing him a letter saying: 'I know you're a man of your word, so I'm expecting your press card in the mail.' "

The Preview

Signs of nervousness are beginning to show up among the filmmakers who have entries in this summers loaded motion picture schedule... [MGM] announced it was moving the release date of 'ROCKY III'...then director John Carpenter, who refused to allow a single still photograph to be taken of the creature in 'The Thing', okayed press screenings of a 23-minute product reel, monster included.

Ebert had mentioned getting postcards from people who hated the preview, and now were told it wasn't a preview of the film, instead it was a 23-minute product reel. Something stinks and we may have uncovered just why the Thing was reviewed so terribly.

I needed to expand my research into older video sources...and what do you know? The first video I found was titled FEAR ON FILM from 1982. It was compered by Mick Garris, who interviewed horror film directors John Landis, John Carpenter and David Cronenberg. All three men are wearing some shade of brown and tan and got to talk about their latest films. What I like is occasionally you can see Carpenter give little knowing smirks and smiles at questions or comments, as though he's saying 'brother, you people have no idea what's about to hit the screen'.

Now unlike most of these old interviews, during the conversation they talk to Carpenter about his upcoming release, and then they show a clip from The Thing... and its still there! What starts to play is footage I have never seen before, an expanded video of the dog-thing autopsy. It's a little clunky and seems to reveal more than the theatrical cut does (at one point Blair mentions the cells are still alive and half the cast stagger back from the table so dramatically I struggled not to giggle). The colours are washed out, the sound is awful and it just looked like cheap video instead of the beautiful Cundey cinematography we all love. This only reinforced my suspicions that something weird happened in that preview.

I tried to be clever, I really did. I have learnt in all my years of research that if you're looking for something unique or forgotten, these items are often hidden under titles that are similar, or at least different enough to not be picked up by your usual research.

I found nothing but a few stills.

Finally, out of desperation I tried the obvious, "The Thing 1982 One Reel Preview", that led me to a clip called 'The Thing - Promotional Condensed Version'. Google it, you'll find it and you can watch what I think is the preview version for yourself.

I believe right here is a major contributor for the horrid reviews for The Thing. Now I'm going to speculate shortly, but before I do, I did ask the producer Stuart Cohen about the reel.

The preview reel you speak of was made by me and was NOT made for, or shown to, the media. It was expressly designed for exhibitors' eyes only, and was taken to eight major cities in late February, 1982 and presented by either David

Foster or myself with lunches following. It was designed to answer this question from them: was this John Carpenter taking the next step, or was this, as one put it, "HALLOWEEN 2 in the snow?". Originally in widescreen and stereo. I write about this on my blog as THE THING product reel, although I was writing from memory, before the reel surfaced...

Now please remember, this is speculation on my part, backed by shards of evidence.

I believe Universal needed to preview the film early and get out in front of that year's big box office releases. Carpenter and team explained the film was nowhere near ready for any sort of preview to get some positive buzz going, worse, they were arguing that they could not let any imagery of the alien get out – especially to the critics who'd give the game away on what they felt was going to be the films big drawcard, the incredible effects. The production team asked Universal to promote the film in a way that no one knew what the alien looked like until they'd bought their ticket and had their bum on a seat.

Step in Cohen, who took what film was ready, added a bunch of unused scenes or alternate camera angle shots that were basically rubbish and built a single reel – roughly 23 minutes long – with bad sound effects and no score. This is what many critics sat down to watch and review. If I'm correct, almost no early reviewer saw the film in all its glory – they saw an extended nonsensical trailer.

Certainly, Cohen says this is not the case, that it "was NOT made for, or shown to, the media. It was expressly designed for exhibitors' eyes only." He's most likely correct, however, there's the little issue of the Mikc Garris interview Fear On Film. This was clearly made before The Thing was released and contains the exact unused footage from the reel. This means it was being used, maybe in a way Cohen was unaware of, but it was most certainly being seen by the media before the films release.

Watch the video for yourself (I believe it's also an extra on one of the Blu-Ray releases, possibly from Shoutfactory) ...it's terrible. There is zero character development and you NEVER see the alien, just those back shots...actually that's not entirely true. There is an extended scene when they burn the Bennings-Thing, but even this is wonky. That great alien moan is missing, it's just an actor kneeling in the snow, mouth open – and then some odd sound like a whale being hit by a submarine starts to issue out of the speaker. We also get that alternate Dog-Thing autopsy scene, and I think here's the source of all those goo and slime comments as it does go on and on. You can see the remains glistening under the bright Fluro lights, and as this really is one of the few shots of the actual alien, no wonder all those reviewers thought the creature looked horrific as there's little in the way of cinema lighting.

If this is what happened, I get the feeling if the reviewers had seen the entire film they'd have understood the build up to those scenes, they'd have known the characters better and just how astonishing the alien effects were.

My point is there's 80% of the film missing, and most of what is on this reel isn't even shots from the final theatrical version. Universal previewed the film too early and destroyed any chance it had to ever find an audience. Watch the video for yourselves and then go back and read a lot of those horrible reviews. They almost all say the same thing. To me that's because that's all they could say, they only saw 20 minutes and there wasn't much else to write about as those 20 minutes are terrible. The movie ends without The Thing titles, just simple block letters and a voice over tagline...*Anytime, anywhere, anyone.* There wasn't even the official tagline 'Man is the Warmest place to hide'.

So, it looks like Universal made a mistake with the single reel review...but that's not their only mistake, and the article from April 26, 1982 in the Detroit free press highlighted this...*he (Carpenter) is obviously concerned about getting lost in the summer product," said a source at Universal, "The Studio sees 'The Thing' as a potential blockbuster, but no one knows much about it".*

This is a note from someone at Universal, and they may have had a point. By restricting any information about the creature, no one really cared and some of those who did take a punt on the film went in somewhat unprepared for what they were about to see...and let's face it, we all know people who have not been able to handle the sheer brilliance of the movie's special effects. This point was very well made by our next reviewer.

Fred Lutz of the Toledo Blade wrote:

"The Thing" although hideous beyond description...not only will it scare the absolute daylights out of you and possibly give you nightmares, it actually has a sense of humour going for it to mitigate the gore and terror...

...Let me say as forcefully and clearly as I can, if you are squeamish, give 'The thing' a wide berth. If you go to see it, be prepared to see human beings ripped open by a bloody monster that can take the form of everything from a bundle of slithering worms to a kind of crab-like monstrosity with a semi-human head.

Yet all this is accomplished with wit, style and intelligence. It is acted by performers who seem absolutely letter perfect, both in their roles as scientists and in their reactions to a puzzling menace...I absolutely loved all of it."

Once the full movie was on screens you get a change. Most of the positive reviews were after people had seen the entire film. Not only did Lutz get it, his review shows the lengths a reviewer had to go to warn and describe the film due to the lack of images the filmmakers and studio publicity department had released. They all but explain the entire film away to warn people why it's great.

Could this be partly why the movie failed? Overly critical but overly descriptive reviews. Maybe it was a mistake to not allow any images of the alien to be released. I know from experience with my first novel that has several large twists in the story – that because I tried to hide these and leave them to be found by my readers that I was hamstrung in explaining the book to potential readers.

Let's recap. Universal, taking on Star Trek, Rocky, ET, decided to advertise this big budget horror film with a cut down, inaccurate, poorly constructed one reel preview for the media keen to review the film…and sadly, we're not even close to being done with how the publicity department bungled this release.

The Edit - or the 'ICK' factor

John sat down with a roughly assembled version of the film between when we shut down at Universal and when we started up again in Alaska. There was little special effects in the film at the time. So John said, "This is a boring movie about a bunch of guys talking." He rewrote a couple of scenes so that they would be shot outdoors. Some scenes shot at Universal that were originally shot indoors were now re-staged outdoors, like the one where [MacReady, Kurt Russell's character] says, "I know I'm human, but I don't know about any of you." Turns out John was right: People love the scenes that we shot outdoors…Masur (Clark) in a 2016 interview.

What we do know is once the film was done, at some point The Thing went through a major edit. Could this be why Carpenter refused to release anything for a preview? He was busy trying to fix the film? The director admitted as much during his interview with David Letterman when he talked about test screenings. We also have the great resource, producer Stuart Cohen's The Original Fan blog (http://theoriginalfan.blogspot.com). This resource covers a lot of the behind the scenes info you don't get from other sources like the blu-rays, so please check it out.

Carpenter cited key issues after this rough cut. One problem was too many scenes of the Outpost 31 men standing around and talking, resulting in a slack pace. Another was The Thing's life cycle being too vague, including its threat to the world if it ever escaped the base. To this end, Carpenter swiftly cut many sequences, including MacCready hanging out with a blow-up doll and Childs (Keith David) and Palmer's (David Clennon) greenhouse where they grew weed. Basically, if a scene could be removed, it was.

This was not the same version as the one-reel preview copy as Cohen notes on his blog they had a staff screening at the Alfred Hitchcock Theatre: *where we had tested the alternate ending for THE THING several weeks earlier.*

Yes, there was an alternate ending – and this was covered well on the DVDs commentary and on various blu-rays. In an interview before the film came out the scriptwriter did talk about his unusual finale. Lancaster explained his thinking to Starlog Magazine.

There seem to be only two endings in these kinds of movies," he observes. "Either the Twilight Zone-type of twist, or the destruction of the monster. What we have in- stead is like a tag. It's a nice comment of partial trust and partial mistrust, fear and a little bit of relief. I liked the ambiguity of it. I thought it would be interesting after all the violence to have this semi-nebulous little ending. I don't know — maybe people will hate it. It may not be a commercial enough ending.

There actually appears to be more behind this alternate ending, and it went all the way back to the script. Fangoria's Bob Martin spent time on location in Canada, chatting with everyone, including producer Stuart Foster.

Fears of studio interference are often raised when a director with an image as strongly independent as Carpenter's becomes involved with a major. We mentioned to Foster a rumour we'd heard...stating that Universal execs were not entirely pleased with the downbeat ending of the Bill Lancaster script. "No, that's not quite it...There was some concern on the part of the producers, on the director's part, and on the studio's part, about the end of the picture. How did we want people to feel when they come out of that theatre? In fact, it was John that kept saying, 'we're dead if they walk out of the picture in a terrible frame of mind, without any hope.' It was John's feeling that there should be hope for survival, and that those that did die, will have died nobly – in order to save their fellow man. John was in the forefront of the fight for an uplifting ending, while the rest of us where in the background wondering, 'well, could someone really survive all this – would it be corny if they did? But there was no dissension about it; everyone was primarily concerned about the audience's experience in the movie theatre. That was all settled to everyone's satisfaction, but don't ask me how. Are there survivors? I'll never tell.

It wasn't just the alternate ending that was dumped, whole storylines were removed, like a scene were Palmer and Childs enter the bases greenhouse as they had pot plants secretly growing there. It would seem everything not tied down was tossed out from this rough cut to make it much shorter and tighter, and yes it does seem a lot of characterization scenes for all the actors were cut. Many of them even complained about this very issue after The Thing staff preview.

Kurt Russel protested to Stuart, *believing that much of the hard work, the relationship work done by the actors from rehearsal was left on the cutting room floor in favour of what he called the "ick" factor.*

The Good Reviews

Yes, most reviewers cut the film to shreds, but perhaps evidence they saw the one-reel 'trailer' initially presented was the numerous positive reviews by those who saw the completed film. Ebert could not have been more wrong and Siskel was correct as there appeared a vocal minority that not only got the film, they championed it.

In 'Looking for the aliens: a psychological, imaginative, and scientific investigation' Peter Hough, after giving the 1951 film a terrible review, was far more positive with '82. "Another attempt was made in 1982, when John Carpenter directed The Thing. It's script and special effects were stunning. The only flaw came at the end, when Carpenter, for unknown reasons, decided to abandon Campbell's mind-blowing denouement.

Phil Edwards for Starburst wrote:

Although the horror effects represent a new dimension in mainstream cinema grossness. The Thing is in fact very measured in its building of suspense. Though there are thrills aplenty and more gore than I can remember seeing in any movie. Carpenter has brought Lancaster's script the solid story telling virtues of a master film maker. After the abysmal longueurs of Halloween 2, it does my heart good to be able to write those few lines. For with The Thing, John Carpenter has truly established himself as a director of the first order. As I hopefully predicted when I reviewed the flawed Escape From New York last year, John Carpenter, with this film, has finally arrived. Miss at your peril!

Marke Andrews of The Vancouver Sun (26 Jun 1982)

When comparing the film to Escape from New York, Andrews wrote. *The Thing is a far better film...If you saw Alien, you know all about monsters emerging from humans. The Thing takes it further, one monster begets another, plasma and slime fly generously around the set, This is gross out as High Art; an unyielding performance by a monster in a leading role...The cast...is universally good, overshadowed as they are by the special effects. Recommended for those with strong stomachs...*

UPI Hollywood reporter, Vernon Scott, wrote an unusual review...I mean, did he like it? Who knows? *Lovers of grisly, gory movie mayhem will see their nightmares come true this month when "the Thing" is unleashed in theatres around the country...Blood, guts, dismembered limbs, entrails, fangs, slime, gizzards, severed heads, indescribable glop, bloody organs and bizarre human-animal forms ooze, seep, peel off and melt all over the screen in vivid, gaudy colours.* He then recorded that: *Preview audiences cover their eyes, scream, groan and moan...The transmutations are horrible to the nth degree, defying description. Audiences will find their skin crawling, their hair standing on end and their stomachs heaving. They will be scared just short of cardiac arrest. "Poltergeist," by comparison, is "Laverne and Shirley".*

Yup, all that sounds right on the head and still I have no idea if the reviewer was reporting all this in a fan or a dire-warning way. One thing that heightens this article over many others was his interview with Kurt Russel, who, when asked why people seemed to be enjoying the film, explained: *Some people liked to be scared to death...and this is the ultimate monster picture. They'll never know what's coming next, but you can bet they'll be horrified.* Russel admitted, *Monster and horror hold no fascination for me...but they're a thrill ride for the public. To them it's a ride on the rollercoaster or a walk through a haunted house. It's the kick of the shock, the unexpected...people like to survive something terrifying in a dark theatre with a whole bunch of other people.*

Russel then goes on to explain the cast and gives a valid reason that should have been used when refuting many of the more negative reviews the film received. *We actors are there to provide story and background for the horror, our real purpose is to play our scenes with credibility to make the monster realistic to audiences.*

It's a great point that most reviewers missed. With such films, it's the creature that's the star, not the various actors in the film.

One guy who got it was Ed Blank in The Pittsburgh Press (25 Jun 1982). *The Thing Bleak, Ghastly but Intelligent Horror Film and was...the cinema of nihilism and paranoia pushed to a ghastly new extreme. Undoubtedly the bleakest, bloodiest movie ever...it makes exceptionally crafty use of craftmanship and is, in ways it might be begrudged, often quite something.* It sure sounded like the guy got it – but then he suddenly turns on the film. *There are more things wrong with the movie then there are right, and anyone would be hard pressed to defend it...about all that can be said in its defence is that some sort of intelligence, however perversely, applied is behind it."* He was extremely wrong about one thing though.

It will make money...

JoAnn Rhetts got it.

If Poltergeist' is the almost perfect ghost story...'The Thing' is as close to the ultimate in adult horror as we have any right to expect. It's a grisly nightmare unspooled at a brutal pace...After 'The Thing,' even the most stalwart adults may have trouble sleeping at night for fear of summoning their own slithering imaginings. But such is the proportion, the awesome beauty and even the humour of Bottin's creatures that the most difficult, painful sight in 'The Thing' is a surgical scalpel applied ever so briefly to a human thumb.

It wasn't just professional reviewers either. Carpenter has complained many times that the fans had also turned on him, well again, not entirely true.

Dear Fango,

I'm a little surprised that The Thing didn't do as well as I'd hoped it would at the box office, it really knocked me for a loop. I guess the public didn't care for Carpenters adult approach to the horror genre.

Your piece on Rob Bottin and his work on the film was way too short. You didn't provide enough details on the spectacular effects Bottin supervised; that's a shame, because The Thing contains scenes of intense horror that deserve too have the unreplaceable coverage that FANGORIA is renowned for in horror circles (Gerry Kimber, Toronto).

One letter that I consider perfect for what the film is and what was happening was by Mitchell B. Craig in Fangoria #24.

Steven Spielberg, the modern Disney-cum-Pavlov, fooled millions into believing E.T. and Poltergeist were films of great worth. And while many believe this, a devout few held in reverence John Carpenter's similar coup this year.

I speak, of course, about The Thing and Halloween III...two of this year's best SF/Horror movies. Both films were ravaged by the Spielberg-entranced critical establishment, most of whom thought the very universe revolved around Carlo Rambaldi's bellybutton. The few who were not yet entranced by Spielbergian sorcery were amply rewarded. The Thing has a wonderful example of something missing in many fantasy films; a mature perspective...

The Release

The story that The Thing was not playing well in front of anyone and had failed to find an audience just doesn't seem to be true, especially in cinemas where the film was given time for word of mouth to get out.

The Baltimore Afro-American reported on the July 17th, 1982, the audience *screamed, pretended to be scared and watched intently every scene down to the last bitter gory minute. Some of the special effects were so overdone that while the audiences did not laugh or boo, they just seemed to take it all in stride being the best medicine to overcome the hot muggy days in Baltimore...* and how was the film doing? *'The Thing' has been drawing full houses for the past three weeks, and there's no accounting for the reason why people revel in all the blood and guts being applied all over the place...and sitting straight up with their mouths wide open.* Three weeks and full houses. One can only imagine what would have happened had Universal held its nerve and allowed people to find the film in the cinema the way they would just a short time later when the VHS version hit video stores.

But that's not what happened. The studio and distributors dropped the film like a rock. Screentime in cinemas was cut and the film started to be withdrawn from as many screens as possible to be replaced with something the studio and operators hoped would make money – and yes, it was often E.T. that replaced The Thing on these screens. This was to increase its sessions and get more of the desperate public inside to watch that monster hit and ease the burden of the ques outside.

What was new to me though was a point Joel Polis made in a recent interview. *The opening of the film was, quite frankly, a real let down for me. It was rushed without much fanfare or promotion to wide release because Universal had another movie that was supposed to open that weekend but was not ready. We were ... so they pushed us into the weekend following E.T.'s history making opening, which was also the weekend before Poltergeist was set to open. The result was disastrous. We were reviewed very coldly and faded from the marquees quickly.*

I was bewildered by all of it. This was my first big movie and I was unfamiliar with movie marketing and promotion, we seemed to have just simply disappeared. Years went by and I got on with my career. I moved back to Los Angeles from New York, and slowly I noticed that The Thing was working its way into a cult classic status. And when the convention circuit for horror and Sci-Fi movies started to grow, I was invited to attend my first "Monsterpalooza" in Los Angeles. That's when I really came to understand what a popular and seminal film it was, and why.

This again explains why the film stumbled. There were complaints the movie never really received a publicity push, and the tsunami...and I do mean tsunami of bad reviews after its preview meant Universal reacted by cutting the film free... as well as its director. Carpenter has said in many interviews that after The Thing was decimated by the critics, Universal fired him from their next project, Stephen King's Firestarter.

DID YOU KNOW: Joel Polis mentioned that he was surprised at the lack of support from the studio to advertise the release. Universal, perhaps because there was so little time to create a serious marketing campaign for the movie as its release had been brought forward did come up with...shall we say, a novel promotion. The studio took advantage of the new video medium, and it was all covered by the Advertising Age, Electronic Media Edition.

Universal pictures is escalating a new, limited program of placing in store windows TV monitors that play movie trailers. The strategy "is to go where the public is", said Universal national co-op advertising director John Butkovich.

The video monitors were placed in about 10 Los Angeles store windows at the first of the year, promoting films like Universal's "The Thing," and by summer's end will be in some New York locations.

Could someone explain this to me? A TV in a store window showing a video that I'm positive had little to no sound was their advertising? If this was it, then Polis was 100% correct, the studio did little to promote the film.

My favourite advertising story for the movie was an accidental one. Fangoria ran a competition for readers to draw what they thought The Thing looked like. The magazine not only received thousands of entries, through some mix up many of these were sent to Universal studios. Instead of just throwing out these artworks, Universal made sure they reached John Carpenter, who searched through them all and chose his own winner.

The Box Office

Almost every resource you read on The Thing suggests it was Spielberg's megahit. E.T. that destroyed any chance of the movie finding a profit. Yes, that freaky lil' Reese's pieces munching, beer swilling alien seemed to have made all the monies in 1982 – but – having spent months going through every contemporary record, I think I've another suggestion why the film bombed.

If sci-fi fans had come out in large numbers, The Thing should have still done okay at the box office – but they simply didn't. The reason for this may well have been a total and utter lack of support from within the industry. I'm not kidding, read any fanboy magazine from the day and they are almost wall to wall stories about Star Trek and the Wrath of Khan.

TREKKIES (you fool no one with that trekster rubbish) seem to have been well and truly burnt by the first Star Trek movie just a few years earlier. Star Trek the Motion Picture was expensive, long and dull. Yes, it had some decent effects, but lord that movie is hard work.

The *Enterprise* crews second outing, Wrath of Khan, was also released in 1982 – and this film, full of adventure, space battles and returning an old villain from the TV series was everything the original movie should have been. The film had trekkies salivating for its release. If you look at any magazine – especially sci-fi mags like Starlog or Starburst at the time, they're trumpeting the upcoming film and covering every single aspect of its creation. With pages and pages just dripping with Trekkie joy – this left very little room for a brute of an alien invasion movie that refused to allow any images or information to escape about its creature to 'keep the secret'. Yes, we have articles and interviews, but compared to how many at the same time were made for Star Trek, well, the Sci-fi world just didn't support the film the way it should.

There's no doubting that 1982 was the year of E.T. Costing around 10 million, the monster soon took in over $240 million and kept earning as it was re-released and whole families went back again and again, and that's not counting the enormous piles of cash created by the movies merchandising. Robert Creenbercer wrote about the bizarre year and noted who made what and why films succeeded or didn't.

When it came to E.T.'s box office success, the author noted this money was *…a figure representing 18% of all money spent at movie theatres this summer.* That means 1/5th of all box office tickets in 1982 was an E.T. ticket.

Star Trek II set the new record for the first three days in release (Friday/Saturday/Sunday) with over $14 million, while E.T. took the 10-day and 14-day records. In all, eight films captured half the summer's receipts.

Now there is a weird moment in this article that I think highlights one reason why the movie is considered a bomb. Creenbercer explains: *Although Universal had several hits on its hands, such as E.T. and The Best Little Whorehouse in Texas, it also released one of this summer's biggest bombs: The Thing. John Carpenter's remake cost the studio $15 million and only brought in $16 million. The film was a victim of the summer product glut and left the theatres very quickly, especially after a round of scathing reviews which attacked its lack of characterization and downbeat storyline.*

Ok, so far this is exactly what we have been told time and time again about the film. It partly failed because of E.T. and bad timing. The article then tied in The Thing with some other 'bombs'. *Other failures included Twentieth Century Fox's Megaforce, which captured a meagre $7 million, and Scott Baio's Zapped, which could snatch only $13,328,312.*

What's weird - and shows that such things are often your point of view - the article explains: *Two small films surprised theatre-goers and studio executives by grabbing big bucks and positive reviews. Australia's sequel to Mad Max, The Road Warrior, broke on a regional basis beginning on Memorial Day. By Labor Day, it had roared in with an impressive $21,840,775. Hailed by many critics as the summer's sleeper hit, the film packed houses around the country.*

However, according to boxoffice.com, MAD MAX 2 grossed $23,667,907, while The Thing made $19,629,760. Yes, that's less - but when it comes to box office revenues, it's not that much less, yet one is being called a sleeper hit while the other is a bomb. One reason for the difference is likely that Mad Max was financed and made in Australia, so its budget does not really cut into its ticket sales as that money had already been recouped in its massive Down-Under release. The budget of The Thing still had to be recouped from its ticket sales.

One piece of information you also don't normally get is just how many screens all these monster movies in 82 played on - which clearly helps the bottom line. Wrath of Khan was released on 1,621 screens. The stats of one film shocked me to my booties - E.T. was only released on 1,116 screens - though as we know, this quickly grew as its popularity soared and other failing films were removed and their near empty cinemas filled with E.T-ites...ET-philes?... a movie that made people cry over a stupid piece of plastic (a direct quote from my grandmother at the time who took us to see it). Firefox found itself on 881 screens, Megaforce...MEGA-FREAKIN-FORCE- that horrible movie I recall seeing ads for on the back page of just about every Marvel comic in the early 80s was released in 1,193 cinemas.

The one movie that Thing '82 is always compared to as they were both sci-fi films, released on the same day, apparently bombed and both are considered true classics was Blade Runner, Ridley Scott's film was released on 1,295 screens.

The Thing was released on 881 screens, far less then almost every other film – and was quickly removed, where most of the others got to play on and on and find an audience. This was 1982, so it wasn't a modern film with You Tube review channels releasing their thoughts within a day of its release. In 1982 you had a friend come to school and tell you about a film and then you bugged your parents to take you to it so you could see it as well. You cannot discount word of mouth – and apparently The Thing had a massive wave of this effect in regions where it was allowed to play longer than a week and its ticket sales grew.

In most regions the Thing was never given a chance to find its audience – and we can see proof of this when it was finally released on video. That movie your one friend saw in the cinema was now on the shelf and you could rent it and you loved it!

The Video - Revision Part Two

Famous Monsters: There seems to be some renewed interest now that people are able to rent movies from the video store and watch them at home. Do you think THE THING might find a second life there?

John Carpenter: Well, VHS is new. I had home video back when it was 3/4 inch, before it was consumer friendly. I've been collecting for years. But you never know. THE THING is over with and I've just got to move on (FM #92).

Clearly disappointed with the box office take, Famous Monsters' question would prove to be valid as it did not take long for The Thing to find its audience. Video stores were spreading across the planet like the alien hoped it could, and in every single one of those stores was a copy of The Thing. Pan and scan, picture jumping from the physical tape being paused and rewound by almost every single viewer on the weird gross parts – the tape became a must watch for horror fans when they went to pick out a few titles for that weekends viewing.

I first saw the movie when I went to a friend's video/slumber birthday party. Ok, we were like 14 or 15, so sleepover doesn't do it justice – it was more like a 'stay up as late as possible, pour as much junk food and soft drink into our gullets gross each other out with as many farts and bad jokes as we could – lie about any sexual conquests none of us had had at that time, and watch scarier and scarier videos as the morning approached' party. I cannot be sure, but my recollection was we didn't put on The Thing until around 2 am...prime horror territory. That woke us up let me assure you.

Video tapes could also be purchased at the time, though usually at an extraordinary - no, that word doesn't portray how much they cost - at a horrific price. Some videos were $100 in the early 80s – that's roughly $300 today. Even in

1990 a copy still cost $35 and here we see one of the great successes of The Thing that is not usually talked about.

Now finding records like this is tricky, but hey, it's me folks…I'm good at my job. Videos had become so popular and so important in 1982 that Billboard – that magazine that ran for years telling you about how your favourite Duran Duran song was charting – carried a top 100 video sales and rentals page snappily titled the '*bestselling videocassettes compiled from retail sales, including releases in both Beta and VHS formats* (Beta…wow, we really are at the start of the video craze).'

Billboard 11 Dec 1982 lists that weeks #1 in both categories is (no surprise) the Wrath of Khan…hey, its Trekkies man, they have good paying jobs and can afford the quadrillion megabucks to buy a cassette. The next big film topping both lists – Star Wars. Now coming in at #6 on sales and #4 on rentals is (drum roll) – THE THING. Yeah baby, beating out every other 1982 release (I don't think E.T. or Blade Runner had been released yet) was our little horror movie…just months after it was pulled from cinemas and still under the reflection of all those horrible reviews. Something had changed, and that was word of mouth. People had begun talking about this movie they loved, but no one could see it as in wasn't in cinemas anymore, so when it finally hit the video shelves people everywhere voted with their wallets.

Four months later Billboard declared The Thing had dropped to #11 in sales and #18 in rentals. However, almost everything above it is a recent release monster video hit like Jane Fondas work out (I'm not kidding – that thing tops every category for years). Now listed was the UK's charts and The Thing was nowhere to be seen – however Escape from New York was a solid #13. So, where was The Thing?

The Video Nasty

As previously mentioned, I visited England in 1997 and bought the widescreen version of The Abyss from a HMV store. Imagine my surprise when I got home, popped the video into my player and found missing that one scene when Mary Elizabeth Mastrantonio's Dr. Lindsey Brigman drowned and, in the process of being resuscitated, her shirt ripped open, exposing her breasts. Turns out this stuff was not unusual in the UK.

The first wave of Hollywood films, especially those from Universal in the 1930s were a world-wide phenomenon, with Dracula and Frankenstein being some of the year's biggest money-makers. Increasingly the storylines in these became adult orientated with more graphic scenes of horror and violence, triggering reactions from parent groups who began calling for bans or some sort of category title placed on such films. In England the government created the 'H' for Horror classification, driving kids out of the theatres and cutting profits substantially.

In my book Horror this happens again when US horror and crime comic books flood the country after WW2, and in the 1950s this issue was actually debated in parliament. Again, the nation started to classify and ban certain comics and created the 'Obscene Publications Act 1959' to stop the filth. Heavy English censorship reappeared in the 1980s with the rise of another home media, video tapes.

In England the National Viewers' and Listeners' Association (NVALA) popularised the term for these movies as 'Video Nasties'. Cheaply made, easily purchased horror films depicting serious violence and sex scenes began to flood the market because these movies didn't have to go before the British Board of Film Classification (BBFC). Turns out there was a loophole in film classification laws as home videos didn't count and weren't required to go through the review process.

Things changed when 'Go Video' distributors thought they'd be clever by sending a truly nasty movie, Cannibal Holocaust, to one of these censorship groups to encourage them to speak against the title and thus increase sales when everyone rushed out to purchase the film they would be told they shouldn't watch. The censorship group went ballistic, attacking the movie and flooding the nation's government ministers with complaints. The 1959 Obscene Publications Act was triggered but found to not be adequate for this new media, so Conservative MP Graham Bright introduced a Private Member's Bill to the House of Commons in 1983. Thus, a new law, the Video Recordings Act 1984 came into effect on 1 September 1985 (yes, those dates are correct…ah, bureaucracy).

It became a criminal offense to supply unclassified or adult classified videos to under-aged people, and it wasn't just the cheaply made videos that got caught in the net. A great resource for this story is the website 'hysteria-lives.co.uk', and Neil Cristopher's 'The Video Nasties Furore – The prosecution of the DPP's 74' records:

In one of the more comic episodes that took place during the video nasties debacle, Hampshire Police seized copies of Carpenter's classic paranoid horror movie and a Magistrate, after clearing the accused video dealer on 8 counts relating to films on the banned list, ordered the copies of this destroyed!!! Fortunately, no-one else seems to have followed suit, and the movie is (and always has been) freely available on Video. Interestingly, the growing reputation of this film was built entirely on it's video release…

Films like the Exorcist and The Thing – led to a massive underground movement of people trading and selling such videos in a weird black-market industry reminiscent of Hogan's Heroes.

A study was commissioned to see the effects of these films and laws in the early 80s, and when it came to adult classified films they asked children to list their 'favourite' and 'most remembered' titles. They listed *Poltergeist, An American werewolf in London*...and number 5 on the list was *The Thing*.

In England today these underground copies are popular among collectors, and their existence has once again come under the ire of the British Board of Film Classification, with one member of the board complaining:

It is not really illegal to own these videos, and many of them have over the years been submitted for classification. But we believe Trading Standards, the enforcement authority for this matter, may take a dim view if they are being traded for money. Every video recording being exchanged for money does need an official classification.

So watch out everyone in England, the coppers may be raiding your house and confiscating your video collection sometime in the future.

The Home Library

Obviously with such a high price point, not many people were buying videos in the early 80s. It wasn't until the 90s when the first DVD players arrived that things got better. Even the earlier laser disks were very expensive, and I only knew a few people that owned one, and they really chose specific movies they cared for to own because of the price. In fact laserdisc as a format was so inconsequential I couldn't find any records about disc sales.

What I know personally is the very first DVD and Blu-ray I purchased was The Thing - and I had to buy my first DVD player from a porn store because apparently porn is always at the cutting edge of new media technology. By now Universal understood they had a serious cult film on their hands because these discs came packed with features - including possibly the greatest commentary track ever - and those who know understand exactly the part I'm talking about (que Russel giggling and saying wait...wait...wait...) and for those who don't know, watch the film again with the commentary, you won't be disappointed.

Records show when the film was released on Blu-ray, in 2010 they sold 8,777 units for nearly $100,000. But in 2021 the new release sold some 650,000 units and made around 7.5 million. All this for a forty-year-old movie that bombed.

With the movie now available to anyone with a video player to watch, this access and surprising popularity magically seems to have given reviewers a chance to change their minds on its quality. Some were a little backhanded, for example John Brosnan wrote a review on Carpenter's latest film in 1986, Christine.

...It also confirmed to me that, despite being highly over-rated earlier in his career, John Carpenter is becoming an excellent director (I admit I've revised my opinion about his The Thing too; it's a much better film than I originally thought).

He proves this in Christine with his fine handling of the actors, in particular with young Keith Gordon...

It was "a much better film than I originally thought", well that's a ringing endorsement.

An example of a complete turnaround was Rolling Stone's top 100 movies from the 1980s (released in 2022). Coming in at an impressive 13 is John Carpenter's The Thing. The interesting point is what Rolling Stone said about the film when it was first released, claiming it couldn't *hold a candle to Howard Hawks' trailblazing 1951 classic 'The Thing from Another World'.*

Thanks to video stores a generation of video-a-holics grew up loving the movie, and Gen X is not afraid to tell the world just how great it is – and many of us now run pop-culture websites and magazines.

Over time the quality of the film shone through. With the rise of the internet, reviews and articles have been written about '82 as fans and journalists pull the film apart into its individual elements. Even that ending, considered one of the worst things ever put on film in 1982, has been redeemed. When TOTAL FILM posted its 25 best film endings in 2019, among the mega-Hollywood-monsters like Casablanca, Godfather, Silence of the Lambs, the Graduate and The Sixth Sense was our beloved The Thing, that ends *in a wonderfully ambiguous finale that stays with you long after the credits have rolled.*

Culture Vulture in 2021 also created a list for the best endings on film, and at #12 sat The Thing, which they noted was: *a perfect encapsulation of the horror of isolation, which makes it an especially cutting rewatch during a pandemic. The Thing ends with MacReady (Kurt Russell) facing Childs (Keith David), unsure if he's the monster, but rightfully suspicious. They share a bottle of liquor, aware that neither can do anything about their predicament, stuck in the icy tundra of Antarctica, staring down their assured deaths.*

The Thing was now a video hit, but did this in anyway help its director? Carpenter was clearly hurt by the reviews, but what seemed to have really got him was the reaction of sci-fi fans.

...it was the fans who hated it, he told Famous Monsters in 1983, *the genre fans hated it. Hated it...And for a bit I've been blacklisted for it. I lost a job. I couldn't find a job. And I didn't quite know what had happened. I thought the THING was pretty good...but I think a lot of fans thought I had raped a classic, that I had done something offensive to the original movie. And they've been unforgiving.*

Was Carpenter fired from Universal's upcoming big budget version of Steven King's Firestarter? Well, the overbudget Burt and Dolly film Littlest Whorehouse in Texas was more likely the culprit for what happened there, though Starburst Magazine (#53) didn't think so. Looking back at how poorly the thing had done, they saw the biggest reverberation of its failure was Carpenter's firing from Firestarter because of his last movies performance?

Poor John Carpenter. *He always was wary of working with the major studios (and, in fact, they haven't helped his reputation that much). But now he's been kicked right in his ... er ... Thing. In a surprise, eleventh-hour decision. Universal cancelled his production of the Stephen King book, Firestarter. Everything was ready for John's October shoot - "perfect" locations in Tennessee and people just queuing up for the honour (and the money) of their houses being razed in the film's pyrotechnic highlights ... when Universal razed the project instead. Threw it right out the Black Tower window in late August.*

Why? Well, the official reason is pure Hollywood double-talk. "Major cast and other creative costs," *says Universal man Fred Brost,* "escalated the budget (rumoured at 17.5 million dollars) to the point where Universal could not proceed with the project as a viable financial commitment."

You want that in English? John's The Thing did not perform as well as expected during its summer release Stateside. So, he's, like had his chance, baby, and flunked it. That seems a trifle tough on John. Sure, the film was a financial disappointment. Yet very little performed that well up against the summer's (and Universal's) runaway E.T. hit... Then again, if Universal had not poured 26 million dollars into its Burt 'n' Dolly Whorehouse movie, the studio would not be feeling the pinch, either.

The article then did make an interesting point. It also goes without saying that if Spielberg had been due to make Firestarter (and rumours are already saying that he might), you can be sure that Universal would have found the budget extremely viable ... and probably would have added a few million in the kitty, as well, just to keep the wonder-boy smiling.

The final word? That's Hollywood for you. You're only as good as your last film. And the knives are sharper than the critics. Particularly when your back is turned.

As for those fans? Horrorhound Magazine (#31) asked Carpenter in their 2011 interview about his growing fanbase, and his reply goes right to the modern recovery of the film.

HH: So, what would you like to say to those fans?

JC: Absolutely, to my heart, flattered and delighted that people love The Thing. And I am happy that they found it... because they found it in home video. They didn't find it in the theatres. It just makes me feel great! It feels good."

The Directors

The Thing was a big budget sci-fi horror release, really the first since Ridley Scott's ALIEN just a few years earlier. Its success or failure could have serious consequences to the future plans of a lot of directors, so you bet they were watching the film with a professional eye. In 1982, Ridley Scott, whose own film Blade Runner seemed to be failing at the box office, was asked about Carpenter's film.

Its interesting that in America now there seems to be a reaction against films that are too graphic or have downbeat endings. The Thing, for example isn't doing well while E.T. is. With The Thing people are objecting to the graphic nature of it and the fact that you don't get a resolution to who is the Thing.

I think the ending of The Thing was confusing, puzzling. I think in one sense, a cardinal rule is whatever you do, whether it's downbeat or not, you must have some kind of final resolution. I think The Thing is a very well-made movie, one of his (Carpenter's) best made movies to date. In fact I'm hoping to work with Rob Bottin on the next film I'm doing. It's been written for a year, but it's just moving into production. It's a Dark Ages fairy story. If we do the film together, we both want gentler aspects of the creature world. I actually think Bottin is the best at it. There are things going on in The Thing that are quite remarkable (Starburst #51). That other film was Legend, and by box office receipts it was a bigger failure than the Thing.

1982…what a fucking year for film. Blade Runner, one of the greatest sci-fi films ever made and still leading the pack when it comes to futuristic cyberpunk, yet as great as Ridley Scott was it still failed. Scott was also far from the only director to trip up that year and who'd been watching The Thing.

Today, Michael Mann's name is synonymous with quality and action. If 1992's The Last of the Mohicans isn't near to perfect, well then no film is…and the bastard followed it up with 1995's Heat – which still has to have one of, if not the greatest gun fight scenes ever. In 1982 Mann's golden future was still ahead, but he did have a small supernatural horror/thriller coming out called The Keep. A Starburst Magazine interview the following year indicates Mann had seen what happened to Carpenter's gory film and wanted to relieve any concerns the scarred public might have with his own flick.

… You will see hardly any red blood at all in The Keep. I'm not interested in gore. I want to make something that is powerful and the point in doing something different like this is that if it is fresh and new in approach it will effect an audience much more. I want to effect them with my impression of death in the same way they were affected by blood the first time they saw it. I'm exploring new channels of shock primarily for that reason. Let's face it. The Thing was the ultimate prosthetic movie so that isn't going to be an area to consider anymore. It was gratuitous and not very exciting speaking personally. The Keep is a new way of frightening you…

Sadly, for Mann, if you think audiences and critics reaction to The Thing was bad, it was far worse for The Keep. Gene Siskel, film reviewer for the Chicago Tribune, wrote:

Stay away from The Keep, one of the most inaudible movies ever made. Oh, sure, you can look at the pictures, but without the dialogue it's going to be most difficult to figure what's going on. Apparently, the score was so loud he couldn't hear the actors.

Just like The Thing, The Keep was based on a short story, and its author, F. Paul Wilson, was so disappointed by the film that he wrote it was *Visually intriguing, but otherwise utterly incomprehensible.* He then produced a comic version of the story: *Because I consider this visual presentation of THE KEEP my version of the movie, what could have been ... what should have been.* It would seem the shadow of The thing would fall over horror movies for years to come.

A decade later the world of science fiction was gearing up for another sequel – one that would also change the way movies would be made in the future. In many ways James Cameron had taken up the crown Carpenter had lost, becoming Hollywood's new hot young director who they believed would conquer the world. Just like Carpenter, his first big hit was the impressive small budgeted 1984 sci-fi/horror – The Terminator. He followed this up with a sequel to Ridley Scott's own Thing clone (ALIEN) by making ALIENS – arguably the greatest sequel of any film. He then broke new technical ground with his movie The Abyss, that also seemed to struggle finding an audience.

In 1992 Cameron was finalising his work on the sequel to his own hit film. Terminator 2 is a beloved film that many claim was superior to the original...and those people are all wrong. Personal opinion – T2 is not a great film. Its watered down (remember, Terminator was a sci-fi/horror in the vein of The Thing and ALIEN) – that almost scene for scene remakes the original film – only with less heart and edge. I could write a book about my issues with T2, so let's just leave it with ...I understand that younger fans grew up with T2 as their Terminator, and that explains why so many likely prefer it (as they saw it first and then watched the technically less impressive Terminator) – but make no mistake – Terminator is a fantastic film and T2 is its poor imitation.

Ahem...anyway, my point is Cameron was a media darling at the start of the 90's and in one interview gave away a very interesting fact (Gorezone #20).

Writer-director James Cameron returns to his science-fiction creation with a bigger budget, a bigger salary' and two of the '80s' most ambitious movies added to his resume: Aliens and The Abyss. Addressing the audience, Cameron adds that the T-1000 was his initial vision for the first Terminator movie.

"Even though I didn't call him the T-1000, that was my original idea," reveals Cameron. "Originally, I had the idea of a liquid metal robot from the future that could take on any form and coloration that it wanted—this would have been back in 1981. And before I actually got to writing the script, I realized two things; One,

I had no conception of how to do it, even though it was a cool idea, and two, John Carpenter was making The Thing, and I had heard they had gone back to the original concept of the story 'Who Goes There?', with the idea of a shape-changer. I had no idea what they were doing with that movie, so I abandoned that concept and went in a different direction. Now I've come full circle after figuring out how to do the effects."

In 1982 Cameron was creating a fluid, shape-changing Terminator, but word coming from the set of The Thing emphasized Carpenter was already doing that. Also, right here with these two films we have the opening chasm between past and future film making. The Thing is considered the height of practical effects. Never before and never again will a film contain so many impressive 'in-camera' effects. On the other hand, after the Abyss, the world began to turn away from practical to ever improving digital shots – and at every stage Cameron would be at the spearhead of this technology. Be it Titanic or the almost entirely CG movie, AVATAR, this all began with T2, a movie that had been held back long enough for technology to help create a liquid Terminator – and this was partly because Cameron didn't want to copy Carpenter's The Thing.

Note: James Cameron began his film career as a special effects artist and had actually worked for John Carpenter on Escape from New York. Amongst other things, he was a matte artist, and I do believe he painted the New York city skyline when the helicopters come in to pick up a briefcase the Duke had taken from the US President.

DID YOU KNOW? Before we leave this franchise, I'm not sure how you feel about 2015's Terminator Genisys? Personally, I thought it was a worthy attempt at Back to the Future two-ing the story. The effects of the T-1000 were made by British effects company Double Negative, who were later also responsible for the T-3000 and T-5000 Terminators. The animation design and technology were similar to how the T-1000 was rendered in T2, only with more advanced fluid simulations. To properly depict the liquid metal being dissolved by acid, not only did Double Negative's artists study acid burning through aluminium but the Terminator's final distorted forms were inspired by The Thing.

The Awards

For a film that apparently no one supported, The Thing didn't do too bad in certain awards in 1982. The Thing was actually nominated in a number of categories in the 10th Saturn Awards; Best Horror Film, and Best Special Effects. The first was won by Poltergeist, but criminally E.T. won best FXs. Yes, E.T. was amazing, but most of its effects have aged horribly…unlike The Thing, which is considered the greatest practical effect movie ever.

Another crime that year, Best Supporting Actor went to Richard Lynch in The Sword and the Sorcerer, beating out Rutger Hauer's portrayal of Roy Batty in Blade Runner.

The Thing also lost at another awards ceremony, the 3rd Raspberry awards. Ennio Morricone was nominated for the Worst Musical Score, which was eventually won by The Pirate Movie's Kit Hain.

The Soundtrack

Why was Morricone up for a Raspberry award? Well, its sounds funny today, but the reaction to the soundtrack released at the time of the film fared no better when it came to the critics. Writing for Starlog, David Hirsch noted that *without the heroics of Kurt Russel or the hideous shape-changing monster, the music for this film is unbearably dull… If there was any kind of main theme for this film, I couldn't find it.*

Being nominated for a Razzie may have hurt, but I do believe Morricone had the last laugh as he won an Academy Award for Best Original Score in 2016. I'll leave it as a 'surprise' for the next chapter what film that was for.

The 40th

Update: as of July 2022, The Thing was released for a short time in specific cinemas to celebrate the 40th anniversary. Records are still coming in, but it seems sales were so strong, that even with only a few sessions of the film shown on 700 screens, it cracked the weeks top 10 Films at #9… well done everyone who went. Sadly, no cinema in Australia decided to join in, and I even contacted my local chain to try and get one happening. They just weren't interested.

When these initial sessions were shown without the original movie format, there was a fan outcry. More sessions and screens were added, with the film presented in its original aspect ratio of 2.35:1. Now I looked everywhere for stats on how well the re-release did and found not a single box office tracker had recorded how much the movie made in 2022. The only one I found was it made $662 in New Zealand, but the international takings have to be pretty decent as I know many of you went and watched it on the big screen. So, keep an eye on the Facebook page and if I ever find that info, I'll pass it on.

The Reunion

In 1982 a very special screening of John Carpenter's The Thing was held at a cinema in the San Fernando Valley. Everyone ever attached to The Thing franchise was invited, but only a few came. The screening had been specifically arranged by journalist Ted Newsom for the surviving members of 1951's The Thing from Another World. Watching the film that day were Kenneth Tobey, Robert Cornthwaite, George Fenneman, William Self, the director, Christian Nyby and the husband and two daughters of the late Margaret Sheridan. Tobey later recounted:

"Everybody enjoyed seeing each other," Tobey remembers, *"and we had a lot of fun. it was a packed house. We answered questions from the audience, posed for photographs and signed a lot of autographs. They even had a cake with a flying saucer buried in the frosting.*

After taking a few publicity group photos, the former cast were asked what they thought of the '82 version, and their interviews later appeared in Starlog #64. Considered the star of the '51 version, Tobey began:

Kurt Russell is a damn good actor, and gave an excellent performance as MacReady. The special effects were absolutely remarkable. I've never seen effects like those in a film before. Rob Bottin is obviously very talented. In fact I met him when we were interviewed together on TV, and he's a very sweet guy. I haven't seen any of John Carpenter's other movies, but I think he's a very good director, although he was somewhat limited by his material. He showed a wonderful aptitude for handling the dramatic scenes, and I'd like to see him do a straight drama next. I'd also really like to see Halloween now.

I could find nothing about Tobey ever catching up and commenting on Carpenter's monster indie hit. He did have some positive things to say about the film he'd just watched though.

Carpenter really built up that opening sequence. It was right on target. As soon as I saw the dog running, I knew what was happening. I knew it portended something bad, and I just ached for that poor animal.

And his favourite part?

I thought the most exciting scene was the blood test. When Russell put the heated copper wire in the dish and the blood jumped, I leaped out of my seat. That reminded me of our scene where I opened the door and the 'thing' was there, and we closed it on his arm. The blood test was the most exciting scene in John Campbell's story 'Who Goes There?', and I always wished we could have done it in our picture.

Cornthwaite, who played Professor Carrington agreed in a 1992 interview (Starlog #178). *The special FX were terrific, and the fact that they went back to*

Campbell's original short story was a good idea. I remember someone handing me the short story early on in the shooting and thinking, "Gosh, this is an awfully good idea. I wonder why they departed from it?" It was not all positive though. *But, back to the new Thing, all the gruesome special FX in John Carpenter's film sort of became overwhelming to me. I was not interested in the people.*

Tobey's comments married Cornthwaites.

On the other hand, while I appreciated that Carpenter tried to put Campbell's story on film, I now realize that was an almost impossible task. I doubt if the story could be told in visual terms. Because of the internalized drama I think it could only be told in narrative form, where everything doesn't have to be shown. The way Carpenter did it he ran into some trouble, because he had to had so many graphic special effects.

From the 50s to the 80s version, there was an almost unbreachable gulf between the effects and even the explicit nature of films. Tobey's reaction resembled so many critics of the day.

The effects were so explicit that they actually destroyed how you were supposed to feel about the characters. They became almost a film in themselves, and were a little too horrifying. The emphasis on effects took away from the human story that has to be told in order to capture the audience's sympathy. When you make a monster movie, the audience has to be able to root for somebody. Usually they root for the humans. In this one there was nobody to root for, because you didn't know who was human and who wasn't. And with Russell wearing a beard and parka, sometimes you couldn't tell the actors apart. He also did a little speculating. *I also thought it was wrong for the ending to be so inconclusive, instead of showing good winning out over evil. I don't think it was fair to do that to the audience, unless it was just to set up a sequel?*

There were far more negative comments on the way. '51's controversial director', George Nyby was also in the audience. I think it's fair to say he wasn't impressed and famously was quoted saying: *if you want blood, go to a slaughterhouse. There are other ways to be effective. How many times can you see something split in two or three and remain scared? And why end with a downbeat ending? Are those guys going to freeze to death now? All in all, it's a terrible commercial for J&B scotch.*

As for the rest of the cast. Robert Nichols was asked if he ever saw the '82 film. *No. [laughed] – I was warned against it!*

Could some of this be down to bitterness from the original cast for not being involved in any way with the remake? Carpenter had talked about the possibility of hiring someone like Tobey for his version in Starlog (#60), and in so doing mentioned another small link between both films.

I really like Kenneth Tobey and think he's a neat actor, but I didn't quite see him in any of the roles. For a while I thought about casting George Fenneman, who came up with the way to kill the 'thing' in the earlier version. As a matter of fact, I went to school with his son Cliff. But then I decided against it, because people know him too well now as being Groucho Marx's announcer on You Bet Your Life.

The voodoo bull stuff

There's one bastard copy of the '82 film that doesn't get talked about much and has recently become available for everyone to be horrified by. In 1987 many TV stations started to broadcast The Thing across the world. Right off the bat I'm going to admit I don't ever recall the movie being on TV, and I lived in Canberra, Australia where we only had one commercial TV station for most of the 80s. If it had been on, I'm sure I would have seen it.

Let's have an old-guy moment. Kids today won't know the weird world of censored public TV many Thing fans grew up in. It wasn't just at the cinema or in books and comic that outraged groups like church organisations and governments once tried to censor. Our TV stations – if they ever bothered to air horror – would release a heavily edited version of the film that often didn't resemble anything like the original release.

Psycho TV

The popularity of Psycho rolled on for years, and in 1966 CBS paid nearly half a million dollars for the rights to televise a modified version of the movie. Three days from its first broadcast on September 23rd, 21-year-old Valeria Percy was stabbed a dozen times in her parents' home under extremely suspicious circumstances. Her twin sister was Sharon Percy (wife of then US senator, Jay Rockefeller, the great-grandson of 'that' Rockefeller), and she was the daughter of future Illinois senator, Charles H. Percy.

In deference to the family (or her father, who was in the middle of an election), CBS pulled the movie from its schedule. To this day Valeria's murder has never been solved, and after paying so much, CBS never actually aired the film (HORROR: The First Time America's Paranoia Infected the World). *Yes, it became that ridiculous.*

I've had it with these monkey-fighting snakes on this Monday to Friday plane!

They censored everything. Nudity, graphic scenes of horror, bad language, and yes, they edited and censored The Thing. In 1986 CBS released The Thing '82 on their TV channel and what people got to see was a very, very, very strange version of the movie.

What screened was the usual compromised adult film you'd get on tv in the 80s. Even played late at night, just about everything was edited out. To begin they cut a huge amount of the body gore – but that's pretty much a given. Most of those iconic scenes were just gone. They also edited the language. Now The Thing doesn't have a lot of swearing, but it's there. Some editors will just bleep the word, others will mute it, but Like Snakes on a Plane, for the Thing they decided to redub words that sound similar, thus matching the mouth movements of the actors on screen. This has led to a lot of mirth over the years and a lot of lines I think everyone should start using every day.

'Stinking couch?', 'Blast you?', 'it's weird and it's ticked off, and yes, "voodoo bull stuff".

The weird part is what they added. Not only did CBS seem to move a few shots around, maybe to cover some of the holes they cut out of the film, but something I don't think anyone has ever mentioned before is the introduction they included.

On April the 4th, 1987, viewers at 11:30pm watched as the CBS logo started sweeping across their screens with that horrible late 80s music bopping out of their speakers. I have read some notes that claim it was on at prime time or even earlier on some affiliate stations, but I honestly have no idea if that's true.

Computer graphic titles, looking a little like TRON, rolled past, announcing the 'CBS Special Movie' was about to begin and that classic 80's movie trailer announcer – you know the one, deep gravelly voice, sounding like he's talking around the half-chomped cigar hanging out of the side of his mouth - explained the exact same thing you've been reading for the last twenty seconds on your screen.

"Tonight, it's a CBS Special Movie…"

It's what occurs next that truly staggered me. Like a terrible modern film trailer, a montage of very short snippets from the film start flickering across the screen – and these are not just character shots or images of the film's locations – nope, you got full shots of The Dog-Thing growling away, the Blair-Thing, the spaceship in the ice, flamethrowers torching aliens, and even at the end the sequence with Mac freaking out when he drops his hot needle into Palmer's blood sample with sound effects and everything. They show it all…

they give everything away literally seconds before the movie begins as the title The Thing is slowly spraypainted across the trailer. That has to rank as one of the weirdest decisions ever, and you can watch the entire intro on YouTube.

Historically this wasn't anything new by the way. One review for The Thing '51 in Australia's The Voice explained how the alien was: *discovered by a scientific expedition lodged at the North pole. It is fished out of the ice and Captain Hendry...runs into conflict with the scientific group...who tries to make contact with the visitor. 'The Thing' commits two murders, turns off the heating system and threatens to extinguish the whole expedition. Hendry sets out to destroy the unwelcome and dangerous intruder. Several attempts to do so fail, until electrocution is used, and 'the Thing' goes out of exsistence...*

...well, I guess you didn't need to see the film afer this review gave the entire plot away.

The TV version does have one unique feature that you won't find anywhere else, a narrator. Perhaps CBS was trying to negate some of the criticisms placed on the film during its initial release in '82, for example the lack of character development, perhaps explaining what occured every time someone new entered the screen.

The narrator introduced each character, explaining who they were and where they came from. So, we get way more information about the world of The Thing, but it all plays like an episode of Unsolved Mysteries. What you heard was almost word for word taken from Lancaster's original script.

- Windows: hates being a radio operator, hates being here, can't wait to get back to the states .
- MacReady: A top helicopter pilot who work for Hughes Aircraft as a test pilot until he got into a confrontation with top management and resigned to take this assignment .
- Childs: a mechanic who went from trade school to the airline's, none better.
- Gary: a 30-year army man who worked up through the ranks to become an officer. Likes the job of station manager
- Clark: he's in charge of the dogs doing a study on the effects of extreme cold on animal behaviour.
- Dr. Copper: Graduate of Harvard Medical School. received his training at Massachusetts General Hospital. A personal tragedy in his life sent him on this adventure.

- Bennings: Meteorologist, an old pro, many papers published in his field.
- Blair: a pioneering microbiologist whose research on DNA helped lay the foundation for genetic engineering. Many discoveries in the field of cellular growth.
- Palmer: Second-string chopper pilot. Crack mechanic who hopes to start up his own business as a mechanic upon completion of this assignment.
- Norris: Geophysicist. Was a professor at Caltech. Has an incipient heart condition.
- Nauls: Inventive cook, a product of what's interested in the Antarctic (Huh? What does that even mean?).
- Fukes: Assistant biologists who work with Blair at the Rockefeller Foundation.

Weird, but I understand the thinking. The movie not only made little money on its release, it had been savaged by most critics, with almost every one of them complaining there was no characterisation. Honestly, I was a kid when I saw the film and I don't ever recall having an issue. This movie never spoon-feeds you anything – evidence it's not only the near perfect horror, but a damn good detective/mystery movie.

I will say, despite its issues this version does explain why they were all there. *These men were commissioned by the United States National Science Institute to gather data concerning the physical and natural sciences of the continent of Antarctica.*

Even crazier, the ending was new and completely changed the point of the film. After the famously ambiguous scene between MacReady and Childs as the camp burns, we then get a shot (apparently the following day) of the dog on the ice fields, implying that regardless of all the humans' actions, the Thing survived.

The narrator ominously returns at this point and warns the audience to "be on guard" and "watch those around you" because you don't know what "tomorrow will bring." I'll give the voice over actor credit here, somehow, he doesn't cackle maniacally after saying all this.

DID YOU KNOW? It's often mentioned there were three endings written and partly filmed for '82? One, the ending we got and the one Carpenter had to fight for. Another, partly filmed, was Mac being rescued and ending with him in a helicopter taking a blood test, proving he was human. A third was Mac slumping down in the snow by himself with no Childs showing up. This was filmed and it tested poorly as it made absolutely no sense.

There were more. The fourth was actually the first ending, one that only ever existed on the page. Lancaster ended the film with both Childs and MacReady turning into the Thing, and later are seen on a rescue helicopter heading back to civilization.

However, there was a fifth that many authors have missed…and I just told you about it, the TV version.

The Thing returns

Our final connection between '51 and '82 is a little weird. Just like the earlier film (and the Harris song) the phrase 'The Thing' once again entered the public mind set and became the go to for anything mysterious going on. For example, The Bladen Journal (2 Dec 1982) reported how an odd mass began growing on one farmer's barn. Clearly an insect nest 'The Thing' was like nothing seen before and soon was enormous and full of dangerous wasps.

'*The Thing' resembled a hornets nest, but it wasn't…it had 12 layers or cones inside a thin outer shell made up of something that looked like cured tobacco…*" and was full of thousands of black, winged insects. The owners noted *every time we opened the door in the building, the things would start singing. It was so frightening.* One day the farmers woke up and the nest was empty and they kept 'The Thing' as a trophy of this weird time.

The Book

If you're reading this you're most likely more than a fan, you're a collector. Sadly, there's very little original merch out there for Thing fans. There's soundtracks, posters and for '82 there was the novelization of the film.

Most sci-fi fans are aware he's the king of movie novelizations, but is Alan Dean Foster the most published author ever? At this point he has well over 100 novels to his name, an astonishing amount, with many of these being novelizations of big 70s and 80s films. He wrote E.T., The Last Starfighter, Clash of the Titans, Starman, Alien Nation, Outlander, Alien, and many are unaware Foster also ghost wrote Star Wars. He also wrote the novelization of The Thing '82.

Famously, Foster wrote his version of Alien and The Thing not from having watched any part of the film but from the script. In fact the makers of Alien deliberately refused to give the writer any information or images of the xenomorph. They understood the novelisation often was released before the film and that this could ruin the visual, horrific surprise they had install for their audience. When I asked the author about this and what his favourite novelization was. Foster explained: *Alien. Because I wrote most of it at night and scared myself silly. Also, because Fox wouldn't show me any images of the Alien (read "the Thing" entry in my book, "The Director Should've Shot You" by Centipede Press).*

Because FOX studios refused to release any information on the Xenomorph other than an early version of the face hugger...in my mind this sounds like you were dealing with your own mini-version of The Thing – that you had a faceless Alien that was installing high levels of anxiety and paranoia in everyone involved. Can you tell us a little of that process? *You use a lot of adjectives and few nouns. I.e., "the horrible gibbering monstrosity lurched and stumbled toward him" conveys plenty of horror without actually describing anything. It's not easy to bring off.*

When it came to writing The Thing, how did the process begin and did you go straight off the script or 'Who Goes There?" *I got a copy of the script, as it was at that point in time, some stills from the sets, and I started writing... Straight off [the script]. I remember the original story well enough that I didn't have to reread it.*

Did you add anything of your own to the storyline? Or is that sort of thing not done when writing an adaptation? *I make changes and additions where and when I think it's appropriate, and when I am allowed to do so. Can't remember specific instances for The Thing, but I'm sure I did so.*

Did you see the film when it was initially released? Did you have any sense if the film was going to be a hit? *I thought it would make its costs back. Beyond that, I thought it was a bit much for the general audience. I had the same feeling after seeing a rough cut of The Wild Bunch.*

Do you recall any of your thoughts, for example, that a scene you had written for the book was no longer there? *I was too busy enjoying the film to notice, except for the ending, which was quite different.*

Have you ever read a script and write the book, then seen the film and been bewildered at the differences between the page and the screen? *Not really. The copy of the script I get is usually while the film is already in production, so while there are always changes, at that point drastic changes are too expensive to make. Terminator Salvation being an exception.*

Did any film turn out better than you imagined as you went through the script? *Alien (because of the Giger reveals). Star Wars (because I never expected they could get what was in the script up on the screen). Starman (the film much more propulsive than the screenplay; plus Bridges's and Allen's acting).*

When it came to the Thing, what sort of artwork/description were you provided with and, thinking back as an artist, did you prefer/enjoy the challenge of not being able to unleash the bizarreness of the movie THING on the page? *I would rather have had some pix of The Thing, to better describe it for the reader. Same as with Alien. But who knows if that would have made for a better read?*

Because Foster was working from the script there are a few differences between the film and the book. The following are some of the more interesting ones.

When exploring the Norwegian camp, the guys discover audio tapes that contain a recording of a Thing attack. Childs and Mac also meet at the end of the book after destroying the camp and play chess, but the one scene I feel deserves a highlight is what happens to the dogs because it may explain an issue we've all had with the movie.

Almost everyone whose watched the film more than once was left scratching their heads over some scenes, such as MacCready throwing dynamite at the Palmer-Thing after it bursts out of the rec-room while on fire. We've all asked, "is that the smartest idea? Surely now there are pieces of Thing all over the place that can later infect someone?"

Now I'm not saying this is the case, I'm just making an educated guess. One difference between book and movie is what happens to the camp's dogs. In the book, after the kennel attack the same surviving dogs are shown to be infected as they had bitten off small pieces of the Thing during the fight. The dogs then take off and are chased by MacReady, Bennings and Childs, who later find the dogs transforming. A fight ensues, Bennings is killed but the others destroy the dogs and return.

The scene (in the script) suggests the Thing is far more infectious than the film version, so perhaps this explains why no one seems concerned with small pieces getting around after blowing them up. Yes, they might be individually alive, but perhaps it takes more than a small piece for total infection in the film? Practically, if you are close to a large explosion the concussive force can rupture biological cells, so perhaps the Thing is literally shaken to death by an explosion?

Movie novelizations rarely are reviewed, but 1 did manage to find a very disturbing assessment in Fantasy & Science Fiction (1982) #63. The reviewer Algis Budrys spent little time examining the book but unloaded on the movie which it was based on.

Of all movie and television novelizations being published, the ones scoring best with readers appear to be in the genre of the fantastic, so this year there is more than enough to read. Bantam Books jumped the gun a bit when they released Alan Dean Foster's novelization of John Carpenter's The Thing ($2.75) in late winter. Perhaps *they were counting on Foster's sterling track record (he probably has written more best selling novelizations than anyone else) but, in any case, his story is a cross between John W. Campbell's original short story "Who Goes There?" and the Bill Lancaster screenplay...*

Nothing too bad so far, though I will point out what the filmmakers were concerned about with the novel is exactly what happened. The book was released in 1981 – well before the film, thus making their decision (just like with ALIEN) to not send any information about the creature, ensuring Foster couldn't give anything away, the correct one.

When describing the action of the book and film Budrys, I believe, oversteps the roll of a reviewer. Now I have no issue with someone not liking something and writing a negative review, but surely the position means you have a certain amount of responsibility. Just because you personally did not like a product, surely that does not give you any right whatsoever to give away an ending to your audience who may well enjoy the piece. I think what Budrys did next is unforgivable...especially as it seemed to have been deliberate.

... What do I care what I give away about this piece of garbage? — the surviving humans may have killed the alien, but assuredly going to die themselves. In a final scene which is one of the most inept recent pastiches on the reliable finale about the indomitable human spirit, the most intense feeling generated is that Carpenter has planted the seeds of a sequel fully worthy of Halloween II.

What an irresponsible dick!

The Reprint

Starlog Magazine seemed to have been the main supporter of '82, carrying interviews with most of the talent connected with the film. In the same issues the magazine also received permission to reprint Campbell's original novella. 'Who Goes There?' appeared in three issues, (#58 to #60), and its main contribution to Thing lore was the inclusion of the artwork highlighting scenes from the story. The artist was Nicola Cuti, and his images are reminiscent of the original art from the stories first printing way back in 1938. They are dark, heavy images just like Hans Waldemar Wessolowski's original art.

PART FIVE
After 1982

The Comics

The mid-1980s were a magical time. Movies like Dark Crystal, Labyrinth and The Never-Ending Story were in the cinemas, while tunes like The Riddle by Nick Kershaw blasted out of our boomboxes. Seemingly to cash in on this, in 1986 Marvel Comics released the Graphic Novel 'Hooky'. Penned by Susan K. Putney and with artwork by the horror master, Berni Wrightson, Hooky was a Spider-Man story set during a magical war in the strange realm of Cloudsea. Here were floating islands, flying ships and a shape-shifting villain called the Tordenkakerlakk. In the story Spidey helps a perpetually 12-year-old sorceress called Marandi Sjorokke fight the monster – which constantly changes shape and is mostly a mass of limbs, heads, and eyes on stalks with mouths appearing with far too many teeth. Wrightson was most certainly a master of horror, but I find it impossible to imagine he wasn't at least influenced by Mike Ploog and Rob Bottin's similar work just a few years earlier.

There were also sequels to The Thing '82 in comic form. Dark Horse comics in 1991 was picking up as many franchises as they could to try and match MARVEL and DC. Rumour is the author, Chuck Pfarrer, pitched his storyline to Universal as a direct sequel to the Carpenter film. When they weren't interested, Pfarrer turned it into a short-lived comic series called 'The Thing from Another World' to make sure there was no confusion between it and Marvel's ever lovin' blue-eyed Thing.

Set 24 hours after the film ended…you know what, let's have the master explain the film. Yes, the comic made it into the hands of John Carpenter, who was quizzed about making a possible sequel by Erik Bauer for Creative Screenwriting #1.

Sure. I'd use the Dark Horse comic book series. There's a three-book series they did in the '80s which started with MacReady and Childs coming across the ice, getting discovered by a ship, and being brought back. It's a great story that ends up in a submarine. It's really cool. I'd just do that. It's all there. Big budget, though. But again, it's always the story. That's the big thing. You have to come up with a great story.

After Pfarrer's story there were more comics released over the next few years and they aren't exactly the hardest comics to find, but now that I've mentioned them all those completists out there are currently eBay-ing as we speak, so go find them before the price skyrockets.

The TV

It's hard to describe how big the X-files was in the early 90s. Think Walking Dead and Game of Thrones rolled into one. I recall everyone having an 'I believe' poster on their wall and setting their VCR to record the latest episode religiously. The Watercooler talk for the next few days would be all about what had happened and how Scully was being a pain and still a disbeliever despite the evidence she'd just seen, and the ongoing trope of Mulder losing his gun every time he pulled it from his holster.

I wasn't a fan. Why? I just found the show frustrating as hell. They almost uncovered an urban legend to be true, almost found an alien, almost did a lot of things if they had walked one step further or looked behind a tree at the right time (I'm not kidding, so many storylines ended with them simply walking away when the answer was right in front of them). I loved the satellite show, Millennium, in fact the standing joke with my girlfriend at the time was I wasn't to be disturbed when watching Millennium (and Babylon 5 for that matter) …it did weird things to me.

In 1993 X-files was growing in popularity. I recall my friends even having a TV party once a week to watch the latest episode for the first season. Each episode increased the viewership of the show as word of mouth spread. Around 8 weeks in Scully and Mulder found themselves shipped to a scientific outpost in frozen Alaska, where everyone has died except a dog. Luckily the dying scientists left the cryptic message 'we are not who we say we are.'

What comes next is exactly what you'd expect. The investigation uncovers the original team had been taking ice core samples from a meteorite strike, and from this a parasite in the shape of a worm has escaped and is then discovered inside the dog after a blood test. This creates symptoms like the bubonic plague, and very soon we discover many of the investigators are also now infected. People start acting strange, Mulder becomes paranoid - in fact the paranoia in the episode amps-up as no one seems to trust anyone else.

In their book, 'Monsters of the Week: The Complete Critical Companion to The X-Files' the authors explained the story was based on Who Goes There? and The Thing, yet the episode *still feels distinct*. I'll leave it up to you, the reader, to make up your own mind about that, but I think you can guess how I felt about the episode at the time.

The truth is out there – the official guide to the series by Brian Lowry, Chris Carter and Sarah Stegall, also mentioned that *there are certain similarities in this episode to The Thing and to the John W. Campbell, jr., novella. Who Goes There? on* which *The Thing was based, in as much as "Ice" traps characters in a confined space with a killer who may be any one of them. Still, the idea for the hour actually started after Glen Morgan read an article in Science News about "these guys in Greenland who dug something 250,000 years old."*

I take umbrage with the word 'certain'. The episode is about an outpost where everyone dies except a dog, that then infects another group of scientists who uncover what the first group were working on was something they uncovered buried in the ice. This turns out to be extra-terrestrial in origin (ok, a meteorite instead of a spaceship), but life is found in the ice next to the 'vehicle', brought back and infects the team. It turns out doing blood tests helps uncover the alien that's now hiding inside some team members, creating a rising sense of paranoia…I would say there's far more than a 'certain' amount of similarities.

This episode explains my frustration with the show. The X-files was a department of the FBI looking for evidence of Extra-terrestrial life…AND THEY FOUND IT. That's it, show over. They have in their little specimen jars proof positive of alien life on earth, but rather then trigger an investigation into this alien creature through obvious scientific means, they walk away and decide never to investigate. Worse, the show seems to suffer from amnesia for the rest of the series about the alien life they'd discovered…sigh.

OK, Mulder asks to return to investigate further but is informed the station had been destroyed – yet if you were truly looking for alien life, and then finding a seemingly hostile alien capable of infecting the world, would you just walk away?

NOTE: There are some very real links between The Thing and the episode. Watch it. If the exterior shots look familiar, well, there's a reason for that. The production designer for the episode was Graeme Murray – who in 1982 worked as a set decorator on Carpenter's The Thing. For the episode he placed unused film from The Thing in the outside sequences.

There's also been other TV shows referencing the franchise, but most of them are just hinting at links between them. South Park ripped off the blood test for an episode about a headlice outbreak (Lice Capades), while Futurama's 'Murder on the Planet Express' has more than a nod to the films. There's a great list collected on the Thing IMDB page if you want some more.

This leads us to one of the most popular TV series of the last decade. I don't think I need to dwell too much here because it's obvious there'd be no Stranger Things without The Thing. I think we've all seen the movie poster hanging in the Wheeler family basement, and how many times was the movie itself on a TV or part of a conversation? The Demogorgon – a dog-shaped monster that can stand in a humanoid form, whose head splits open like the petals of a flower to reveal its mouth… is almost exactly like a certain wolf-dog in a certain movie.

In season 4 we have a major part of the show in an arctic tundra outpost, trapped with an unseen monster in a claustrophobic prison. Notes from the Duffer Brothers before the season release explain... *Meanwhile, back in the states, a new horror is beginning to surface, something long buried, something that connects everything...* we even have most of the cast caught and wrapped up in Thing-like tendrils at one point. The shows name is even Stranger 'Things', and we could go on, but I think the points been made.

Another series leaning heavily into the franchise, AMC's The Terror, is based on a novel by Dan Simmons. This shows still new enough, and oddly unknown enough, that I don't' want to give too much away because everyone should watch it. Set around the Franklin Expedition looking to sail above Canada and find the famed North-West Passage...historic spoiler: they don't make it. This stories about the horror the crew uncover during this journey, but again there's lots of books with numerous nods to the Thing franchise, so why does this one stand out? Well, the novel contains an interesting dedication: ...*with love and many thanks for the indelible Arctic memories, to Kenneth Tobey, Margaret Sheridan, Robert Cornthwaite, Douglas Spencer, Dewey Martin, William Self, George Fenneman, Dmitri Tiomkin, Charles Lederer, Christian Nyby, Howard Hawks, and James Arness.*

Any of those names ring a bell?

The Clone

The opening shot is a spaceship hurtling from deep space towards the Earth. We then cut to a helicopter, introducing a team of men in an alien landscape. They're investigating another similar group of men who have been butchered, and soon, one by one, they're killed by an alien that at first cannot be seen, and later only partly seen. In fact every time we encounter the alien it looks different and the paranoia just continues to ramp up. Finally, the few survivors set up traps and try to kill their enemy, we even get a face-to-face between hero and creature with a nice little 80s tough guy quip, and then an almighty explosion and the film ends with the two survivors finding each other in the rubble and we're left unsure if they're alive.

John McTiernan's Predator has so many similarities to The Thing that I'm having trouble believing they're a coincidence. Yes, Predator ends with Arnie on the CHOP-PAH, but he could easily be dead, and remember, at least one Thing '82 script ended with Mac on a helicopter....wait, isn't one of the Predator characters also called Mac?

The Movies - a New Century

The story was first published in the 30s, with the first film at the start of the 50s. How many franchises have then stretched 50 years into the new century? Tarzan, Superman, Batman...arguably the Phantom. My point is, not many.

The first imitator was a 2001 horror film from Germany. Deep Freeze (or Ice Crawlers in English), is a film based around the old trope of a Geotech company heading to Antarctica (violating just about every UN treaty I can think of) to look for oil. There are ice tremors, someone's died, investigation teams are coming to find out why and maybe shut everyone down. There's scientists, miners, investigators, an ancient trilobite attacking the unwary, all clearly based on The Thing, but so are dozens of films like Leviathan (1998), The Last Winter (2006), Blood Glacier (2013) and Black Mountain Slide (2016) ... so what makes this one different? Let's watch the film together shall we dear reader as yes, there's a copy available on YouTube...ready?

Opening shot – a camera panning over snowdrifts and a bleak landscape. Within 10 seconds we get a shot of a very, very...very familiar base in Antarctica. Yes, just like the X-files episode, somehow the producers of this movie got their hands on unused shots from The Thing '82 and have cut snippets throughout the film.

Let's jump four minutes forward and the titles start to fade in and out while music, not dissimilar to Morricone's famous theme, plays and we get a montage of shots – some directly lifted off the Thing... and right there we get Mac's hut.

Oh, gentle reader, there's more. The characters decide to kill the creature by blowing it up, and of course the usual Hijinx ensue with people getting knocked off. Finally, the creature shows itself in all its monumental glory, and there's a few quips thrown, the explosives are ignited and the camp – interior shots of Outpost #31 – explodes, and yes, they use the final Thing scene of the burning camp's flames reaching high into the Antarctic night sky.

There's very few reviews for Deep Freeze – with most summed up with 'MEH'. A few reviewers have noticed the use of the exterior Thing '82 shots, but as far as I can see I'm the first to notice they used the interior shots as well...so you know... yay me.

It's always about the blood

Possibly the most accurate version of Campbell's 'Who Goes There?' was the 2002 radio version for BBC's 'Chillers: Four Tales of Terror' series. Award winning radio producer, Mike Walker, assembled a small team of actors and created a British version of the story, with MacReady sounding Scottish to me.

It's a great version, well made with fantastic audio performances. It's also astonishingly tight at only 28 minutes, and yet seems to contain all the stories beats, including the blood test. I'll admit there are two things I struggle with every time I hear it, though. The first is the cast, they sound a lot like the crew from Red Dwarf, but it just takes a few minutes to shake that off and you can just sit back and enjoy.

The second thing? Well, it's what I call the squeaky dog-wheel. When the Thing attacks the dog kennel there's one sound effect that's irritating as hell…and my gift to you is you can hear it for yourself as the audio copy is readily available all over the place.

The Cheating Bitch

One criticism placed on the movies was the lack of female rolls. We discussed '51, but those who study '82 know this isn't strictly true…and no, I'm not talking about the cut scene with the blow-up doll. For a film that's eminently quotable, we began this section with one scene that everyone seems to love – MacCready playing a chess computer.

As many of you know, the actress Adrienne Barbeau not only appeared in Carpenter's films like Escape from New York, she also played the voice of the Chess computer.

Well let's jump forward a few decades to a release that, just like the Dark Horse comic series, was an official sequel to the '82 movie.

When we first heard that The Thing was going to morph into a game we were pretty sceptical. It is, after all, one of the finest and scariest pieces of celluloid in existence and the ZONE boys (and girl) were of the opinion that something this good shouldn't be messed with…Then we heard that UK-based development house Computer Artworks were behind the title and we got straight on the phone and demanded an audience with them (PC Zone #113).

Apparently the crew at Computer Artworks decided early on a game based on '82 was pointless as there'd be little suspense in such a well-known story. Instead, they looked at what could have happened just after the film's iconic ending.

Their game focused on the US team - specifically Captain Blake of the U.S. Special Forces - sent to discover what happened at Outpost #31. Not only did Carpenter officially endorse the game, he appeared in it, as did the two survivors from the movie, Childs and MacCready.

PC Zone interviewed the games producers about how this evolved.

Universal approached us...and we jumped at the chance to work on the title. The fact that it is 20 years old doesn't really come into it. It is a classic horror movie that still manages to scare and shock. [Universal] *were very good to work with...They told us to come up with original ideas. It wasn't like a Harry Potter license. There weren't strict guidelines, as long as we retained the quality of the original work.*

The game follows the rules set out in all the previous versions of the story. The troops come under attack as they start to unravel what happened. Controlling Blake, the player makes their way through a series of problems and solve puzzles and achieve goals – however – the player must ensure they retain the trust of the other characters because if they don't, they'll begin to lose faith and may even start to think the player (Blake) is the Thing.

...Chris. "Given the great sense of tension and suspense in the film, we wanted the player to have to work to get the best out of their team members. The idea is that the NPCs have trust and fear. Trust is based on the player's actions...and on the NPC's perception of how likely it is that the player is infected. Fear is based on the environment and possible enemies. At the extreme, an NPC that loses all trust in you may open fire on you, seeing you as a definite enemy.

Once again paranoia is the theme and the game's very good at instilling that into the player. Unlike '82 the game was also a moderate success, selling well over 1 million copies. I know I bought one for the PlayStation 2 and still have it in my collection.

Let's leave the final word on the game to the P2's official magazine.

PC2: Did you pick anything up from the original black-and-white movie?

CHRIS: To be honest, no. John Carpenter's interpretation was much truer (in my opinion) to the original short story than the 1952 version, so we based our research on that. We preferred it since it focuses more on suspense and tension.

Before we finish with computer games there's one more title that's sneakily been taking over the world unseen, much like a certain alien we all love. 2018's 'Among Us' from the game studio Innersloth is an online multiplayer game where one player is the alien – but only the person who's been randomly chosen knows this. The 'imposters' mission is to then kill the other players, while the humans win by completing assigned tasks or figuring out who's the alien by the way they're behaving ('hey buddy, why you always trying to get me alone ya' perv?'), and ejecting their slimy alien butts out the closest airlock.

Apparently, the original version of the game was far more brutal and much more Thing-like, but the co-creator, Forest Willard explains: *We found this was too stressful and didn't leave much time for detective work ...*

2013's Dead Space 3 is apparently also inspired by Carpenter's The Thing, but I've never played it, and the kids haven't played it, so I've no idea how true this is or not.

Whiteout 2009

At first I thought this was a stretch, that having not seen the movie in a while I was maybe mis-recalling the connection between both films. There's of course instant similarities because both were set in Antarctica, populated by people in parkas running around in blizzards, etc. However, as I started to watch the movie again it soon became clear there was a whole lot more.

Opening scene, we time travel to Antarctica and watch as a vehicle crashes into the Icey landscape to be buried. We then travel to modern day and a feast of Antarctica vistas and the base. OK, expected, but the way everything is filmed recalls Carpenter's style. Almost every shot is a longshot with a vehicle in the distance moving to show immense scale. Even when we have people exiting buildings or vehicles, it's those same Carpenter angles, and I swear we even get the iconic scene fadeouts The Thing's infamous for.

As for similarities in the story? Let's see... there's a murder mystery, a body with two faces found in the ice mutilated in a seemingly impossible way. A sassy pilot is needed to fly into the increasingly stormy Antarctic wilderness to where the body was found. There's a distant camp that cannot be contacted, all the while moving through the base's uniform corridors is a faceless killer in a fur-lined parka. Who could it be? The paranoia amps up, a whiteout is on the way, the music becomes long pulled out string sections wailing into the freezing atmosphere that occasionally sounds similar to a certain Morricone soundtrack.

The movie strives for the paranoia of not trusting those around you, with an attack on the main character, Carrie Stetko, by the mysterious murderer. Is the person standing next to me the killer? Then there's the flashback when Stetko talks about how her old partner let their prisoner escape and tried to kill her for a massive bribe.

"What I can't get away from is that Jack had turned, and I didn't have a clue...".... OH COME ON...

We then get a flashback scene of someone abseiling down into the crashed plane from the opening, and damn if that image isn't exactly the iconic cover from The Thing, though without the light shining through the parka hood.

Just like The Thing, Whiteout failed to find an audience and is considered a box-office flop. It also received a lot of negative reviews – almost every single one drawing comparisons between both films. Perhaps because of this, there aren't too many makings of or interviews to tap into – but the few that exist have the cast and crew explaining how no other film looks like this and the extremes of filming in such conditions. To me it seems they're make an extreme effort to not compare both films. However, if you watch Whiteout its clear the filmmakers never went to the same lengths as Carpenter or even Hawks as it was mostly shot on green screen. Instead of filming in a cold building to get steamy breath, they just digitally added the breath later...and you can tell, again proving the problem with digital effects. They age almost immediately.

The Ghosts

I liked it. I did no research before I saw the 2011 prequel, I went in cold. I had no idea what it was about and was pleased to see the direction they went. A prequel, well I'll be dammed, and not just a prequel, they're telling the story of the Norwegians. Well, that's ballsy. Is it perfect? Hell no. Did they make bad decisions that I'm pretty sure they instantly regretted? Hell yes. Despite all the issues, I liked it.

The first time I investigated the film was when I researched this bit, so excuse me if this is old knowledge, but it was all new to me. Now like '82, there is ample information on the Blu-ray, especially the commentary track, so I won't repeat much of that here. Ok, one thing I will repeat, outpost31.com gets a mention when the director and producer comment they used work by the fans to figure out the dimensions and layout of the Norwegian camp.

The story is simple. Fans of '82, producers Marc Abraham and Eric Newman had remade Dawn of the Dead and were looking around for their next project. Universal had The Thing on their books. They were soon joined by director Matthijs van Heijningen Jr, and the team convinced Universal to make a prequel, not a sequel. Why? Well, one simple reason is they weren't Americans. As Europeans, they'd always been fascinated about what happened to the Norwegians in '82 and this was a chance to tell their story.

In 2010, Patrick Goldstein and James Rainey interviewed the producers for the LA Times. This is a great resource because it's from before the film was released. Newman explained their thinking. *I'd be the first to say no one should ever try to do 'Jaws' again and I certainly wouldn't want to see anyone remake 'The Exorcist... and we really felt the same way about 'The Thing.' It's a great film. But once we realized there was a new story to tell, with the same characters and the same world, but from a very different point of view, we took it as a challenge. It's the story about the guys who are just ghosts in Carpenter's movie -- they're already dead.*

The original idea was to have MacReady's brother heading to Antarctica, but this was quickly dropped for the same reason a woman (Kate Lloyd) was chosen to be the main character. The entire production had a massive Mac-shaped shadow over it. Any male actor, no matter how accomplished, no matter how cool, was never, ever...ever going to live up to MacReady. They also had a different ending, with Kate making it onto the crashed spaceship and discovering, much like Alien, the dead pilots and that the Thing was an escaped specimen they were carrying.

I'd be a fool to not understand there are some very serious opinions about this film, and I'm not trying to invalidate them. What I'm trying to do is pass on maybe a different perspective that some of you may not be aware of.

I will point out that many fans simply never gave '11 a chance and went into the film looking to rumble. I can say that with absolute confidence because, going through the message boards on posts about the trailer or pre-release convention panels, people were getting nasty, and they hadn't even seen anything yet. I said near the beginning of this book that Thing fans are something special, that they generally don't bicker and fight, but are more helpful and supporting then most genre fans. Well, not so much when it comes to the prequel, and it only got worse once the film came out.

Yes, one of the biggest issues is the computer graphics. The film had originally been planned to be mostly practical. In October 2010 IGN reported how the director explained that he pushed really hard to use practical creature effects rather than CGI -- to which the Comic Con crowd responded with notable applause... and apparently they did film many effect scenes practically...but it soon became obvious they couldn't do them all. In reality '82 had a year of preparation to design and create all their practical elements, '11 only had three months. Most scenes still have practical effects, but they have been 'enhanced' with CGI – and I think here is where people have been tricked. Because you can tell a CG effect, it's easy to think the entire effect is CG and not just the tiny embellishments on the practical elements. It seems the movie is maybe 70/30 practical, and that means it feels almost 100% CG because those enhanced bits are so easy to spot. As we mentioned earlier, the problem with CG today is that it's very quickly outdated, and our ever-experienced eye picks it instantly.

NOTE: It's mentioned in several places how the team from '11 approached John Carpenter and talked to him about what they were thinking, and he gave them their blessing. I'm not saying that wasn't the case, but I did find this question that had been put to the director online.

There are rumours going about that you a) gave the producers of The Thing Prequel your blessing and b) you were being lined up for a cameo role - is there any truth to these rumours or are they just lies? A. And the rumours are not true.

Right here is how miscommunication can quickly become a fact. It's clear Carpenter was talking about his possible cameo, but but if you read that comment too quickly it would be easy to think he never gave '11's creators his blessing? Again, I tried to contact the man but so far no luck.

Things they should get credit for. The team went back to Campbell's original story and populated the camp mostly with scientists (as an Antarctic outpost does have), unlike '82 and '51 which had very few. They also wanted real Norwegian actors, partly for realism, but also to heighten the paranoia when these characters spoke Norwegian and instantly cut the English speakers out of a conversation. The cinematographer also used old style camera lenses to keep the look of '82, while they really strove to match the camp with the ruined, burning set from Carpenter's film.

In some of the transformations they specifically worked hard to get the actor changing to be involved – and you can see on their faces and in their eyes the distress as they feel their body ripping apart as the Thing takes over and there's simply nothing they can do. Watch the scene when Juliette, the only other female in the movie, is taken over. Watch her face and her eyes. You can see the horror and fear…and not just in that scene. When they open the door to burn the Juliette-thing in the corridor there's a brief look at her head hanging off the back of the creature, and its pure fear and pain – she's still there, feeling every change and there's nothing she can do about it. Same when Kristofer is being devoured by the arm-thing and you can see his single eye. That look indicates he's aware and freaking out.

When Carpenter was asked about this idea on outpost31.com, he explained… *we stayed away from explaining how the Thing imitates a person. Secondly, I don't know if a person knows he's a Thing or not. I assume so, but it brings up complex, existential questions that perhaps would get in the way of a simple premise. Best not to ask.* Good on '11s creators for giving this one a go.

You should also watch the extras on the Blu-ray because here you get to see what the practical effects team was doing before the CGI took over. They were doing some nice work and you get an idea just how much had been practical.

DID YOU KNOW? The end title sequence is far more than a simple homage to '82. Yes, they used the same title font and score while filming the exact type of helicopter and rifle, but as the Norwegians are beginning their chase of the thing-dog across the glaciers and snowfields, there is actual footage from '82 mixed in.

Result

Reviews were actually pretty decent, with many liking the idea and pointing out '11 was far more than just a nod to '82, it was a well-crafted horror, with good timing, a decent pace and imaginative sequences. None of this helped. With a budget of $35 million, The Thing prequel made just over $31 million world-wide. I don't think anything more needs to be said except, to write this I went back and watched the film a few times, once for the storyline and once with commentary – and I have to say I really enjoyed it. Like the original, it gets better with viewing because you, the viewer, start to like the characters more and begin to catch all the subtle turns it has as you try to explore who and when people may have been taken.

I know a lot of you out there are not going to agree with this, and that's the way it should be. You don't have to like everything. My point here was to reveal that the film makers really went in with good intentions and they pulled off a lot of great stuff, so maybe give it another chance.

DID YOU KNOW? In Antarctica's base camps, at the end of the season, with everyone heading home there's an annual tradition for the skeleton crew being left behind of back-to-back-to-back viewings of The Thing from Another World (1951), The Thing (1982), and The Thing (2011). That's awesome.

The Penguin

Just a quick note. Also in 2011, clay animation specialist, Lee Hardcastle, was stuck in a hotel room for a while and made a little fan film of The Thing '82 based 'NOT ON PINGU'. 'Thingu' was later uploaded onto You Tube, where it became a sensation among the Thing community and currently sits on 1.29 million views. It's not only brilliantly crafted, with great sound and visuals, it even reproduces a lot of the little technical aspects of the movie's special effects (like the dog-thing skull dropping when it splits), but in clay. Well done Lee, who I did email for a chat, and replied just as I sent in my final edit, so I managed to sneak it in at the last minute. *John carpenter tweeted me when it came out and it was flagged by the owners of Pingu and taken down, and someone at Amazon prime used a still as a thumbnail for Pingu on prime…*

…so remember for every legal reason you can think of, the penguin is NOT Pingu.

Canon

For sci-fi fans, the idea that various storylines within the media they love being related to each other is important. You can see this with the arguments over what's 'canon' in franchises like Star Wars, Star Trek or the Marvel universe. Well, in the new MonsterVerse franchise that includes Kong and Godzilla - a seemingly unrelated movie makes a surprising appearance. The world's dormant Kaijus/Titans are watched over by outposts of the Monarch company, and in one film it clearly shows Antarctica's Outpost #32.

The Thing is now officially within the storyline of Godzilla and King Kong, leading to some exciting speculation. What if the Thing infected Kong? Or Godzilla? We Know Ghidorah is an Alien…so does it know of the race The Thing came from?

The way once unrelated media seem to be referencing each other suggests that if the next Thing movie does well, there could be a place for the Thing in future MonsterVerse films. Imagine the Predator coming to earth to hunt the last Thing. What if they knew how dangerous it was and that's why it was here in the first place? Hiding on one of the planets the Predator only occasionally visits?

I'll take you one further, ALIEN's xenomorph became the hero of the universe because it's the one creature that can't be taken over by The Thing. The Xenomorph has acid for blood, and so any attempt at a physical incursion will end in disaster for the Thing. The Alien as a hero monster…I'd like to see that…or maybe the reverse could be true. A plague of Xenomorphs and the intelligent alien known as The Thing presents itself to humanity to help fight and stave off the disaster. I'd buy a ticket to that as well.

The future seems bright.

That's not dog. It's imitation… part 2

With the video store generation now grown up and making their own films, it's obvious The Thing has become a serious source of inspiration to many. In the last decade there's been no studio that has owned the box office more than MARVEL, and for a long time one of its shining lights was the film director James Gunn. Many don't like comic movies, but Guardians of the Galaxy converted hordes of the haters.

Recently Gunns' had a little hiccup in his skyrocketing rise, leaving Marvel to make The Suicide Squad and follow up TV series Peacemaker for DC. For Gunn this all started with a film in 2006 about worms.

'Slither' is a horror/comedy featuring a meteorite striking a small town, and the alien life onboard – parasitic worm like-things bent on utter world domination - begin attacking the town's residents. The infested soon transform into tentacled critters.

The in-jokes fly thick and fast, and if this doesn't already sound like a cross between the original tentacled Alien from Who Goes There?, The Thing and the X-files episode Ice, well, there's always the town's mayor.

Jack MacReady was named after both the Thing's heroic main character and Big Trouble in Little China's slightly less heroic side-kick, Jack Burton (hey, he's the side-kick who doesn't know he's the side-kick. His buddy Wang did most of the heavy lifting in the film when you think about it). Further, an abandoned building has a sign out the front, 'Auctioneers & Funeral Home' owned by R.J. MacReady.

Far more of a remake was 2009's The Thaw. In this film a bunch of scientists in the arctic manage to unearth a woolly mammoth from the frozen tundra. As the corpse begins to thaw the ancient parasites that killed the mammoth are released and start causing havoc and mayhem.

One scientist decides to infect himself and carry the parasite back into the world to unleash it on a humanity that refuses to do anything about climate change. Luckily the survivors discover his plot and attempt to stop him. All we're missing is a dog – which then turns up when we think the disaster has been avoided. A hunter and his mutt find a dead bird, which the dog tries to eat, and out of that bird comes more of the parasitic bugs.

Some reviews only point out the similarities between the movie and the X-files episode 'Ice' (both have parasitic bugs), but as we know, the tv show was based on Thing '82 and the original Campbell story.

Reservoir Dogs

Yup, Reservoir Dogs is based on The Thing, or at least part of it is. We all know Tarantino is one of the world's leading cinephiles, and like many of us he grew up, not so much watching as devouring movies. Now there's books and books on Tarantino and his history in the cinema industry, so there's a lot of information out there about what influenced his various movies. When it comes to Reservoir Dogs, Stanley Kubrick's The Killing and 1952s Kansas City Confidential were a great inspiration…however if you recall, in November 2021 Tarantino was a guest on the Late Show with Stephen Colbert, who asked him about his favourite adapted films:

I'm a huge fan of the original short story or novella of 'The Thing'… do you enjoy the Thing?

Tarantino gets that enthusiastic look that only Tarantino seems to get. *I love both of them. I love the Howard Hawk's The Thing and John Carpenters…*

Now Colbert lights up. *I love John Carpenter's the Thing because it's my happy place. If there's something wrong in my life, I go watch it. If my kids see me watching The Thing, they ask if everything is okay?*

Tarantino then unleashed the following.

It's a weird happy place, but it's a beautiful adaptation of the feeling of the novella. Actually, one of the reasons The Thing holds a special place in my heart, is I love horror movies. I'm a big horror fan. I don't get scared at horror movies. I respond to suspense, what's going to happen next… I can jump at a boo scare, but that's not terror. I don't get scared in movies. The Thing I got scared in. Tarantino then expanded…*I was scared and it made me want to put it under a microscope about why I was actually frightened during that movie, and I think the reason is this, its because if you know the movie, part of the situation is these men are trapped in this situation in the artic research centre, and so, one or more of them are possibly this Thing that's going to devour all of them, and no one knows if you are the guy I've known forever or are you the Thing?*

Colbert nods, engrossed.

The movie makes the paranoia of that so palpable, Tarantino explained, *so real, it's like it's almost another character in the movie, just the sheer paranoia of it... They're trapped in this shelter. So, the paranoia is bouncing off of the four walls, bouncing, bouncing, bouncing, the fear of the paranoia...bouncing, bouncing, bouncing, until it has nowhere to go except through the fourth wall of the audience, and I started feeling exactly how they felt.*

Colbert: *Which I think is an enormous indicator of great art. It changes how you look at the art.*

Tarantino: *By putting that under a microscope and realizing, okay I'm affected by 'The Thing', for that reason, and I figure out why it is when I started writing 'Reservoir Dogs'. I was like, I need to have that aspect that's in 'The Thing'. I need to trap these bastards. I need to trap them in this warehouse, and no one can trust anybody else, and I want the paranoia of what's going on in that warehouse to bounce across the walls and hopefully, like in 'The Thing,' it will go out into the audience.*

In an interview with Michel Ciment and Hubert Niogert, Tarantino expanded on this idea.

...a film that actually really did that was John Carpenters remake of The Thing. In some ways its exactly the same story as my movie. A bunch of guys are trapped in one place that they can't leave. In the Thing, the tension and distrust and betrayal and paranoia those guys had going toward each other on that little outpost: it went right through the audience. I felt it, like a character in the movie, and it was freaking me out. That was what I was trying to achieve with reservoir Dogs. I was hoping that lightning would strike twice, and I could make an audience feel paranoid, creeped out, not knowing who to trust.

Premiering at the 1992 Sundance Film Festival, Reservoir Dogs was picked up by distributor Miramax Films after it became the festival's most talked about release. It was then sent to various film festivals, where it received rave reviews... well, that's what you generally read. It turns out the film was not only heavily influenced by The Thing, it suffered many of the same attacks upon its release.

I'm only going to use one here, Roger Eberts, because of its similareties with his originalThing review.

Now that we know Quentin Tarantino can make a movie like 'Reservoir Dogs,' it's time for him to move on and make a better one. This film. the first from an obvioulsy talented writer-director, is an exercise in style.... the movie feels like its going to be terrific, but Tarantino's script doesn't have much curiosity about these guys. He has an idea, and trusts the idea to drive the plot... As for the movie, I liked what I saw, but I wanted more...It was made on a low budget. But the part that needs work didn't cost money. It's the screenplay. Having created the characters and fashioned the outline, Tarnatino doesn't do much with his characters except to let then talk too much, especially when they should be unconscious from shock and loss of blood.

So, expects more of the director in the future, not enough work on the characters and suddenly does not seem to have an issue with over the top violence/blood, thus giving it a mostly positive review. I wonder what he would have given it if he knew the film was based on The Thing?

The Hateful Eight

To the rising strain of a deep bass heavy orchestra an image fades in of a bleak landscape. Lonely mountains covered in snow and ice with mighty white clouds rolling across them partly concealing a lapis lazuli sky. The isolation of the landscape is palpable. As image after image of stunning winter landscapes scroll across the screen with the blue filter of a sunless vista, the music starts to turn into a heartbeat, with the long, single note of straining violins.

Sadly, I missed Hateful Eight (H8) at the cinema and had to watch it when the Blu-ray was released. All I knew was this was a Tarantino western, and so one day when I had the house to myself I put the movie on, sat back and was struck almost right away at the similarities with The Thing. At first it was obviously the shot of a vehicle rushing across a wide, frozen landscape – ok, it wasn't a Norwegian helicopter, but a stagecoach pulled by a puffing team of horses. As the vehicle moves on, we get shot after shot of arctic-like vistas.

Next was the music. We immediately know there's a link when the film's composer was listed as Ennio Morricone. Not only did Morricone write the score for The Thing, it became obvious H8 was more than just a homage when the actual 1982 soundtrack began filtering into the picture.

A quick search found a screening of H8 with a Q & A sessions after the film with the director and one of Hollywood's big guns, Christopher Nolan. This interview is perfect as it covers behind the scenes stuff and originally I was going to print it here and, just like one of those old read-along-records, you could find the interview and read along... but, no, I'm not going to do that. Space is growing short, and while editing I noticed its almost a giant single ramble of incomplete sentences and ums and ahs...in other words a typical Tarantino interview. Instead, you're getting the highlights.

Nolan got straight into the influences of H8 with a funny line:

...obviously there's a danger asking you about influences and getting a lot in response...as I watched the film when I saw that Ennio Morricone had done the music I was thinking, 'oh okay, obviously a great history of westerns'...but in watching the film suddenly thought about The Thing, and I wondered as you were a fan of that, whether with Kurt Russell in it, they were just a couple of things that I felt were a homage?

QT: ...look. in particular the Thing is probably the one movie that is the most influential on this movie ... and actually Reservoir Dogs was very much influenced by The Thing...

Nolan: ...and the question I'd ask you is whether Morricone had done all the music for the film?

QT: Well, it was interesting because we'd flirted with working with each other for a while but this thing felt like the one to do. I had a little voice in my head saying, 'This material deserved an original score.' And I've never thought that way before...I didn't ever want to trust a composer with the soul of my movie...

Nolan: ...what was different here

QT: I don't know. I think it was the material... And so I took the first step, which was getting the script...translated into Italian, and I sent it to him, and he read it and his wife read it and he really liked it and his wife really liked it...I did mention the little voice ...that said the movie deserved a score of its own, and so then we started talking and he thought that I hadn't started to shoot yet, little did he know I'd already shot and would need the score in a month...

...he's like, "well, this is not gonna work. I'm working with Giuseppe de toro and he just finished shooting the other day and I've got to do his score, I mean this is not gonna work. I was told a lot of things that aren't correct. I'm really sorry."

...and I go well so am I...and I go okay, well tell me what you thought about the script? And so he starts talking... "so I had this idea for a theme...that I thought was kind of intriguing..".

...A theme that you said you heard in your head, um, what was it? and he goes, "... I see a theme that's moving forward... but the important part of the theme is the fact that it truly suggests the violence that will follow eventually."

Well, that sounds pretty good... I already talked to him about the Carpenter... music for the Thing and then he told me a story...

"...he came and showed me the movie...then I wrote a whole Orchestra score, and I wrote a whole synthesizer score because I knew that was what he was used to. And I gave him everything and the only thing he used in the entire movie was the synthesizer main title, so...all that music that's on the soundtrack album the Thing has never been used in a movie, ever, so what I can do is, I'll write the theme, I'll give you a mixed version of the theme, I'll give you a version of the theme that's just brass. I'll give you a version of the theme that's just strings, and then with the

other Thing...music. Now, you have your original score that's never been used in a movie before."
...and I go, wow, that sounds fantastic...then all of a sudden ten minutes of music became 17 minutes of music, became 35 minutes of music... and so with that and the unused Thing portions that I used is my original score.
Nolan: *Wow*

Wow, indeed...now go find the interview and watch. You'll see why this is edited down. It's a great story and we even know what John Carpenter thought of his score being used in such a way. The 2016 magazine Little White Lies (#067) interviewed the director and asked him about it.
See, that's just weird. The Thing was the first movie I did for a major studio, and they didn't want me to do the score. So they brought in Ennio, which was amazing for me because he's one of the greatest film composers of all time. I don't speak Italian, he doesn't really speak English, but we worked pretty closely together, and it worked out great. I have no problem with the fact he ended up using some of the music he wrote for The Thing on another movie.

Morricone had finite time to devote to The Hateful Eight, but ended up writing a good thirty minutes of score to be sliced and diced and shuffled around. He suggested Tarantino round out the film with unused Thing cues. *One of those borrowed cues was an aggressive string movement titled "Bestiality"—another, "Eternity," an anxiety-inducing synth piece. But Tarantino went a step further and included a cue that actually did appear in The Thing* (tasteofcinema.com). 'Despair' is the track playing when MacReady and the others find the alien ship buried in the ice, and it's one of the few complex pieces with a full orchestra creating a swirling instrumental.

What no one seems to have noticed is the exact same thing happened with John Carpenter. Before The Thing, Carpenter had always written his own music, and for his first studio film the company suggested bringing in a professional to write his score – and it was the exact same man Tarantino used three decades later.

If you recall in the last chapter we mentioned Morricone was nominated for a Raspberry award in 1982 for the years worst soundtrack, but then in 2016 he won the academy award. Guess what film he won it for? Morricone's Hateful Eight music, based on The Thing, won the academy award for best original score.

Finally, in the same Nolan interview Tarantino admitted to screening The Thing for his cast and crew on the set of Hateful Eight.
QT: (MacReadys') *a bad guy. That concept of a character became very interesting to me, and I thought about what if I could take eight of those characters and trap*

them in a room during a three-day blizzard where, if they try to leave, certain death. So, they have to deal with each other. They all have a back story, we can't trust a thing they say, and we can't trust anything that they say... and we just have to figure it out as we watch the story, yet there is no... moral centre. There is no hero that you can gravitate towards... the Thing cannot be ignored, it's the only movie that I showed the cast...

Nolan: Smiling at the thought. *You didn't show it to Kurt Russel?*

QT: *I did show it to Kurt Russell. He loves The Thing, so he loved watching it with the cast because he was just 'that's my baby.'* Tarantino then goes on to tell the same story he told to Colbert.

Playing chess

Watching H8 again I'm struck how often we get The Thing vibes. For example, when the men are trying to stash the horses in the distant barn (looking a lot like MacReady's hut sitting some distance from the main compound), we get the very familiar bass/heartbeat thump of Morricone's Thing score. This is also reflected in the earlier film when Clark is walking the alien/dog to the kennels.

There are also a lot of the still camera shots Carpenter became famous for in his 1982 movie. Framed doorways or windows, with action in the distance and stillness in the fore ground with a camera that seems cemented to the spot.

This happens again when the men decide to peg out a rope from the main house to the barn and the outhouse so that everyone can find their way around when the blizzard hits. Minnie's haberdashery resembles Outpost 31, with ropes and snow and bleak, blue tinged landscapes. I may be repeating myself, but I feel H8 is close to a remake.

Example. Once everyone is indoors the paranoia starts to go through the roof as we learn most characters either have a history, or know each other through their shared history – and often none of this is for the betterment of the party. As the blizzard howls and everyone starts eyeing each other, Kurt Russell's' John 'The Hangman' Ruth pulls those he thinks he can trust aside and gives a speech almost identical to the one he gave in 1982 about how one or more are not who they say they are and if we're not watching them carefully it could be the death of us all. The scene's even shot in almost the exact same way.

Instantly the paranoia amps up in the room, the camera moves, and group dynamics are set almost exactly like those from the Thing. Those participating in the conversation standing in what you take to be a circle, but is instead a straight line, and Tarantino again shows he's a serious student of Carpenters'.

Next - The Hangman takes the guns from everyone he doesn't know or trust and has the stage driver OB taking the dismantled weapons to the outhouse.

Already we're getting MacReady vibes from the driver as his gear is hauntingly familiar to the helicopter pilots - down to that odd large brim high crested hat and those odd aviator sunglasses MacReady wears. Seeing this figure walking through a series of buildings with ropes hanging between them and night fallen and the blizzard howling, and mysteriously with those same buildings backlit by some enigmatic blue light (it makes no sense when you think about it – where the hell is that light coming from?) – we feel like we're back at Outpost #31.

Better, when OB returns to the main building we get a great shot directly along the rope line – exactly like a Carpenter shot of MacReady's hut or the storage building Blair was locked inside and with Nauls staggering back by himself.

Infighting ensues among the group, conversations are had, loyalties seem to shift and we're fed titbits, encouraging the viewer to start questioning who might be a killer. And then there's the camera work. Shots of action happening behind characters backs, or something in the foreground in crystal clarity while action in the distant background is also in focus – a unique way of filming that Carpenter mastered in 1982.

When the survivors realise there's at least one compatriot of Daisys' in the room, they get them all to line up along the far wall. The shots similar to when MacReady comes up with the blood test and has everyone else line up under pain of a flamethrower to the face while he explains how they can find out who's a Thing?

Finally, we end with two characters, suffering, dying and looking at each other. Is there anyone else still alive? Will any of them survive? H8 ends exactly the way Carpenter ended his film in 1982.

It wasn't just the cinematic look and themes that Tarantino homaged. Both previous Thing films had been set in the cold, and to get that look they filmed in a cold storage warehouse. Cold as this was, to enhance the breath the actors were encouraged to drink a hot beverage before a take to make their breath even hotter and steamier. Tarantino used all of these tactics in the exact same way as Hawks and Carpenter. One of my favourite shots is when Warren drinks some coffee and the steam from his mouth and the mug rises around his head and from under his hat – just awesome.

The Thing in a Cave

I swear, you think you're done and you find something else. I'd put the first draft aside for a few days to clear my mind so I could begin the lengthy edit process, and a streaming service suggested a movie after something else I'd recently watched. The Outsider (2020) was a miniseries made by HBO and based on a Stephen King novel. I'm no fan of King and would not have watched it, but I didn't know until a few episodes in it had anything to do with the writer. I don't want to spoil anything for anyone who's now going to watch this show, but to me, it's the Thing in a cave. There's paranoia, the cops think they might be tracking an entity that seems to pass itself on through blood and possibly shapeshifts. You don't know who is who and where or even if the thing is gone? The show takes its time, and honestly, I liked it, but to me it hits so many Thing beats that it had to be placed here.

The Toys

Merchandise for The Thing is rare, with only a handful of action figures being released over the years by specialty makers like MacFarlane Toys and recently NECA. Sure, there's some great garage kits, but you need to go back to 2000 and McFarlane toys Movie Maniac line, which began when the company licensed movie properties at the end of the 1990s. Wave after wave of these popular figures came out, and this included the Norris-Thing, the Spider-Head Thing and the final Blair-Thing.

The Movie Manic line ended over a decade ago, and many of the people who created these figures then broke away and started their own company, NECA. These folks are making some truly staggering action figures for numerous franchises, including The Thing. As of this moment they have released two MacReady figures and I am currently waiting to order the online release of the 3D THING movie poster action figure, which looks amazing, and I believe will be insanely collectible (at the time of editing – yay, I got one).

There was a second company that produced larger figures at the same time as MacFarlane. State Of The Art Toys (or SOTA) were in business for only a short time, but lucky for us they produced two amazing figures, one was a diorama of MacReady entering the dog kennel with the Dog-Thing inside, and another was a large scale Thing-Head. All of these figures are pretty rare, so if you see one grab it as you may never see one again.

I can find no evidence any figure was released for the prequel.

The Last Word?

There's always plenty of rumours for a Thing sequel, for example Fear Magazine in 1989 announced: *STOP PRESS: Remember John Carpenter's The Thing! SFX man Rob Bottin is trying to get The Thing II off the ground. I don't envy him the job...*

The strangest was a George Clooney mini-series, but there have always been rumours of Thing sequels and I'm running out of space in this book to go through them all. Instead, what I'd like to talk about is the recent revival of Carpenter's connection to the Thing.

The director clearly has always thought of himself as a rock star, and one of my favourite things is the video clip for the single he released from Big Trouble in Little China (we got biggggg trouble...in little Chiii-naahh). There are volumes of interviews with John on how his Hollywood career all but stalled after 1982 – and how he returned to being an independent film maker. His pain is palpable, but what I love is how he's recently found himself. Today you can go to a Carpenter live concert, where he plays the songs he's created for cinema over the last 50 years. In 2016, Little White Lies magazine interviewed the director about the recent interest in his music. *I can't explain it, it's just luck I think. There seems to be a nostalgia for an old synthesiser sound, which probably has something to do with it.*

When Den of Geek Quarterly Magazine (2021) interviewed the director about enjoying his new career, Carpenter answered: *Ah, man, are you kidding me? It's a dream come true...* When the interviewer pointed out this new interest was helping revive his older films, the director agreed... *it's the greatest. And plus I'm doing scores to the new Halloween movies which is really, really fun. We just finished up Halloween Kills and it's great.*

These recent Halloween scores have won several awards, such as the ASCAP award for top movie soundtrack of 2022 and the Fangoria Chainsaw Award for Best Score. As for the soundtrack to The Thing, the vinyl re-release by WaxWorks records sold out instantly and today demands huge prices online. The website notes: *Waxwork Records worked for two years to ensure that such a highly anticipated and sought after vinyl soundtrack re-issue would meet and exceed expectations of the biggest fan of John Carpenter and his sci-fi / horror tour de force that is THE THING. Features include the complete Ennio Morricone soundtrack re-mastered from the original master tapes...*

The soundtrack for '51 also got its very first release a few years ago, covered in Film Score Monthly.

SCORING THE THING FROM ANOTHER WORLD WAS Dimitri Tomkin, one of cinema's most famous composers, who nonetheless was known for his popular melodies rather than an aptitude at science fiction. Tomkins roaring, bellicose score for The THING (26:50) featured unusual instrumentation—particularly the electronic theremin—that terrified audiences along with the film's titular villain. The score became the blueprint for the '50s "monster" movie genre, although Tomkin never attempted another one like it... MASTER TAPES TO THE Thing are long lost, but the complete score survived on monaural acetate transfer disks in Tomkins personal collection, and that source has been used ...

It a great time to be a fan. Giant industries and companies are on the wane and micro industries and passion companies using underground or fan-favourite properties are on the rise. This ensures items like soundtracks and action figures are constantly being released, even decades after the media they're based on disappeared. With the Thing 40th anniversary there's likely going to be a lot of re-releases like this, so keep an eye out, you may find yourself a real treasure.

The Return

Richard Stanley made his bones releasing sci-fi/horror films like Hardware, which garnished praise and support across the globe. He then lost a lot of this goodwill when Fleetway Comics sued because the film plagiarised their story SHOK!, that appeared in the Judge Dredd Annual 1981.

Somehow Stanley got his career going again and was hired to direct 1996's 'The Island of Dr. Moreau', and if you think reaction to The Thing '82 was bad, look into that horror of a film. After a mutiny by the cast and crew and the studio doing everything possible to undermine him, Stanley was fired and John Frankenheimer took over. I was reading an interview with Stanley when he said:

I think that John Carpenter's The Thing is the pre-imminent masterpiece of the genre. It's probably the greatest monster movie ever made, and certainly the most Lovecraftian ever made despite not coming from Lovecraft material. I'm certainly a huge Carpenter fan and we kind of homage The Thing with the multi-headed alpaca monster.

Well, that got me...what freakin' Alpaca Monster?

After a rough career Stanley managed to direct again, this time 2019's 'Color Out of Space' – a sci-fi/horror of serious Lovecraftian origins starring Nick Cage. This explains why I missed it. Let's face it, for the last decade we've all been ignoring Nick's low budget films. So, about an hour ago I finished watching the film and yup, there's a freakin alpaca monster that's a serious tip-of-the-hat to the Dog-Thing.

As for the film, it's not bad and there are serious Thing vibes the whole way through...check it out and let us know what you think on our Facebook page. I'm curious to know how many Thing tropes you find?

The Songs

When I first read that Ministry had borrowed sound effects from The Thing, I was a little sceptical, and listening to the song 'Burning Inside', I couldn't hear it...so I went back and re-read the reference and noticed they were talking about just the warning klaxon that can be heard in the movie whenever anyone pulls an emergency cord. So, going back with a good set of headphones, this time I caught it. You can hear at the start of the song the clear sound of that klaxon used in the film - and there's also a little snippet from Carpenter's Prince of Darkness score. This, however, is not the only song that has sampled the film.

Named after the giant sandworms in Dune, the punk/metal band Shai Hulud released 'If Born From This Soil Man' in 1999. Now their songs not only contain a lot of pop references, they are beyond growly – I'd call it more barky – but when you listen to the song you can hear a few snippets from movies, including Kurt Russel from The Thing. The song also has a line 'A likeness only in structure, not in mind' surely has to be harkening back to the movie.

I've got to say, I have trouble hearing Russel in the tune. I have no problem hearing the references in 'Hellebarn' a 2000 song from German black-metal group Nagelfar, from their last album, Virus West. Throughout the song they've sampled a lot of the movie, including the sounds of the Dog-Thing as it's in the kennel.

> *This is the thing about people*
> *You never really know what's inside*
> *Somewhere in the soul, there's a secret*
> *Hysteria grows where it was invited*
> *This is the thing about fiction*
> *How everything feeds on its paranoia*
> *...Live it up for the path of resistance*

These are just some of the lyrics from Sufjan Stevens & Angelo De Augustine's piano driven song called '(This Is) The Thing'. It's a lovely, fun song with great harmonies from their 2021 album, A Beginner's Mind, and the song's dripping with Thing references. In fact every single song on the album is based on a cult movie like Mad Max, Clash of the Titans, Hellraiser III and Night of the Living Dead.

> *An ancient danger*
> *Frozen in time*
> *Unearthed by inquisitive minds*
> *An evil life-form, devious design*
> *An imitation*
> *In man it dwells*
> *No one the wiser, who can tell?*
> *Born again into another living shell*
> *...Find in who The Thing resides*

In 2021, British thrash metal group EVILE released a new studio album, Hell Unleashed, and vocalist/guitarist Ol Drake comments: *The 3rd and final single...*

is not only based on my favourite movie of all time, but it's a strong contender for my favourite song off the album...

If you know of any other songs based around the Thing, drop us a line at our Facebook page, I'm sure there's a lot of fans out there that'd be interested. In my research I found a lot...and I mean a lot of versions and remixes of Morricone's theme, far too many to list here, but they exist, and some are actually pretty good.

The Game

Who would have thought that in a world with every conceivable type of computer game and more streaming platforms then you can shake a stick at, that many of us have decided to put aside part of their week so they can sit at a table for a few hours with their friends, eat pizza and knock off a boardgame or two?

Recently there's been a rush to release games based on media properties, and The Thing has joined them. The first to appear was the unauthorized 2010 card game that, as you pull a card from the deck the game unfolds.

The first boardgame was 2017s The Thing: Infection at Outpost 31 (Mondo Games) and 2020 'Who Goes There?' (Certifiable Studios). All are based on '82 or the book and play is situated around outpost 31. Players being a character and the games secretly infecting players through the rounds with those human surviving to the end winning and the THING winning by defeating the remaining humans. The last one also has collectible figures based on the films characters as extras to purchase, and they're pretty great. I'm not going to say much more as the games are still available, so grab one because they are serious fun.

Did You Know? Certifiable Studios created their game through a Kickstarter campaign and was after $54,097 to finance the game. They ended up raising over $612,000.

The Fans

If you've got this far, you're a fan. Have we come up with a name for ourselves yet? A thingite? A Thing-a-ma-bob? A Thing-ster? As mentioned, this franchise has some seriously knowledgeable fans who have undertaken epic adventures. Many fans have made it a pilgrimage to head out to the glacier where they filmed '82 – many bringing back parts of the set and even pieces from the Norwegian helicopter that blew up in the opening scenes. Like truffle dogs they poke around, searching for hidden titbits of information they can share with the fans. They have run conventions (thingfest) and host FB pages like The Thing, Outpost 31, John Carpenter's The Thing, The films of Director John Carpenter, The Thing Legacy.

There are websites like THE THING wiki, which seems to be growing with new titbits.

Dean Houghton (admin of The films of Director John Carpenter) explained: *I absolutely love the thing for what it brought to the table in special effects, plus it's made by my favourite director John Carpenter, who I recommend to anybody who loves that sort of thing*.

Peter Abbott is the fan that other fans talk about and creator of 'The Thing 1982 fan group' and has met up with cast and crew from '82 and was even included in special features on some Blu ray releases for the film.

To be a fan of The Thing, where do you start, well for those (un)fortunate to be old enough I guess it started in the summer of 1982 on its release in the United States or later that year in the August for the U.K., that said it wasn't till the summer of 1983 in the U.K. at the tender age of 10 that my father brought it home on its VHS release, I remember it being a hot summers day and being sat on the couch by the patio doors while my father placed the cassette in the player stating "you're going to like this one" ...knowing full well that I wasn't a huge fan of horror films at the time, more so anything Zombie related but gore in general but I was already a fan of John Carpenter movies after seeing Assault on precinct 13 and Escape from New York so o was kind of expecting the same kind of film, and so it started, I felt quite comfortable watching at first due to the beautiful filming location and the fact there was a dog in it...who knew!, but that was soon lived...when the kennel scene hit it was like a sledge hammer and the dogs face splitting like a banana was truly the most horrific thing I had ever witnessed on screen and I wasn't sure I'd make it through the rest of the film after my father compounding my fears with his comment of "son, that was a mild scene".

Cut to many years later and the film had become an obsession/passion, it had become imprinted in my brain from such an early age and I became a sponge for information on the making of it, the actors, the production crew and of course John Carpenter, on formation was very limited for many years other than reading literature in magazines and books but then came the internet...it was the early 2000's that I came across the most incredible website called 'Outpost #31' run by my now good friend, Todd Cameron, Todd had created this site for fans of the movie to visit and i was astonished just how much fan base this film had, I thought I was alone, but by far the most incredible area of this site was photos of Todd and his friend Steve Crawford visiting the filming location in 2003 and that was me hooked on keeping in touch with all these incredible people. Time rolled on again until the summer of 2016 and when visiting Canada my fiancé suggested we head up to British Columbia and find the location ourselves, we took the flight up to Terrace and drove 4 hours to the town of Stewart where cast and crew stayed (as well as

Hyder) and with the help of Todd's information on finding the location in 2003 we hit the spot, and more importantly coming across the remains of the Norwegian helicopter that was blown up at the beginning of the film, what a find and what a feeling to be stood in the exact same place where this film was made that had made such an impact on me for all those years....

We're fast approaching mid-2022 as I finish this final chapter and again there's news in The Thing world that a remake is on the horizon – and astonishingly it may be another Carpenter film. At this moment the future looks bright for the franchise...but isn't that always the way when it comes to The Thing. It's all about paranoia and mistrust. Sure, these new stories may appear, but then again we've all heard this story before and nothing ever comes of them – so until we meet again in a cinema somewhere with a heartbeat base line playing through DTS speakers and a plastic garbage bag is set alight to allow the words THE THING to blaze across the big screen, I hope you enjoy the book half as much as I enjoyed researching it. I thank everyone who answered my weird queries, and I hope we remain the great fan base I know we are.

Be polite, be happy, share what you know, and please share with me if I missed something, and remember it isn't Fuchs...but it may be someone close, so trust no one.

THE THTHNG

In 2023 we will also get to watch the ultimate fan project. THTHNG : Desolation Unknown is a fan-made film about to be released, and I caught up with creator Kelly Porter.

Our original concept was what if an A.I. made its own sequel to John Carpenter's "The Thing". We liked how the AI image making tools were trying to imitate reality and we started to troubleshoot breaking the tools in order to get them to make horrific imagery because a lot of the prompts that would describe what we wanted it to create would be flagged and not work. So we had to trick it using prompts like "dark sanguinous fluid" to get it to make blood. Me and Robbie Martin are the ones working on it, and have been over the last year using all of the AI related tools we could get our hands on. It has changed a lot as we have progressed through the project and it is the first in a trilogy of movies. We wrote all of the dialogue and plot ourselves, but used different "A.I" tools to create the voices and the music as well. I am a visual artist and QA engineer and Robbie Martin is an electronic musician and a journalist.

Epilogue

The Fossil

The turtle's body steadily rose towards the glittering ocean surface, its huge flippers beating and stroking like oars, almost grabbing and pulling its immense bulk through the water. Eyes adapted to piercing the deep in search of food like jellyfish and squid open wide, catching and focusing on a dark shadow moving beneath. Its owner serpentines into view and seems an amalgamation of several creatures. Its body also has wide, paddle-like flippers that help swim and turn with near-impossible swiftness. Its long, snake-like body writhes and undulates, powering a broad tail with half a fluke, creating even more speed and agility. All of this hangs behind a head straight out of somebody's nightmare. Enormous, curved teeth protrude from a blockish, triangular skull, capable of impacting against prey with tremendous force. Things get even worse when that skull opens up, revealing not only those banana-size teeth – but impossibly a second row of teeth inside the mouth like the Xenomorph from ALIEN. Also like that hideous creature spawned from the dark mind of H R Giger, this interior jaw can move back and forth to help pull prey inside the mouth.

It's hard to argue that speeding towards the turtle was a creature of nightmare.

There was once a monster hunting prehistoric Antarctica. It didn't come in a crashed spaceship and find itself trapped in the ice, no, this monster was born and died there. I've been writing natural history articles for twenty years, and normally I'd point out you don't like to call any animal a derogatory name or use negative terms. There's no such thing as a bad snake and sharks don't infest a coastline…they live there. If anyone is infesting the beach its humans. But this is a book about horror stories and monsters, so hopefully I'll be forgiven the little hyperbole back there. All I wanted to do was highlight that there was once an enormous predator that swam the oceans of Antarctica when it was part of the much larger supercontinent, Gondwana. This animal was indeed an amalgamation of other creatures, and its head looked every bit like the final shot we got of Carpenter's Blair-Thing before MacReady throws his dynamite and dive rolls to safety (see final note coming up).

In 2011, the very same year the THING prequel was released, palaeontologists exploring Antarctica's tiny Seymour Island found something unique. When it comes to eggs, none come larger than those from *Aepyornis* - the elephant bird - that once roamed Madagascar…or so we once thought. Those bird eggs were the size of a serious watermelon. Well on Seymour Island these scientists found an egg from the Cretaceous, some 66 million years ago, that was the size of a football. The dimensions weren't the only thing unusual either as it seemed to have had incredibly thick skin…not shell mind you…skin. This egg belonged to an aquatic reptile that laid soft eggs like turtles' deposit in the millions along the worlds beaches every year. The egg was also 5 times thinner than a bird's shell and far less complex in its structure.

Seymour is something of a palaeontology paradise as most of its exposed rocks are from either the late Cretaceous or early Eocene, meaning they either contain the last animals that lived during the dinosaur age or the first animals from the following age of mammals.

Was this an enormous turtle egg? Not according to these palaeontologists. Certainly, there were enormous car-size turtles swimming the Mesozoic oceans – but these palaeontologists believe this egg belonged to something else.

By comparing the fossil egg to others, scientists believe the mother was at least 23ft long, and likely laid the egg after holding it within her body until the very hour of hatching. The airbreathing baby reptile would immediately pull itself out of the egg and swim for the surface to take its first breath. Anything else meant certain death for the baby.

When the fossil was first found the scientists weren't sure what it was and carried the rock back to camp and showed it around. No one could agree as to what it was there either, so it received the nickname of Antarctica's arguably most famous cinema creature, 'The Thing'.

The fossil was sent to the National Museum of Natural History in Chile, where it sat on a shelf for years until Julia Clarke visited the storage room, saw the specimen and suggested it was an egg. Next, every test you can imagine was performed on the fossil, including CT scans to see if there were any remains still inside. This would obviously explain instantly that A, it was an egg, and B, maybe reveal what sort of creature had laid it. Sadly, the scan proved it was empty. These tests did prove to everyone's satisfaction that it was indeed an egg though, the first vertebrate egg of any kind to be discovered in Antarctica and the largest soft-shelled egg known to science, as well as the second largest egg ever recorded.

It's owner? most likely a mosasaur, a giant marine reptilian predator that was one of the very last major animal groups to evolve during the dinosaur age. They were closely related to modern snakes and monitor lizards like the Komodo dragon. The species was named *Antarcticoolithus* or the 'late Antarctic stone egg'.

This Thing once patrolled the oceans off Gondwana, ambushing prey from below while carrying the eggs of the next generation within their bodies, waiting to be expelled alive, ready to kill and survive a hostile world with teeth and subterfuge.

Note: One last bit of fun. That final, toothy Blair-Thing got me thinking the alien could be extremely old and maybe even had visited the earth before? So, I sent a message to the guy who designed the Thing to see if I was onto something.

Phil: Hey Mr Ploog, I hope all is well...Could I ask, did you use any dinosaur ideas in your THING designs? Always thought that last monster had a definite tyrannosaur look to it.

Sarah (Mike's fb assistant): Mike says that he only wishes he was that smart! Ha! No t-rex or dinosaur thoughts at all. He was creating and winging the designs as he was drawing.

Damn, I thought I had something there.

Just shows you can never trust these Things.

Author's Thanks

I'd like to thank all those interviewed for taking the time to talk to me about their work. It's truly appreciated.
I'd also like to thank the fans of The Thing, who have been generous in sharing information and being so supportive.
I'd like to thank my school yard friends for hosting a VHS slumber party and putting on THE THING after midnight and scarring me for life.

Last, to Katherine for making me smile and being so understanding as I fell down the rabbit hole researching this book.

Phil Hore

www.ingramcontent.com/pod-product-compliance
Lightning Source LLC
Chambersburg PA
CBHW031926240526
45464CB00023B/1715